BIG RED
CONFIDENTIAL

INSIDE NEBRASKA FOOTBALL

ARMEN KETEYIAN

CONTEMPORARY
BOOKS

CHICAGO · NEW YORK

Library of Congress Cataloging-in-Publication Data

Keteyian, Armen.
    Big Red confidential : inside Nebraska football / Armen
Keteyian.
        p.   cm.
    ISBN 0-8092-4580-9
    1. University of Nebraska—Lincoln—Football—History.
I. Title.
GV958.U53K48   1989
796.332'63'09782293—dc20   89-35391
                                            CIP

All photos courtesy of the Journal-Star Printing Co.

Published by Contemporary Books, Inc.
180 North Michigan Avenue, Chicago, Illinois 60601
Manufactured in the United States of America
Library of Congress Catalog Card Number: 89-35391
International Standard Book Number: 0-8092-4580-9

Published simultaneously in Canada by Beaverbooks, Ltd.
195 Allstate Parkway, Valleywood Business Park
Markham, Ontario L3R 4T8 Canada

To James Hinga . . . who first lit the fire

CONTENTS

ACKNOWLEDGMENTS

This project came to life over a four-year period. From concept to completion, that meant doing everything from casually observing football games on a Saturday afternoon, to combing through court records, to conducting more than 150 interviews with people associated in some capacity with Husker football.

The seeds of this book were first planted back in the fall of 1986 and grew rapidly during one chaotic week in November 1987. I spent several weeks visiting Lincoln and other cities in 1986 and '87 reporting on the NU football program for *Sports Illustrated*, for which I served as a full-time investigative writer and reporter from June 1982 to September 1988. Additional reporting and, in many cases, rereporting of original *SI* interviews was conducted during an eight-month stretch from October 1988 through May 1989. The entire book was written in the fall of '88 and spring of '89, after I had left *SI* to pursue other interests—including this book.

This particular interest, it turns out, could not have been pursued without the support and cooperation of a great many people. Some are named herewith; many are not. The very nature of certain sections of this work—and, at times, its controversial subject matter—placed several people close to the program in a situation where they requested anonymity in order to speak freely. That is the main reason why this book contains an inordinate amount of sourcing, with references to former players, former coaches, ex-girlfriends, and sources close to a particular situation. In some cases names were omitted simply because I saw no compelling reason to subject the speakers to any more public pain, questioning, or embarrassment than they and their families had already suffered.

Finally, a heartfelt thanks to some special friends who helped make this book better. Thanks to the men who cover Husker football on a daily basis: Michael Kelly, sports editor of the *Omaha World-Herald*, and two of his key staff members, Lee Barfknecht and Steve Sinclair; and the sports stalwarts at the *Lincoln Journal-Star*, Mike Babcock and Ken Hambleton. Gentlemen, I appreciate your sharing not only your thoughts and experiences but also the professional courtesies extended to me. Thanks too to former Contemporary Books executive editor Shari Lesser Wenk, now a literary agent, for believing in me and my idea; current Contemporary associate publisher and editor Nancy Crossman, for crafting a better book; copy whiz Nancy Nasworthy, for making sense of stray thoughts and constructing, when necessary, cleaner, sharper language; and my agent, John Ware, for his unwavering support and counsel.

But, most of all, my love and gratitude to:

Martin Francis Dardis, investigator extraordinaire, father figure, and journalistic partner at the magazine for the last three years;

Sandy Padwe, for all the battles fought and lessons taught;

Jack Tobin, the best "paper" man in the business, who willingly and patiently taught me the hidden and priceless value of the public record;

and, more than anyone, my family—my darling wife, Dede, and daughters, Kristen and Kelly, and our guardian angel for the last six years, Mary (Mimi) Henderson—who all lived "the book" with me during so many days and nights.

PROLOGUE

State Senator Ernie Chambers (Omaha) sits behind a desk drowning in a landslide of legislative books and documents. Not that he cares, mind you, since Early American Messy seems to be the dominant decor in his sparsely furnished first-floor office in the Nebraska State Capital Building, a 400-foot-tall award-winning phallic structure erected on the southwest edge of downtown Lincoln. A stocky, energetic man with powerful arms and a minister's voice, Chambers is known as something of a political maverick in these parts. A barber by trade, he regularly attends sessions in Nebraska's Unicameral, the state's unique one-house, nonpartisan legislative body, dressed in T-shirt and jeans. In the past, Chambers has gone as far as sending a letter to Libyan leader Col. Muammar Qaddafi seeking assistance in "providing housing and educational opportunity" for black Americans; and he has railed about the rights of white farmers and black athletes. Image aside for a moment, Chambers has also built an impressive and admirable legislative record in nineteen years of public service. Most recently he has gained national attention as not only a sharp critic of the hypocrisy of college

1

sports but also a man attempting to institute significant change.

It was Chambers, for example, who pushed for the passage of a state law in 1984 prohibiting Nebraska colleges from lifting athletic scholarships from injured players. It was Chambers again who has, in every session since 1982, proposed a bill that would "provide that football players at the University of Nebraska at Lincoln be treated as university employees"—in effect, requiring that players be paid stipends ranging from $500 to $1,000 per month for their contribution to the $10 million industrial-athletic complex that is Husker football. In April 1988 the measure passed the legislature with the stipulation that at least four other Big Eight schools pass similar bills before it became law. No matter, Governor Kay Orr vetoed the measure, deeming it "not the appropriate format" to speak to the NCAA.

In February 1989 Chambers cosponsored another NCAA-related statute. If passed, LB397 would force the NCAA to follow due process in its disciplinary procedures, giving a school like the University of Nebraska a means to take the organization to court if it ever imposed sanctions without due process—which some local folks argue is exactly what happened back in 1986 when the NCAA came snooping around town.

To be sure, Chambers tends to overdramatize the plight of the players, describing them as virtual field workers "sweating and laboring under a broiling sun, or shivering from the nibble of the icy teeth of winter, soaking the earth or artificial turf with their youthful blood." But nowhere is there a more serious student of the Tom Osborne Era—seventeen years and counting. So when Chambers speaks, as he did one fall evening from behind that cluttered desk, long after the capital's lights had dimmed, you listen.

"People used to say Nebraska was like a program that came straight from heaven—like the Ten Commandments, unblemished," Chambers says. "So when the players were found guilty of these past violations, all the people here, instead of acknowledging the rules . . . wanted to condemn the NCAA for imposing any kind of punishment. But before that, you should have seen how they wrote letters about all those other crooked schools and crooked coaches and, thank God, we've got Tom Osborne and a Holy Joe program like this that never does anything wrong.

"People connected with the program come off sounding very sincere, very innocent, very naive. But you have to remember these are savvy men of the world. Osborne and [Athletic Director Bob] Devaney and the rest of them over there have to see the same things the students see."

Chambers shuffles some papers on his desk before continuing. "I have never tried to get the school put on probation, nor have I ever tried to get a player to lose [his] eligibility," he says. "That's not my intention. It's a big, corrupt business, and it's here to stay. . . . I would not say what I say if I didn't know it for a fact. I know what I'm talking about. I know people who give money and things of value to the players. I know players by name given things by merchants for catching a good pass or touchdown. I know of a player who was paid a certain amount every time he caught a touchdown pass.

"There is no way that things can happen on campus with reference to these players . . . and the coach not know. I think usually he's careful when he says—like most coaches do—that 'I have no direct knowledge.' Said in such a way, technically speaking, it may be correct. But in a sense of people being aware of what goes on in their environment and their bailiwick—everybody at the university knows. Everybody knows.

"The cars, the money, the drugs—they are not secrets on that campus. The athletic establishment will pretend they don't know these things are happening, but they know. And they won't do anything about it until somebody calls their hand. And the first thing they'll do is deny it. But because Tom Osborne is viewed as a god in this state, they want to shut their eyes, stop their ears, and stuff the mouth of anybody that would want to speak about it, so they don't have to face the reality that Tom knows as much about what goes on in this program as coaches do in any other school. And if he doesn't, then he is extremely naive and ought not to be allowed on a public street by himself. How can people be given credit for being so wise, and not know what's going on right under their nose?"

Chambers takes a hollow breath. Sweat builds on his brow. "What we have is a coach with a Holy Joe image who says 'I don't do anything wrong. I don't tolerate anything wrong.' Yet the program functions on a par with all similar programs in the country. That's why I'm disgusted about Nebraska. It's the most hypocritical school you can find."

SUNDAY
NOVEMBER 15, 1987

6:54 P.M.

Bobbing down the aisle of United Airlines flight 495 from
Chicago's O'Hare to Lincoln, Nebraska, comes a giggly gag-
gle of college-age girls all dressed in assorted states and
stages of red. In twos and threes they break off from the main
body of laughter to huddle and chat near assigned seats,
stashing travel bags with the words *Nebraska Swimming* on
the side into overhead compartments. The other passengers
on this jammed flight, mostly male and buttoned down,
snicker a time or two, peering up from newspapers reporting
Letterman's reunion of Sonny and Cher and the continuing
investigation of former White House aide Michael Deaver.

The captain comes on over the intercom. By the time he
finishes introducing the cabin crew and updating the passengers on Lincoln weather—fifty degrees, fog and intermit-
tent rain—the athletes have settled snugly into their seats,
like movie patrons just before the previews begin. A pretty
blonde slips into seat 15B. Somewhere over Illinois this tall
wispy-haired teenager—who's wearing a red Nebraska
sweater—mentions that her name is Allison Barker and that

she's nineteen and a freshman butterflyer. Her team just finished second in a big meet against North Carolina, Penn State, and Southern Illinois. As she says all this, her green eyes glow and the sound of her voice informs you she's from across the ocean. Cambridge, England, says Allison. "One of my coaches there knew the coach at Nebraska," she explains. "I've been there only three months. It's not what I expected it to be. Pretty slow. I'd seen New York and California on TV. I thought it would be like that." She laughs. "No, I'm not disappointed," she says. "I like it now. I like going to football games. I don't understand it; it's a bit confusing. But I like sitting in the stands with the other students. Everything is geared toward football; they don't really concentrate on swimming. But this week is the big game, you know. I'm really looking forward to that."

The Big Game. Depending on one's cultural and athletic bias, that can translate to Harvard vs. Yale, Army–Navy, Pitt–Penn State, Cal vs. Stanford, Florida–Florida State, Alabama–Auburn, or, heck, even Slippery Rock–Edinboro. Yet somehow over the years, one major college rivalry has transcended time and place, down and distance, becoming, in effect, the personal yardstick against which certain college football fans measure the value of their lives—and in which football players, in the words of ex-Oklahoma linebacker Brian Bosworth, "reach down inside and figure out what kind of guy you are." A football game that, for a few hours, can provide welcome relief to devastating droughts or dried-up wells. One game, unlike any other: Nebraska vs. Oklahoma.

"To me," former OU star quarterback Jack Mildren once told *USA Today*, "Oklahoma playing Nebraska is the prototype of excitement, drama, the struggle, the fans, the worries . . . everything there would be in a great football game."

The history book says that entering 1987 the two teams had met 67 times since 1912, annually from '28. Nebraska had pretty much owned the Sooners, lock, stock, and oil barrel, the first 22 years (16-3-3), including—and this hurts—11 shutouts. Oklahoma proceeded to pick itself up off the dirt—and rubbed Nebraska's nose in it—winning 34 times in the next 45 years, 16 straight from '43–'58, to lead the series 37–27–3 overall. Six times since 1973, one of the teams had come into the game ranked first or second in the nation; every year but one since 1970 either OU or NU had been ranked in the top five in the country; 40 times since World War II the Big Eight Conference title had been at stake, including the last 27 years in a row. Nice stats, if you're a numbers freak.

But the game everybody still talks about, which stirred the pages of history, The Game, was played in Norman, Oklahoma, on November 25, 1971, Thanksgiving Day, on national television. The dance card read No. 1 Nebraska vs. No. 2 Oklahoma, and when the music finally ended, it was a tune destined to play forever in the hearts and minds of college football fans everywhere. Mildren vs. Jerry Tagge at quarterback. Greg Pruitt against Jeff Kinney in the backfield. Johnny "J.R. Superstar" Rodgers and—perhaps the greatest single play in Husker history—his sudden, shocking 72-yard first-quarter punt return for a touchdown. Eighty million people watching on TV. President Nixon calling both the winning and losing coaches. In the end, a game replayed over and over on home videos, like a Hitchcock thriller, a game chosen by a national panel of sportswriters as the best college football game ever played. The Game of the Century. Nebraska 35, Oklahoma 31.

Well, come Saturday, November 21, 1987, at 2:45 P.M., to be exact, it appeared that the gods of college football had conspired to grace this rivalry again. For the first time since '71 Nebraska and Oklahoma would enter the game undefeated and ranked first and second, respectively, in every major poll. The stage was undeniably set. The best two teams in the country in a nationally televised showdown for No. 1, the Big Eight title, and a chance to play defending national champion Miami in the Orange Bowl. And what teams they were:

Nebraska, 9–0, the nation's total offense leader (524.6 yards per game). Second in scoring (43.6 points per game) behind Oklahoma (46.2). Second in rushing behind the

Sooners (390.2 yards). Featuring its fastest and most athletic front five ever, a seasoned and elusive quarterback in junior Steve Taylor, and a hungry, high-spirited defense led by brash-talking (some would say trash-talkin') All-America defensive end Broderick Thomas. A loosey-goosey Nebraska—kicking ass, taking names, and generally acting like no Nebraska team had ever acted before.

Oklahoma, 10-0, a Ferrari in cleats. First in rushing (429.8). A young but turbocharged backfield. An offensive line manned by five returning starters, two All-Americas, all built along the lines of a major kitchen appliance (averaging 6'4", 283 pounds per man). The nation's total defense leader (205.4 yards allowed per game). Smooth as raw silk but Tyson-tough and, as always, loose and a little bit arrogant.

Yes sir, ladies and gentlemen, step right up to Game of the Century II.

Deepening the drama were the intriguing histories of the two head coaches. Both took over their respective programs the same year—1973, and now, after fifteen seasons, a single victory separated them, possessors of the best winning percentages among active Division I coaches: Barry Switzer (147-25-4, 85 percent) of Oklahoma and Tom Osborne (146-32-2, 82 percent) of Nebraska.

But that's where the road split; they had near identical records but vastly different backgrounds and beliefs. Switzer, born in the backwoods of tiny Crossett, Arkansas, on October 5, 1937, grew up in a backwoods house without plumbing, phone, or electricity. His dad, a convicted bootlegger, was murdered. His mom eventually committed suicide. Their son didn't know the full meaning of running water, electricity, or indoor plumbing until he attended the University of Arkansas, where he played center and linebacker for three years and made captain his senior year. In his fifteen seasons at OU he had cultivated a reputation as an effervescent, wisecracking rogue who played it fast and loose on and off the field—as did his teams, which seemed to embody their coach's anything-goes attitude. How far Switzer had gone was the subject of considerable public debate. The NCAA had investigated OU in 1973 and put the team on probation for two years. In 1984 the Securities and Exchange Commission filed charges—later dismissed by a federal court—against Switzer for alleged insider-trading abuses. And the NCAA Committee on Infractions had just authorized another detailed probe into charges of improper car loans, illegal recruiting offers, and scalped complimentary game tickets.

But most Oklahomans pushed such indiscretions aside and lavished praise on Switzer for what he did better than anybody else—win football games. Particularly in the case of Nebraska, where Switzer was seen as a miracle worker, having whipped the Huskers 11 of 15 times since '73, including 3 in a row entering the 1987 contest. Three of those 11 wins ('76, '80, and '86) had bordered on black magic, materializing as they did in the final minutes of play.

Switzer had also won 3 national championships ('74, '75, and '85), and flashed a huge, glittering "No. 1" diamond ring to prove it.

On the other sideline was arguably the cleanest coach in college football, a mild-mannered Methodist, a man whose program was considered above reproach, the ideal blending of both academic and athletic excellence (a five-year graduation rate near 80 percent)—a model for countless other schools across the country. Whereas Switzer's ethics had been called into question, Osborne appeared to wear a halo above his head. Stolid and stone-faced, he embodied the cherished midwestern ideals of honesty and integrity, so much so that folks were known to call him "Preacher Tom" for his profound faith and unflappable inner strength. He seemed to live the words that were chiseled at the top, southwest corner of Memorial Stadium: NOT THE VICTORY BUT THE ACTION. NOT THE GOAL BUT THE GAME. IN THE DEED THE GLORY.

Osborne hailed from the heartland—from Hastings, Nebraska, the third of four generations of men whose quiet dignity and steely resolve could be traced back to the pioneers who pushed their way across the plains. Perceived as an "uncommon man" in the minds of many Nebraskans, Tom Osborne stood totally committed to the physical and mental—and spiritual—development of his players. "A builder of men," says Bernie Altsuler of Omaha, a Husker season-ticket holder since 1946. Osborne: A man whose "approval factor"—according to local newspaper polls—annually rated higher than the governor's. A man so powerful that, as one former player put it, "There seems to be total state agreement that he stands just a bit above God."

Tom Osborne had certainly achieved his share of coaching glory. Although he would be the last one to mention it, he was entering the Oklahoma game as the winningest college football coach of the 1980s, his decade-long record of 81–4 included more wins than such media mavens as Switzer, Joe Paterno, Bo Schembechler, and Jimmy Johnson. Yes, under its squeaky-clean coach, the Big Red Machine had piled up an average of 10 victories a season. Moreover, his teams had played in a bowl game every year he had coached, won 5 national rushing titles, produced some 30 All-Americas, and won or shared 6 Big Eight titles.

But what few folks inside the state—and precious few outside—understood was that beneath this flinty, disciplined demeanor, this snow-white mantle, lived a man of deep mystery and devilish contradiction, one caught in a catch-22 of conflicting emotions.

Yes, in many ways, Tom Osborne, hometown hero, Nebraska born and raised, was quietly struggling to gain control of his life. To wind down and not take life so seriously. To jog and laugh away the stress and strain of being the "Supreme Being" in a state that deifies its football team, to "do it right," as he likes to say, in a system plagued by criticism and corruption. Here was an offensive genius who viewed football as a chess match while off the field played mind games with the best of them; a "realistic perfectionist" (his son's observation) driven by a traumatic and perplexing past; a man dogged—nay, haunted—by his only major football failure, the inability to supply his supporters with the one drug they craved most—that most natural of highs, a mythical national football championship.

No, to football fans outside the plains states, what the redheaded, fifty-year-old Osborne symbolizes is a state of mind—the unbridled passion, power, and pride that is Big Red football. The special knot Nebraskans have lovingly tied each and every fall for almost a hundred years, a bond built on the belief that Saturday, not Sunday, is the day of worship and red, blessed red, is the color of courage, of commitment, of choice. All in a state where the soil is rich and so are the memories of Lyell Bremser, legendary voice of the Huskers for forty-five years, shouting, "Man, woman, and child! Look at those Cornhuskers roll!" A state where simplicity reigns and, should you get the urge, you can start your day with a bowl of Big Red Corn Flakes or move on to your maker with the words "Go Big Red" proudly etched on your gravestone.

Nebraska. Fields of winter wheat. Cattle country. The Oregon Trail. Pony Express. Boys Town. The sweet smell of summer corn. Warm, weathered faces. And, of course, the most righteous image of all—that of the mighty Cornhuskers dressing in their red-carpeted locker room, feeding at a training table fit for a king, studying in a $1 million academic center, growing bigger and stronger and tougher in the home of Husker Power—the gleaming $5 million, 13,300-square-foot Strength and Conditioning Center—practicing in a new $3 million indoor facility and, finally—hallelujah!—bearing witness in front of a 76,000-member congregation in Memorial Stadium, clapping and cheering to high heaven. A scene so inspiring that awestruck recruits, seeing what it's like to live in the third largest city in the state—which is what Memorial Stadium is on autumn afternoons—can only gaze around the stands and gasp, "They sure live for red around here, don't they?"

That they do. Of course, so the stereotype goes, there's little else to live for. No beaches or mountains to escape to. No sun-splashed resorts. No professional sports franchises of any kind to dilute the sporting dollar or chill a football fever. No other Division I schools competing for local talent. Even the university's own basketball team, the only logical source of comparable athletic excitement, struggles near the bottom of the Big Eight. "It's the only show in the state," says Bud

Pagel, an associate professor in the university's journalism department. "It's the one combining force that allows us to feel important."

But most important? Why, those who start—and star—on fall afternoons. Not so much football players as they are survivors of a finely tuned, fiercely competitive, complex program where depth charts run ten deep, strength and conditioning have been elevated to art forms, and acres of athletes battle each year. About 60 percent are in-state kids, walk-ons mostly, prized players from places like Kearney, Gering, Broken Bow, and Burr, who grow up dreaming of wearing the scarlet and cream. The remaining 40 percent define what Nebraska football has become in the late 1980s: the second home to speedy blue-chip black athletes from the inner cities of Chicago, Los Angeles, Houston, and New Orleans. Defensive backs, linebackers, running backs, split ends, strangers in a strange land, all struggling to adjust— socially and otherwise—in predominantly white Lincoln. Trying to cope. Struggling to understand the pain, the plea- sures . . . and the pressures of big time football in a state where, as one former player found, "you get brainwashed. Nebraska football is everything—you eat, sleep, and drink it."

Just what are the hard truths about Husker football and the man who symbolizes it? The perfect program? The cleanest coach? Myth or reality? The truths, it seems, lie somewhere in between, for indeed the Holy Huskers have "sinned" in recent years. Season tickets have been sold for thousands of dollars, star players have snorted and smoked cocaine; others have turned to steroids to maximize size and strength, boost- ers have paid backfield stars for yards gained and touchdowns scored, and federal authorities have investigated cocaine and steroid rings operating in and around the football team. And since 1984 the local police have cited player after player for speeding, assault, theft, and other serious crimes.

The fog has mixed with a light rain, blanketing downtown streets in a misty shroud. The city's version of a night-light—a giant red N—glows brightly above an entrance to Memorial

Stadium, the concrete confines quiet but foreboding, a re-minder that come Saturday, about 5 percent of the state's population (1,594,000) will squeeze inside for an NCAA-record 156th consecutive sellout, screaming "Go . . . Big . . . RED! . . . Go . . . Big . . . RED!" until their lungs seem to burst.

In the shadow of the stadium stands the nerve center of Nebraska athletics: the South Stadium Office Building, a modern two-story structure set just off 10th Street on the western border of campus. Nebraska, or UNL (University of Nebraska–Lincoln) as it's officially known, is a public land-grant institution. Chartered by the Nebraska Legislature back in 1869, it boasts such distinguished graduates as authors Willa Cather and Roscoe Pound. Today more than 25,000 students attend, majoring in agriculture, architecture, the arts and sciences, business administration, engineering, and journalism, all the while browsing the art gallery, museums, and planetarium that add color and quality to university life.

The late hour finds the parking lot at South almost de-serted save for a few sports cars and one aging, wood-paneled Ford Country Squire LTD station wagon. The wagon is parked in its usual spot, hugging the sidewalk nearest the door, its front bumper kissing the sign that reads "Assistant Athletic Director." It's Osborne's car, his spot, the "Assistant Athletic Director" his "other" job for the past nine years.

Red double doors pull open. To the right is a long hallway lined with administrative offices. To the far left, a bank of ticket windows. Dominating the main-floor decor, however, are eleven glass trophy cases of various shapes and sizes. All are filled with pieces of Husker history, tributes and trophies awarded to those who have served the school ever since the first ball was snapped way back at NU in 1890, when under the direction of Dr. Langdon Frothingham, a faculty mem-ber, the Huskers shut out the Omaha YMCA, 10–0.

. . . A picture of coach Frank Crawford (1893–94) . . . a leather game ball inscribed November 14, 1914, Nebraska 35, Kansas 0 . . . a black and white photo of the 1970 national championship team . . . the "World's Longest Telegram," yellowed with age—signed by more than 46,500 fans from

"Cornhusker Land," who sent it to Miami on December 31, 1970, to be presented hours before the New Year's Day game against LSU. *To: Coach Bob Devaney. From: Norbert T. Tieman, Governor, J. J. Exon, Governor Elect. Congrats and Best Wishes to the Finest Coaching Staff in America. You are Number 1 with us. We are Very Proud of you. Go Big Red.* . . . Silver trophies from the Cotton, Sugar, and Orange bowls . . . marbled replicas of the Outland and Lombardi awards won by linemen Rich Glover, Dave Rimington, and Dean Steinkuhler . . . Mike Rozier's 1983 Heisman . . . dozens of Big Eight title trophies . . . All-America certificates honoring the likes of Rodgers, Kinney, Tagge, Larry Jacobson, Rich Glover, Willie Harper, John Dutton, David Humm, Vince Ferragamo, Junior Miller, Jarvis Redwine, Jimmy Williams, Roger Craig, Rimington, Steinkuhler, Rozier, Irving Fryar, Danny Noonan. The glory days—and men—of Nebraska football.

Names and faces aside, the watershed moment of modern Husker gridiron history undoubtedly occurred in 1962 when a dynamic, demanding coach by the name of Bob Devaney rode in from Wyoming. In the previous five seasons, under coach Bill Jennings, the downtrodden Huskers had won just fifteen games and never once reached .500, slipping to the bottom of a barrel that had seen the team post only three winning seasons since 1941. Tickets were a dime a dozen. Farmers tended their crops on Saturday.

Enter Devaney. First-year record: 9–2. Second year: 10–1, a Big Eight title, and a 13–7 victory over Auburn in the Orange Bowl. In the next nine years, from 1964–72, the legend-in-the-making put Husker football on the map, winning or sharing the conference crown 7 times and—Glory be!—earning 2 national championships. When Devaney finally retired after the '72 season, missing in his attempt for an unprecedented third straight No. 1 ranking, he left behind a storied past: a 101–20–2 won-lost record at NU and a .829 winning percentage; and this bit of news: he was passing the coaching baton to a handpicked successor, his meditative, methodical offensive coordinator, thirty-four-year-old Tom Osborne.

Now, fifteen years later, what's known around Nebraska as the Devaney-Osborne Era stands without equal among college football coaches. To wit:

▸ 26 straight winning seasons (neither coach has ever had a losing season)
▸ An overall record of 247–52–4
▸ 17 straight years in the wire service (AP or UPI) Top 10
▸ 19 consecutive seasons with 9 or more wins
▸ 18 straight bowl game appearances

Moreover, under Devaney-Osborne the program prospered into one of the most profitable in the nation, annually grossing more than $10 million in revenue from ticket sales, radio and television, and other sources—enough to support seventeen other intercollegiate sports programs. Sources of six-figure revenue included the heavy-hitting 400-member Touchdown Club, the Husker Awards program, the mom-and-pop Extra Point Club, and the 650-member Beef Club, which contributed cattle and cash toward the training table. Nebraska also boasted an active and sophisticated network of out-of-state booster clubs led by the powerful 2,000-member Californians for Nebraska. The California club, founded back in the late 1920s by former football team manager Otto Baumann and 1929 letterman Felber Maasdam, annually chartered planes and brought as many as 600 "Californians" back to Lincoln each season. The club anted up thousands of dollars in rights fees each year to have Husker games broadcast over radio stations in the state.

Upstairs on the second floor of South, preparations for Game of the Century II are in full swing. It's after 9:00 P.M., and defensive coordinator Charlie McBride, fretting over OU's wishbone option attack, is drawn over his desk, fiddling with a pencil and protractor, refining ways to slow down the Sooners. Out in the hall, grad assistants hustle in and out of doors the color of candied apples carrying canisters of film. Red-framed photos of Rimington, Steinkuhler, Rozier, and Rodgers dot the walls. Empty trays of take-out Chinese and Italian food sit stacked with discarded overnight Express Mail envelopes near the stairs. The floor is calm but energized, like a huddle before a key play.

A day-old newspaper is picked up from a table. Suddenly a presence is felt. It's Osborne.

"Good to see you again," he says.

He has aged considerably since we last met, mostly around the blue-gray eyes. His ruddy complexion appears a bit more wan and waxy than 12 months earlier. Tall (6'4") and as thin as a ballpoint pen, his most distinctive feature—the wavy carrot-colored hair—is thinning slightly on top, growing gray and scraggly.

The strain is understandable. In February 1985 Osborne submitted to double bypass heart surgery for two obstructions in his main left artery, no doubt a function of heredity (his dad had died of a heart attack a year earlier) but also of the grueling, stressful pace he kept the previous twenty-five years—the eighty-hour workaholic weeks, the relentless recruiting, the years of swimming in what Osborne likes to call "the goldfish bowl" of Nebraska football.

There were other reasons as well, ones not always aired in public but equally taxing. Simply put, since 1984 Nebraska football as most fans know it—the holy roller image—had changed, taking a sad and shocking turn toward lawlessness, at least by NU standards. Since the early days of 1984— leading right up to Game of the Century II—Osborne had been burdened by an unremitting wave of personal and professional problems that left him shaking his red head, as he did one day during the '86 NCAA investigation, admitting, "I just never, the last couple of years, have encountered a period where it seems so many things besides coaching come up. It's been a very distracting and difficult period to go through . . . It's a tremendously turbulent time."

How difficult? How distracting? How turbulent? Tom Osborne had been faced with:

▶ The crushing 1-point loss to fourth-ranked Miami on January 2, 1984, in the Orange Bowl, a 31–30 upset that cost top-rated Nebraska a national championship.

▶ The death of his beloved father, Charles, on February 13, 1984, of a sudden heart attack.

▶ Mike Rozier revealing to the *Pittsburgh Press* in February that he had received illegal financial aid from "some alumni" and in October of that same year telling *Sports Illustrated* that he had signed with an agent in August 1983, before his senior season and had received $600 a month—$2,400 in all—making Rozier, in effect, a professional.

▶ Charges leveled in December 1984 that Osborne had offered illegal inducements to former USC offensive guard Booker Brown—charges instigated by agent Mike Trope and flatly denied by Osborne, who took a lie detector test to support his innocence.

▶ The August 13, 1985, suicide of senior tight end Brian Hiemer, the day fall practice was to begin.

▶ Rozier being named as defendant in an "alienation of affection" suit filed by Lincoln real estate salesman Chuck Waldron in October 1985.

▶ A series of December 1985 and January 1986 articles in *Sports Illustrated* magazine detailing steroid use by several members of the 1983 and '84 teams, including former Outland and Lombardi award winner Steinkuhler.

▶ A major five-month NCAA investigation in the spring of 1986 into suspected recruiting, ticket, and "extra benefit" violations in the football program.

▶ A ticket scandal involving the misuse of pass-list privileges by sixty NU players that broke three days before Nebraska's 1986 season-opener against Florida State.

▶ The October 1986 NCAA announcement that the football team had been placed on a maximum one-year probation for, among other mistakes, violating the NCAA's "extra benefits" rules. The probation did not affect postseason play, television appearances, or scholarships in football. The university did not appeal.

▸ An August 1987 *Philadelphia Inquirer* investigation that
alleged sports agent Art Wilkinson, thirty-two, of Philadelphia, had built his practice on an "unusual association"
with the University of Nebraska football program, an association that included Wilkinson's obtaining restricted sideline passes for several Nebraska home football games in
1985 and '86—the only agent in the country to have such
access to a college team.

▸ A dizzying array of dozens of player problems—everything
from academic worries to drugs, steroids, traffic tickets, car
accidents, shoplifting, breaking windows, burglary, and all-
out police brawls involving All-America middle guard
Danny Noonan and defensive star Broderick Thomas.

"I'd certainly say we're not perfect," Osborne admitted one
fall afternoon in 1986, during the NCAA investigation. "The
only thing I feel comfortable telling you is, I'm almost positive that in the years I've been here we've never bought a
player. But once they get here, you've got a problem. This is a
football-crazy state."

But how crazy? How big a problem? Osborne said he wasn't
keen on the idea of anyone poking around the "goldfish
bowl," stirring up the waters. At one point that fall the man
who admits to being "a little paranoid" about negative news
became so uneasy that receivers coach Gene Huey, who has
since left the program, asked a certain young Lincoln
woman to lunch, Huey going so far as to volunteer to pick the
woman up at work.

"I need to talk to you in some depth," he told the woman,
who was a major source of information about the program.

At lunch, according to the woman, Huey flipped open a
notebook and began reading from a prepared list of questions. According to the woman, who had known Huey for
nine years, the questions went like so:

"Was the contact in Omaha responsible for tickets?"

"The cars, they come out of Omaha, don't they?"

"Do you know who is supplying steroids to the football
team?"

"Did a reporter mention anything about players getting paid for football games?"

"Do you know anything about [former Nebraska assistant academic counselor] Marsha Shada and her personal life?"

"Who supplied the drugs?"

"Have you ever seen Irving [Fryar] take cocaine?"

"Do you really think Mike [Rozier] and Irving might have thrown the Orange Bowl? Do you think they might have played loaded? Do you think they'd do that? I don't want to think they'd do that. I understand from some of the guys he [Irving] was involved [in gambling] here."

The woman answered to the best of her ability, and when she had finished Huey gently closed his notebook. The next morning, when she arrived for work, the woman noticed a message on her desk:

"Please call Coach Huey."

She called.

"Would you mind coming by the athletic office?" asked Huey.

"When?" said the woman.

"Right now," answered Huey.

"He was very insistent," recalled the woman later.

The woman arrived at South at about 11:00 A.M. As she climbed the stairs toward the football floor, Tom Osborne was standing at the top of the stairs. "Understand," he reportedly told the woman, "we're not trying to do anything deceitful. We're just concerned about the program, about possible NCAA violations."

The woman says she was escorted to a room adjacent to Osborne's office. There, she says, she was introduced to an attorney representing the university. Another woman sat nearby behind a stenotype machine. The visitor says she was asked to state her name, address, and age. The questioning began. When it was over, some thirty minutes later, the university lawyer had never asked about the Orange Bowl game, the contact in Omaha, or anybody getting paid to play. He did, however, pursue this line of questioning:

Did you talk to [a specific reporter]?
"Yes."
Did he talk about tickets?
"Yes."
Did he talk about using booster cars?
"Yes."
Gambling?
"Yes."
Taking drugs?
"Yes."
Steroids?
"Yes."
And what did you tell him?
"I told [him] a lot of things."

MONDAY

8:33 A.M.

Outside The Cornhusker Hotel, at 13th and L streets, it's 47 degrees on a dim, dark morning, a gray film coloring the horizon. Downtown is faintly funereal; only three or four cars motor down O Street—the main east–west artery—making Lincoln appear simpler and smaller than the numbers (pop. 183,000) suggest, but then Lincoln rarely moves to the big-city beat; it's more easy listening, calm, congenial, gentle to the eyes and ears. A city where people stop at crosswalks, hold open doors for each other, and generally give true meaning to the words "Heartbeat of America." A city, to be sure, fortified by a full set of bars and movie theaters, places the college kids can warm their bones when the arctic winds slash through the plains like a saber, sending the temperature plummeting and setting teeth a-chatterin', but small town nonetheless.

The state itself—home to Father Flanagan's Boys Town ("I have never found a boy who really wanted to be bad"), three-time presidential nominee William Jennings Bryan, Henry Fonda, Malcolm X, William F. "Buffalo Bill" Cody, and Cather and Pound—derived its name from the Indian name for the Platte River, the state's principal water source. The exact date of settlement is not known, but archeological evidence indicates that the first pioneers were prehistoric Indians who hunted big game 10,000 years ago. The Nebraska region later became the main highway of history leading to the exploration and settlement of the west.

It officially gained statehood in 1867, 2,000 years after pottery makers called the Woodlands People had entered the area from forest regions to the north and east. They lived near small streams from 100 B.C. until around A.D. 1000, when portions of Nebraska, as we know it today, became populated by villagers sharing small earth lodges, growing corn and beans, and fishing and hunting for wild game. It wasn't until 1750 that white men—fur traders and salt prospectors—encountered the Indians and traded beads, cloth, and metal. In 1803 Nebraska was part and parcel of "America's Best Buy," the Louisiana Purchase. Shortly thereafter its fields and streams were explored by Lewis and Clark (1804), Zeb Pike (1806), and Stephen Long (1819). Fort Atkinson and Fort Karney were built to protect fur traders from Indian and British interference and the thousands of travelers passing overland along the Oregon Trail. Then on March 1, 1867, thirteen years after President Franklin Pierce created the Kansas and Nebraska territories, Nebraska became our 37th state, only to see a bitter quarrel erupt over the location of an official state capital. Forces north of the yawning Platte River supported Omaha or Bellevue; the southern side backed a site in Lancaster County. The latter eventually won, and on a hot July afternoon the village of Lancaster, in the southeastern section of the state, was selected. It was renamed Lincoln in honor of the late, great president Abraham Lincoln.

On this day in the land of Lincoln, before dawn's first light, Tom Osborne had sat down to his standard breakfast of Shredded Wheat, skim milk, sourdough bread (toasted), and decaffeinated coffee before sliding into his Ford wagon and driving carefully to work. He arrived at his parking spot slightly before 7:00, as he does almost every morning, ready for a ninety-minute defensive meeting. Over the next five days he would spend virtually every waking moment—some ninety hours in all—preparing and posturing about what was arguably the biggest game of his career.

In many ways, Tom Osborne had come to a crossroads. On one hand, here was the winningest football coach of the 1980s, respected and secure enough to turn down several tempting NFL offers to remain at NU, where since 1982 his team had finished the season ranked in the top five four times; he'd pretty much done it all, except, of course, for winning that national championship, a point, Osborne admitted, "People get real upset about." But not quite as sore as over this Oklahoma issue. The 3 straight losses. The 4–11 record since 1973. All those last-minute heroics.

No sir, you didn't need a hearing aid to catch the moaning and groaning, the rising resentment over NU's failure to put the Sooners away. How in big games NU had assumed Osborne's passive personality; how, frankly, they weren't nearly as tough, physically or mentally, as other schools. How Osborne was not relating to today's athlete; had outlived his usefulness. Sure he kicked some ass in the seventies and eighties, but what about the nineties? What about the future of Husker football?

Now toss in the scheduled arrival of some 540 media members—250 more than at any previous Nebraska home game—all looking for an angle, prying into personalities, the psychology of the game, and the coaches. It all boiled down to P-R-E-S-S-U-R-E.

"I would hope our consistency counts for something," Osborne once said in answer to his critics. "I can't control the national championship. If some of the teams are better than we are, then there's nothing I can do. The important thing is we have a good football team and play well. That really, honestly, is my No. 1 goal.

"Ultimately, it may sound hokey, but really the only thing of lasting value is what happens to the players. And if I feel that most of them are lesser human beings for having been here, then really, I haven't done a very good job and I ought to get out of it."

One native Nebraskan, now living in California, went so far as to tell the *World-Herald*'s influential sports editor Michael Kelly that if the Huskers lost again maybe it was high time—whether the players became lesser human beings or not—that Osborne started checking the "Coach Wanted" ads. Maybe, said the fan, the time was ripe to "hold a postgame ceremony in which dignitaries give speeches and thank Osborne for his great years, and then give him a motor home and send him on his way."

"We can't live under this man's jinx," the fan told Kelly.

Jinx or not, in fourteen full seasons under Osborne, Nebraska had come painfully close to claiming the No. 1 spot three times. The first time, in 1978, after 5 straight losses to Switzer and OU, Nebraska, finally, prevailed in the regular season, 17–14. Despite being upset 35–31 at home by Missouri the following week, NU earned an Orange Bowl bid and looked forward to playing undefeated (11–0) Penn State for the national title. But Penn State had other ideas and ended up playing—and losing—to Alabama 14–7 in the Sugar Bowl. NU's bowl opponent: Oklahoma. Talk about letdowns. This time the Huskers lost, 31–24.

"Put me as low as I've ever been in coaching," Osborne once said of that loss. "I wanted to chuck it all right there."

He felt the same way after the 1982 Orange Bowl against top-ranked Clemson. A series of bowl upsets early in the day had given the 9–2 Huskers an outside shot at the national title. A convincing win over the Tigers would have done it. But again the Huskers failed, this time by a score of 22–15.

"Toughest loss of my career," Osborne said afterward.

One more chance. Miami, Orange Bowl, 1984. Nebraska entered the game undefeated (12–0), ranked No. 1, and riding the crest of a 22-game unbeaten streak. Oddsmakers installed NU as a formidable 11-point favorite over the Hurricanes. President Ronald Reagan lauded the team as "Not just No. 1 in the country, but . . . one of the great football teams in the history of the country."

And why not? The '83 Huskers had it all: a cool-handed magician behind center in quarterback Turner Gill; a Heisman Trophy–winning I-back in Rozier, who would ramble for more than 4,700 rushing yards, far and away the most by any Husker back in history, and score an NCAA-record 52 touchdowns during his brilliant career; a dashing, flashing wingback in Fryar, soon to be the No. 1 pick of the entire NFL draft; and right guard Steinkuhler, a junior, who would sweep the Outland and Lombardi awards his senior year.

Yes sir, the '83 team was a runaway train, careening along at unstoppable speeds, piling up eye-popping points and yardage totals: 48 points in one quarter, 41 points in just 2:41, 5 games with more than 600 total yards. The "Scoring Explosion," as the team came to be known, opened the season by scoring 44 points against Penn State in the Kickoff Classic. It was 56 the following week against Wyoming, then victories over Minnesota (84-13), UCLA (42-10), Syracuse (63-7), Oklahoma State (14-10), Missouri (34-13), Colorado (69-19), Kansas State (51-25), Iowa State (72-29), Kansas (67-13), and—yes!—Oklahoma (28-21).

At a December "Double Hundred Celebration" honoring the coaching accomplishments of Devaney and Osborne—the only two coaches from the same school to achieve 100 career victories back to back—the dinner turned into a night to remember for the '83 team as well. President Reagan sent his video congratulations, calling Devaney and Osborne "miracle workers" and the team one of the greatest in history. He ended the tape with the requisite message: "Go Big Red."

Bob Hope was on hand, as were U.S. senators James Exon and Edward Zorinsky and Governor Bob Kerrey. So were 3,200 other supporters—including eighty former players—all packing Pershing Auditorium, joining Gordon MacRae as he led the crowd in "God Bless America." Tom Osborne, at the pinnacle of his coaching powers, entered the auditorium to a thunderous standing ovation.

But the cheering suddenly stopped in Miami. In a stunning

first quarter, freshman quarterback Bernie Kosar (later of Cleveland Browns fame) came out throwing darts and piled up 17 first-period points before the Huskers batted an eye. 17–0, Miami.

But Nebraska rallied. Steinkuhler scored on a 19-yard guard-around "fumblerooski" play that faked Miami out of its collective jock. Then, just as the half was drawing to a close, Gill edged over from the one to make it 17–14. But after Nebraska tied it 17-all with less than two minutes gone in the third quarter, Miami stormed ahead, 31–17, entering the final 15 minutes. Again Nebraska valiantly fought back. And after I-back Jeff Smith, replacing an injured Rozier (147 yards in 3 quarters), sprinted 24 yards for his second TD of the quarter, this time with just 48 seconds remaining, the scoreboard read "Miami 31, Nebraska 30."

Now Tom Osborne had a choice—the biggest decision of his coaching career. Most fans figured he would kick the extra point and take the tie; the betting line on the man being he was anything but a gambler. "That's Nebraska," folks would say. "That's Osborne. Conservative. Dull. Nice. No guts."

What Tom Osborne did, however, made for a moment, as Steve Marantz of the *Boston Globe* once wrote, in a *Sport* magazine article entitled "Saint Thomas of Nebraska," that Nebraskans remember "the way people recall where they were and when they heard John Kennedy had been shot." One gallant gesture. One decision that, in the end, helped humanize the big business of college football. Made it a game again, to show the rest of the sporting world that Nebraska— which for all its success had come to represent an impersonal (red) army of athletes—was human too.

In his frank and revealing 1985 autobiography, *More Than Winning*, Osborne closes the prologue with just this moment in Miami:

"Irving!" I shouted. I had spotted Irving Fryar, who had run off the field. "Tell Turner to run the two-pointer." I sent him back in with instructions to call the two-point play we had worked on in preparation for the game.

As our team huddled, the crowd noise was so loud that

I could hear nothing else, but it was also so constant that I stopped noticing it. I was alone with my thoughts. People say that in moments of extreme danger they have had their whole lives pass through their minds. It was kind of like that for me. . . .

The team broke the huddle, moving away from me so I couldn't see the players' faces. I couldn't tell if there was confidence in their eyes or anxiety. *Darn!* I thought. Biggest play of their careers and maybe mine, and down here on the sideline I have the worst view in the nation.

Irving lined up in a slot formation to the right. Jeff Smith lined up in a wing position to the right of him, and our split end lined up outside both Jeff and Irving, giving us three receivers to the right side.

On the snap Irving drove toward the inside, taking with him the strong safety, who was playing him man-to-man. At the same time Jeff ran to the flat area vacated by Irving and our split end. Turner rolled to his right. "He's open!" someone yelled in my ear. The man trying to stay with Jeff was not going to be close enough to cover Jeff before he had caught the ball and sprinted the three yards to the end zone.

Turner released the ball into the night sky. The roar of the crowd crescendoed. And for an instant it looked as if we would connect and score. But the man covering Irving saw Jeff running to the outside, left Irving, and started for Jeff. He slipped slightly, then regained his balance and lunged desperately for the ball. He got two fingers on the ball and barely deflected it, causing it to bounce off Jeff's shoulder pads as he made a futile effort to turn and clutch it.

Some of the players on our sideline, who had twisted their bodies to help Jeff catch the ball, fell to the ground silently. A couple of them pounded the turf with their fists. A few others kicked at the ground or stomped around. I just closed my eyes, leaned over, and put my hands to my knees. When I opened my eyes, I saw the trampled ground and noticed my dirtied shoes and bright red slacks. Then I stood erect, began clapping, and welcomed our players back to the sideline with encouraging words.

It was a difficult moment, to say the least. The team that had won twelve straight games and had been ranked No. 1 in the nation from the Kickoff Classic against Penn State in late August until the Orange Bowl on January 2 had lost by one point. Some thought it was the finest college offensive squad of all time . . . Yet there it was. Time had run out.

And the team that had gone 12–1 for two straight seasons had come up short again.

He could have kicked the extra point, taken the tie, and been awarded his first national championship. Who could have not voted for such a courageous comeback? Two fingers. The difference between everlasting joy and excruciating pain for many Nebraskans. But not Tom Osborne. And before any second-guessers or outsiders set foot in his locker room, Osborne made a speech. Straight from the heart. "For you seniors," he said, "I hope you got more out of our program than just football and I hope you will take something out of our experiences together that will be of value to you later on in life. To you players who will be coming back next year, we'll start all over and go after it again. You have nothing to be ashamed of. You are a great football team."

His players applauded.

On the way to the team bus Osborne released a statement through Sports Information Director Don Bryant: "I couldn't look my players in the eye if we had gone for a tie. I don't regret my decision."

Neither did many Nebraskans. Public polls, phone calls, and letters to the editor and the athletic department all expressed overwhelming support for his courageous, victory-first decision. A lot of coaches talk and preach about playing to win, going for it, the importance of principles, but when it counted, Osborne never flinched. He went for the Goal above the Game. To many fans of college football his deed embodied coaching and personal glories beyond what any ten sports psychologists can string together. "Greatest thing he ever did," says season-ticket holder Altsuler. "He's a winner. No Nebraskan can fault him for that."

"Many people thought the narrow miss of yet another national championship would be devastating to me personally," wrote Osborne in *More Than Winning*. "It wasn't . . . I guess kicking the extra point and tying the game would have given us the national championship, but that wasn't our goal. Our goals were to prepare well, try hard, and be in a position to win each game. To that extent, we achieved our goals in the Orange Bowl.

"My primary goal in life is to *Honor Him*," added Osborne. ". . . When that goal gets twisted to *honor me*, as it often does, whatever I do has a hollow ring to it; I begin to drift, and things no longer seem to fit."

He chose to close *More Than Winning* with this message:

"My prayer had been to honor God. Sometimes prayer is answered in unlikely ways. To some, our loss to Miami was simply a bitter, disappointing defeat. To others, including myself, the game was exciting, well-played, a credit to college football, and, I hope, within God's view of what football and the human spirit should be."

Such principled pronouncements coupled with .817 won-lost records over fifteen years qualify Osborne as an endangered species in modern sports. These very beliefs, this football faith, remain at the very essence of a man, a "private person," who admits, "I don't view the world the way the average player does or probably the average fan. And that creates tension." As sports editor Kelly noted in an August 1987 column: "Many of us have read his autobiography and have heard him speak of his philosophies and have watched him act and react, but how well do we know Tom Osborne? Maybe only his wife and children, and perhaps a couple of old friends, know him well. More important than the public knowing him, of course, is that he know himself. Of that, there is little doubt."

To understand Thomas Osborne—Dr. Tom as he's often called because of his Ph.D. in educational psychology—his drives, desires, and decisions, you need to go back. Way back. To the rugged homesteaders of the 1870s in western Nebraska and Osborne's admired paternal grandfather, Tom Osborne, Sr., a strict Presbyterian minister who put himself through Hastings (Nebraska) College in the late 1890s, played a rugged game of football, then devoted himself to God. So much so that while his wife worked their land he took to preaching in stagecoach towns like Bayard and Alliance, walking the forty-odd miles between the two stops if he happened to miss his ride. A hearty soul, a cowpuncher who knew the language and customs of the Sioux and earned the respect of fellow ranchers, he was later elected to the Nebraska State Legislature but lost the post because he had little stomach for campaigning. He just figured folks already knew what kind of man he was.

During this period, near the turn of the century, the family grew, but unfortunately Tom's income did not. Money troubles were often compounded by physical pain. The elder Osborne developed throat trouble, lost his speaking voice, and was unable to preach for several years. Farming was the only way he could support his wife and six children. Two of his sons, Clifford and Charles, were forced to live outside year-round in a tent because there just wasn't enough room in the house.

Charles Osborne was himself a roustabout and football player who worked his way through Hastings College. But he couldn't fully drain football from his blood. So he carried, in the trunk of his car, a uniform he "borrowed" from college, and five days a week he traveled the state, selling Speedwagons to farmers and businessmen, striking up friendships with high school coaches in hopes of scrimmaging with their teams.

Charles's first son, Tom, was born on February 23, 1937. Tom's childhood memories are troublesome, even traumatic at times. He talks about his father's travels and the severe strain it placed on his mother, Erma, a slim, loving redhead with an eye for antiques. "My mom was lonely and, at times, a little anxious," wrote Osborne in his autobiography. "She was home with me all the time, and she expected a great deal of me."

So, it seems, did his paternal grandfather. The two had met only a handful of times, but the grandson remembers his namesake as a dignified man who carried himself well, who loved the outdoors. "I greatly admired the fact that he was a minister and a man of conviction," Osborne wrote. Young Tom was only six when his grandfather was killed in a bizarre accident—struck by lightning at age 65—which placed an even greater emotional burden on Tom, who remembers being "treated more like an adult than a three-, four-, or five-year-old child is normally treated."

"In some ways this was good and in some ways probably bad," he writes. "I learned a lot about being responsible, but I was never quite as much a child as I might have been."

Osborne's was a childhood irrevocably altered by the events of December 7, 1941. The Osbornes—another son, Jack, had been born a year earlier—were visiting Erma's parents, the Welshes, in St. Paul, Nebraska, a quiet, patriotic community, 90 miles west of Lincoln. Suddenly news of the Japanese bombing of Pearl Harbor broke over the radio.

Charles Osborne fairly leaped from his chair.

"I remember," Osborne says, "my dad kinda jumping up and down in his chair and saying something like 'Dadgum, I'm gonna get involved in that.'"

Charles Osborne was thirty-seven years old, but that didn't stop him from enlisting in the army—an act of commitment and courage no other Hastings man his age made. Charles Osborne left his family for five frantic years; at times, Tom recalls, the family would go weeks, even months, without hearing a word. Erma took a job in a munitions factory and taught school to feed the family and busy her mind. Young Tom, meanwhile, spent a great deal of time with his maternal grandparents in St. Paul and tried—unsuccessfully—to cope with the absence of one parent, the angst of another. To make matters worse, he had what today he terms a "frightening experience" while fishing with his uncle Virgil, who had taken over as the father figure in his life. A crack outdoorsman, Virgil had repeatedly warned his nephew about the slippery footing on the bank of one particular pond. Osborne remembers himself as a young boy going "down and down in the pond. Dark, cold water poured over my head." Osborne survived only because Virgil noticed a familiar hat floating on the pond's surface. Reaching down, he pulled a gasping young boy to the surface.

Growing up, Jack had the sunny smile. Tom was moody. Jack received praise and attention. Tom caught criticism— which, he admits, "I didn't handle really well." The results? Osborne says as a child he felt isolated, on the "outs with *everybody* in our family," an alienation fueled by what Osborne remembers as a "recurring nightmare in which German soldiers took over St. Paul and were marching down the street looking for me." The tension and fear were further heightened by his father's pending return. Osborne admits he "almost resented" how it would affect the family's life, but when Charles Osborne returned to Hastings in 1946, the fears of a ten-year-old child faded to love as Charles spun stories about the war, college football, life during the Depression.

Yet overall Tom Osborne's impression of childhood is one of worry and deep insecurity. "Much of my life," he writes, "has been directed toward proving something—what it is I really don't know—but the roots of that striving, I am sure, lie in the events surrounding my childhood experiences during World War II."

The morning sun rises brightly to the east as Tom Osborne pushes the accelerator of his Ford wagon closer to the floor. The speedometer sits at a steady sixty-five. The hills and farmland that parallel Interstate 80 roll by. Osborne adjusts his sunglasses, cutting the glare. He looks sharp in a blue sport coat, red tie, and white shirt, camera-ready for the taping of his weekly TV show in Omaha. He's asked about his autobiography and the lasting effects of his childhood. "My grandmother really raised me," he says. "Mom was there [in St. Paul] on weekends. My grandmother was very strong, you know, and my mom was understandably quite uptight, and I picked up some of that insecurity at the time. I really started having this feeling I never quite belonged anywhere. . . . My mom really expected quite a lot out of me. I was reading by age three. When my brother came along, it really put quite a burden on her. She expected quite a lot. [In] some ways I was always pretty responsible.

"I think the insecurity of that time led me to feel, somehow, I didn't quite measure up and in order to be accepted I had to deliver. I almost unconsciously became very achievement-oriented. To do things in order to be approved of."

His hands close tighter around the wheel. "I really think a lot of people have a very high need to achieve," he says. "There's a certain neurotic element, and I think when I was a kid, I was in a very insecure environment for a while. Consequently you try to strive and prove yourself adequate."

He strived and strived and strived, proving himself on the playgrounds of St. Paul and Hastings. Charles Osborne had moved his family right across the street from the local college, making it easy for his sons to immerse themselves in serious sport, to watch practice and shoot hoops until kindly school janitors flipped off the gym lights. Osborne turned to organized sports in eighth grade. His height and aggressive nature—a coach had told him he'd never be any good "until you're willing to get your face scratched up"—helped him stand out. By ninth grade he was contributing in football (quarterback), basketball (forward), and track (hurdles).

With success, it appears, came a certain cockiness, which Osborne carried into baseball the summer between ninth and tenth grade. Many of his Junior Legion teammates were two and three years older and didn't cotton to his constant chatter. They took to calling him "Yak," often in a derisive manner. "I resented this," wrote Osborne in his autobiography. It didn't help much that he rode the bench and played poorly (hitting under .100)—his first real failure in sports. Sensitive to the razzing and his own poor play, Osborne, in his words, "crawled into a shell" that summer, a protective coating that, in many ways, he still wears today.

"I decided that rather than opening up and expressing myself as I had earlier in the summer, I wasn't going to take the chance of being vulnerable again," he wrote. "So I withdrew and didn't talk much around those guys, and this developed into a general pattern of being reticent, of keeping things inside myself. . . . This served me well as an athlete, because the emotions and sometimes hostilities I had pent up inside gave me tremendous drive and incentive to play well. At the same time, I developed some unhealthy emotional patterns in not really talking about my feelings, expressing neither anger nor joy. I was a very quiet and somewhat withdrawn person during the rest of my high school career, and I trace much of it to that experience in the summer between my ninth and tenth grade years."

Whatever raging fires burned inside him, whatever hostilities he held within, Osborne channeled those emotions wisely. His junior year at Hastings High he quarterbacked the varsity to a near-perfect year (the only loss, to archrival Grand Island, 21–20) and started as a 6′3″ guard on a basketball team that won the state title. In 1955, his senior season, the kid his friends called "Red" made second-team All-State quarterback, All-State in basketball, started at third base on the summer baseball team, finished second in the state meet in the 440-yard dash, and won the discus, an event he had begun practicing only that spring. For his efforts Osborne was named High School Athlete of the Year in Nebraska, more for his versatility, he says, than for any outstanding performance.

College scholarship offers arrived from both the University of Nebraska football and basketball coaches, but no coach called or visited the recruit. Osborne felt slighted by this ho-hum approach. He delayed his decision, hoping to hear from the one school he had dreamed of attending—the University of Oklahoma. "I think had they offered me a scholarship I would have been excited and very interested," he writes. "But I didn't hear from them. I can't imagine how different my life might have been if Oklahoma had been interested in me."

In the end he chose to follow the path of his father and grandfather at Hastings College. He earned All-Conference honors three years in a row as a quarterback, twice more as a forward in basketball. And still the fires burned. Once, six days after a major appendectomy, he started a basketball game. He overcame painful injuries to his elbows and calcium deposits in both thighs. In the spring he ran the 440-yard dash and won regularly—despite a bitter distaste for the event. In his junior year he was selected Nebraska College Athlete of the Year, marking the first time in state history one athlete had won both the high school and collegiate honors. But by his own admission, Osborne's college sports career tilted badly toward compulsion. Take the 440, for example. He ran it every spring for four years, hating it every step of the way but helpless to quit, mercilessly driven to show people he was the best. Who these people were exactly, Osborne wasn't quite sure.

Off the field, he was an island unto himself, living, studying, and eating at home throughout his four years at Hastings. Friends remember a normal social life, and at one point Osborne was engaged to a college sweetheart. But in terms of conventional college experiences—the drinking, the pranks, the parties, a hangover or two—Osborne ("Straight Arrow Oz" to his buddies) was the odd man out.

Osborne sensed this isolation, that somehow his life lacked "reality and vitality," and went searching for help. So it was during the summer between his sophomore and junior years at Hastings, that he drove to Estes Park, Colorado, nestled at the base of the majestic Rocky Mountains, to attend his first Fellowship of Christian Athletes Conference. There, he says, he found himself surrounded by young, energetic college and professional athletes of every race, color, and creed. SMU quarterback Don Meredith attended. So did his All-America wide receiver Doak Walker. LSU star Jerry Stovall. Olympian Bob Richards. NFL quarterback Otto Graham and running back "Deacon" Dan Towler of the Rams.

Estes Park proved a pivotal experience; it revitalized and

refocused Osborne's life and cemented his heretofore fragile
faith in Christ. From his autobiography: "I can't pinpoint an
exact moment, a particular Scripture verse, or a certain
speaker, but the overall conference made an impact on me
that truly started me on my spiritual journey that continues
until this day."

Upon returning to college he continued to major in history
(and minor in political science) but took time to sample
psychology, math, and the humanities. At the end of his
senior year Tom Osborne was awarded the Bronco Award,
presented yearly to the student who has made the most
significant overall contribution to the college.

In 1959 Osborne was selected in the eighteenth round of
the National Football League draft by the San Francisco
49ers, a splendid feat for someone who was (a) from such a
small college and (b) drafted when the NFL had only twelve
teams and not twenty-eight as it does today. Unfortunately
San Francisco had quarterbacks by the names of Y. A. Tittle
and John Brodie on its roster and thus little room for a skinny
rookie quarterback named Red. So Osborne adapted, switching to flanker back, and lasted until the final cut. The 49ers
offered a spot on the taxi squad, but the rookie refused and
told management he wanted to try the ministry instead.
(Osborne had won a Rockefeller grant, which provided for a
free year of study at a seminary.) The experience lasted two
weeks. He rejoined the 49ers, participated in practice sessions, and occasionally traveled with the team, rooming with
quarterback and future U.S. Congressman Jack Kemp.

Released the next season by the 49ers, Osborne was immediately claimed by the struggling Washington Redskins. The
Skins were no match personnel-wise for San Francisco, so
Osborne saw playing time that year at flanker behind current
New York Jets coach Joe Walton. In the off-season he took a
graduate course in psychology at USC. The next year, 1961,
Walton was traded. Osborne, despite a severe hamstring pull
sustained the first day of practice, an injury that required
weekly injections of Novocain, caught 22 passes, second best

on the team, for 297 yards. But the nagging pain and the
Redskins' pernicious ways (they'd reneged on a promise to
pay back $500 owed him for exhibition games) pushed Os-
borne in other directions. Actually, in old ones. He returned
to his home state, enrolled in graduate school at NU, and
began working toward his Ph.D. He had set his sights on
becoming a college administrator.

The next thing Devaney knows, the kid's in his office asking
for a job. "I hired him as a grad assistant," recalls Devaney.
"No salary, but he could eat at the training table and live in
the dorm." Osborne's contribution: counseling discipline
problems and assisting the freshman coach.

1962-64: assistant football coach. Instructor in educational psychology. Teaching and coaching. Coaching and
teaching. He earned his master's degree in 1963 and his
doctorate in 1965. Now the educational psychology department wanted a commitment, but Osborne still yearned to
coach. Decision time. So it was that he walked back into
Devaney's office in 1967 and requested permanent full-time
status. Devaney, now in his sixth year and 47–8 since his
arrival from Wyoming, said yes. He named Osborne his
receivers coach and gave him the recruiting territories of
Kansas City, California, Arizona, and western Nebraska.

Osborne proved as relentless and resourceful a recruiter as
he was an athlete. Last guy on the plane. One more call to
make, one "final" visit. He simply outhustled and outsmarted
the competition, all the while organizing, listening, and
learning, deciding early on he'd resist succeeding Devaney if
the job was ever offered, especially after witnessing how
loudly the local wolves howled when Devaney posted consecutive 6–4 seasons in 1967 and '68—seasons that included a
12–0 embarrassment against Kansas State, a 47–0 shellack-
ing by Oklahoma, and no bowl invites. It was here that
Osborne saw the cold and callous side of college coaching—
how personal letters to the editor can get, how quickly peti-
tions get circulated, how fleeting and shallow "sainthood"
can be.

He began checking around; by the end of the 1969 season

he'd applied for head jobs at Texas Tech and two colleges in South Dakota. Devaney pressured him to stay, going so far as to install a jazzier offense, junking the unbalanced line/full house backfield in favor of the multiple set system employed so successfully at USC and Oklahoma. And it was Osborne who breathed life into it, meeting with NU quarterbacks, mapping strategy, calling the plays on game day. His stock was rising; ditto the team's. In 1969, the team went 9–2 and beat Georgia 45–6 in the Sun Bowl.

The next two seasons, 1970 and 1971, the clouds parted, the sun shone, and Nebraska went 11–0–1 and 13–0 and won two consecutive national championships. Yet what Osborne remembers most of that second title isn't the glory and triumph, but the emptiness he felt at 2:00 in the morning in the Ivanhoe Hotel in Miami.

"Come on. Everybody's celebrating. Let's *do* something," said Osborne's vivacious wife, Nancy, whom he had met while a grad assistant at Nebraska. Her husband didn't budge.

"I'm going to go crazy," said Nancy. "I'm going to go out and celebrate even if I just ride the elevator up and down all night!"

It was then, Osborne wrote, that he discovered his love of the *process*, the bedrock of his coaching beliefs. It's not the wins, the titles, the fleeting fame that's important, he decided, but rather the process, "the path you follow in attempting to win the championship. . . . The relationships that are formed. The effort given. The experiences you have. And when it's over, it's all over! Everything else, at least for me, was kind of an anti-climax."

10:00 A.M.

Bob Devaney sits in his first-floor office at South Stadium wearing a white golf sweater (with a tiny Husker helmet over his heart), dictating a letter. He smiles through weary eyes, apologizing for his tired-looking appearance, a far cry from some fifty years earlier, when he arrived fresh off the campus of Alma (Michigan) College, chock-full of the kind of can-do vigor that led to sparkling years at four Michigan high schools before he joined Biggie Munn's staff at Michigan State. In 1957 he was named head coach at Wyoming and went 35-10-5 over five years before Duffy Daugherty, who succeeded Munn at Michigan State, recommended his former assistant for the vacant NU job. "A tough decision," remembers Devaney. "Nebraska had terrible facilities at the time, the worst in the Big Eight by a long shot. But I talked to a regent named Clarence Watson. I'll always remember what he told me: 'You only go so far at Wyoming. Come up here and you can go to any heights.'"

Devaney began scaling those heights by opening the 1962 season with a forward pass. As Altsuler recalls it, the ball didn't land within spittin' distance of the wide receiver, but the fans—who'd had their fill of NU's painfully predictable offense—rose up and cheered anyway. A Standing O—for an incomplete pass. For the next ten years they rarely sat down as Devaney's boys won 83 percent of their games, while their colorful coach worked the state like a presidential candidate, slapping backs, making speeches, throwing down drinks, especially over at places like Misty's or the local legion hall, where coaches and fans congregated after home games to drink and dance the night away. "Those Wyoming guys had a lot of fun together," remembers Darryl Brown, a Lincoln real estate executive and Big Red booster.

When Devaney retired in 1972 with his 8 Big Eight titles, his 2 national crowns, Coach of the Year honors up the wazoo, and a lifetime record of 136-30-7 (.806 percent), best in the nation at the time of retirement, he remained aboard as Nebraska's athletic director, a job he had first accepted in 1967. Now in his early seventies and a member of College Football's Hall of Fame, his name gracing the school's sports complex, he downplays retirement talk and says he has never regretted the decision to name Osborne as his successor. "I didn't want to lose him," says Devaney. "Tom always had a great driving force to be successful."

"I did not want to follow in his footsteps," Osborne once

said. "I knew how difficult it would be. But I thought that if I didn't take this job, I might never get one." So Tom Osborne was named Nebraska's head coach at thirty-four years of age, one year ahead of his personal timetable. The potential, he knew, was enormous, but so were the pitfalls. He asked for a five-year contract. He got it at Devaney's insistence.

He rode the roller coaster those first five seasons, struggling with the inevitable coaching comparisons ("The first few years were tough because of the contrast between Bob and myself"), receiving praise for a combined record of 46–13-2, harsh criticism for 5—count 'em, 5—straight losses to OU, including a 27–0 frosting right out the chute. ("Huskers Discover Futility" read one headline.) He was too conservative, too aggressive, too nice. The heady rush of a New Year's Day spent at the Orange or Cotton bowls was replaced by lesser December dates in Tempe (Fiesta), Houston (Astro-Bluebonnet), and Memphis (Liberty). Make no mistake, the heat was on—even at home, where one of his young daughters, Annie, once shouted, "I'm going to move to Oklahoma if we lose to them again!"

It was shortly after yet another butt kicking in Norman in 1977 (38-7) that Osborne says he made a discovery, no doubt thanks to his training in psychology. Page 65 of *More Than Winning*: "It's occurred to me often that many problems in athletics—perhaps *most* problems—result from people having an inappropriate understanding of athletics. The problem with some fans, for example, is that they get their sense of worth, or lack of it, from the athletic team they support. They often have inadequate feelings about themselves, so if the team wins, the fans win. If the team loses, the fans lose and they begin to feel worse about themselves."

The solution? "Having a spiritual dimension . . . a reliance on God's grace," realizing the most important thing in life is "not whether you win or lose football games, but rather your relationship to Him."

Fine and dandy if you were of such Christian faith, but frankly football fans in these parts found it a bit bothersome, particularly when OU did a number (31-24) on the Cornhuskers in the '79 Orange Bowl. Folks were fed up, and Osborne was seething. He'd had about enough of the second-guessing and backbiting. In future years the possibility of coaching the NFL Seattle Seahawks (job offered, very tempting), the New England Patriots, the Houston Oilers, and even the Dallas Cowboys made the Lincoln papers. But the University of Colorado job, which precipitated the trip Tom and Nancy took to Boulder in December, was different: Osborne initiated that contact. And the Colorado athletic department responded like car dealers at clearance time, offering all kinds of inducements. But Osborne stayed put. The reasons, he says, were NU's fine facilities and his loyalty to fans and players. Darrell Brown, a longtime Big Red Booster, said at an Extra Point Club lunch one day that he remembers Osborne asking for some more help in recruiting. "Now," Brown said, "we can pick up a recruit on a Friday night and have him back in time for class on Monday morning."

Fast forward to the '80s. In '84, '85, and '86 Nebraska wins 29 times, loses 7, and plays in 3 major postseason bowls (Sugar twice and an upgraded Fiesta once). Yet in these same 3 seasons—after victories over the Sooners in 1981, '82, and '83—the Huskers drop 3 straight games to Oklahoma, twice at home, destroying any chance for a national championship.

"Sooner magic," crows Switzer after the '86 win. "Our kids just never quit believing."

The wolves began to howl once more. Fingers pointed. Grumbles began anew. The team was so tight it squeaked. Osborne's offense was an open—and boring—book. His record against Top 10 opponents was a dismal 12–19, including 1–11 against OU. "Since I've been here," said defensive end Thomas in August 1987, "all I hear is that it's Osborne's fault. 'Osborne does this; Osborne does that.' I don't appreciate that. Coach Osborne coaches to the best of his ability. He's been a play short, one point short."

"Year after year, we've come close," said senior I-back Keith "End Zone" Jones, a burner out of Omaha, another in the long line of All-America candidates at that position. "We've had the 9–2s, the 10–1s, the 11–1s—all those records. But all of them have fallen short of what we are capable of doing. It's happened so many times, it's almost routine.

"You get out into society, away from the football stadium, and you hear people say, 'Yeah, well you always choke.' You get tired of hearing that, especially last year ['86] after the Oklahoma game. People were saying we were going to choke, and [that] we did. Well, we didn't choke, but we lost the game. It's to the point now we have to prove to the fans we can do it."

In order to do it, one of Osborne's cardinal rules of coaching boils down to this: I'm no baby-sitter. Can't be. Not with 200 of you running around here every year. I'll supervise, set policy, issue directives, provide leadership. But I won't hold your hand. "His philosophy is what a person does in his private life, he can't control," recalls Mark Mauer, an ex–NU quarterback (1979–81) and later a graduate assistant coach. "He hopes his influence, the way he leads his life, will somehow have an impact on what a player decides to do."

It has. In addition to twenty-eight All-Americas, the Osborne Era has produced twenty-three Academic All-Americas—more than any other Division I school—yes, more than the Ivies and Stanford. Hundreds of his players have gone on to successful careers as coaches, doctors, dentists, lawyers, local businessmen. Players like former All-America and ex–Oakland Raider and Tampa Bay center Rik Bonness (1973–75), now an Omaha attorney. "Coach Osborne is one of the most sincere, dedicated, inspirational men I've ever met," says Bonness.

"He seemed a little like, um, Clark Kent," remembers four-year letterman (1979–82) and two-time All–Big Eight tight end Jamie Williams, a starter with the Houston Oilers from '82 to '87. "You know, supertruth, justice, and the American way. I'd always try to catch him messin' up, but I couldn't. He was so pure, so truthful. If he told you something today, you could believe it tomorrow."

"He was good, straight, honest," says former Husker running back Albert Lewis, who later transferred to Arizona after a knee injury. "Coach helped me out. He said he'd call anyplace I needed and put in a good word, and that's exactly what he did."

Other players from both the seventies and eighties paint a different picture of the man.

"Morally aloof," replies one ex-Husker. "He builds a wall between himself and his players."

"Intimidating," says another.

"Out of touch with the modern athlete," says a third. "Most guys just want to play ball, get through college, hit the bar, and pick up girls. Osborne doesn't understand average grades or drinking. That's *Star Wars* as far as he's concerned. He honestly doesn't know why someone would get into a fight with a frat guy at a bar."

Osborne's tight time schedule and laconic personality naturally limit interpersonal communication, so he delegates much of the daily discipline duties and player counseling to his assistants—nothing unusual in major college football these days. "Nothing came to him unless it was necessary," says one former grad assistant coach. "The [assistants] handled everything. Nobody bothered the coach unless it was necessary." But those who suggest he is "aloof" and "out of touch" do raise a valid point. Osborne does tend to be less accessible, to detach himself more than most coaches, to build that wall between himself and his athletes a little higher than, say, a Switzer, Paterno, or Holtz; he consciously seems to avoid kibitzing or social spontaneity. In the mold of a Tom Landry, he tends to observe, to teach, remaining guarded with respect to his feelings—unless pressed—aloof on any subject outside football. So much so, that even after four and five years of strapping on helmets and running his drills, star players like Thomas can only shake their head when asked about their leader. "Every time I went home, everyone would say to me, 'Oh you're playing for the legendary Tom Osborne,'" says Thomas. "You know, 'What a great coach,' 'What's Tom like?' I was shocked. 'Tom is ah, ah, ah, Tom is very nice,' but that wasn't a good enough answer."

There are no easy answers. "He's a hard guy to get close to," remembers a former NU quarterback. "I guess because he figures he's only got you for four or five years and then you're gone. He's not a coach you could slap on the seat and say, 'How you doin', Tom?' He's really under control, very businesslike, a lot like Landry."

Prior to the 1987 season, however, Osborne consciously tried to alter his image, to lose a little of his famous self-control. To mellow out. To relate. During the summer he took far more time off than normal—escaping for four-day fishing trips to Canada, Wyoming, and Colorado and day trips to Lake McConaughy in western Nebraska; in years past he'd have taken only one such excursion. And later in the summer, when twenty top black athletes mustered enough courage to complain about being afraid of venting their emotions and told him, "Coach, we don't know you. People ask what you are like and we don't know what to say," he didn't evade or dismiss their plea. He listened.

A meeting was held at the Hewitt Center, which houses both the team training table and the academic lab. Starting cornerback Charles Fryar was one of the players who attended the forty-five minute session led by senior wingback Von Sheppard. "It brought us closer together," he says. "It seemed like we wouldn't see him that much. As a defense, we didn't see him. He didn't coach us. It seemed like Coach McBride was our head coach. So now he's more on both sides of the ball.

"You know," adds Fryar, "most of us are from cities. Down in Norman they always had a chance to speak out. And here, you know, I guess, during Coach Osborne's reign, his team has always been portrayed as himself. So this year we kinda got together and had a talk with him. He said emotion is good, to use emotion, but not to run our mouths and not be able to back it up."

Back it up they could. In preseason polls in both *Sport* and *Inside Sports* magazines, the Huskers were ranked No. 1 in the country. The Associated Press, meanwhile, slotted them right behind top-rated Oklahoma. This would be the year

Osborne, the mags predicted, would find the missing link, claim that elusive national title, a thought that even the coach conceded had crossed his mind.

"Yeah," he said when the polls came out, "I'd like to win one."

Certainly this team was capable, with ten starters (six offense, four defense) returning from a squad that had finished fifth in the AP balloting the year before. Jones, who had led the conference in rushing (830 yards) and touchdowns (14), and Thomas were returning All–Big Eight picks. There was improved speed at split end and wingback and a smallish but speedy defense anchored by Thomas, defensive tackle Neil Smith, and strongside linebacker LeRoy Etienne. Question marks? An inexperienced offensive line (one returning starter, preseason All-America guard John McCormick), Noonan's replacement at middle guard, and Taylor's erratic play. At 6'0", 195 pounds, the junior quarterback was unquestionably a gifted athlete, fleet of foot, nimble, and strongarmed. But his numbers (42 percent completion rate) and error-prone play—particularly in big games—were worrisome, especially in the face of the Cornhuskers' toughest schedule in years. As many as six legitimate Top 20 teams were on the slate: UCLA and South Carolina at home, Arizona State and Oklahoma State with Heisman-hopeful Thurman Thomas on the road, improving Colorado in Boulder. And, of course, you-know-who in Lincoln.

The first two weeks were a breeze. NU opened the season by blowing past Utah State, 56–12, then showed its true mettle by dusting third-ranked UCLA, 42–33, as Taylor threw for 217 yards and a school-record 5 touchdowns, breaking the old mark held by Gill, Ferragamo, and Humm.

Starting fullback Micah Heibel (6'1", 225) was one of that game's many heroes. He ended up being featured in the *Sports Illustrated* story about the game, an account detailing how Heibel, in typical Big Red fashion, had blocked hard and "dug for extra inches." The story also noted that after the game Heibel took the stage at Chesterfield's on 13th Street and sang with his band, Brain Hammer, a parody of a fictional heavy-metal group called Spinal Tap. "We don't do 'Sex Farm,'" said Heibel, "but we do 'Hell Hole.'"

To many *SI* readers Heibel (rhymes with *bible*) was just another number—No. 48 to be exact—in a long line of cherub-faced, corn-fed, wide-bodied blocking backs who seemed to roll off the Lincoln assembly line every year. Another of those local hotshots who spurned other schools to stay home and star for the Huskers. Which, in this case, was about half right. Heibel, a *Parade* All-America, All-State, and Nebraska Defensive Player of the Year as a senior linebacker at Lincoln's Pius X High, had stayed home, all right, nixing a scholarship at Notre Dame to take his chances in Lincoln. And a chance was about all he was offered. But like so many other hometown heroes, he took it, finding the experience rewarding but rife with hidden pressures. "I don't think there's anyone out here who hasn't wanted to quit at one time or another," he said.

The simple reason relates to numbers. At Nebraska you can't ignore the numbers, the depth. In practice they come at you in waves, red, white, yellow, and black jerseys stampeding past like cattle to auction, dozens and dozens of fresh faces each and every year. Bigger, taller, tougher (or so they think) than last year's model. All hoping to catch an eye, to crawl over some other blue-chipper on the ten-deep. Yes, to play at Nebraska—to make it like Heibel—requires extraordinary attributes. Patience for one. Pride. Talent. And above all, Perseverance. "A player might get two, three years of development before he even plays," notes strength and conditioning coach Boyd Epley. "The end result is more depth, more people ready to come off the assembly line, so to speak."

So to speak. For in Osborne's world, building a better Husker is like preparing for Oklahoma or Kansas State—or even landing a trout. To coin a phrase, it's a process. Players must be indoctrinated, educated, strengthened, programmed, before they are ready. That's why true freshmen or sophomores—particularly non–skill position players—rarely walk right in and contribute. It took Heibel four years to see serious game action. Converted to fullback out of high school, he started on the undefeated freshman team in 1983. He moved up to fourth string during spring ball the following year before, like 90 percent of all Nebraska sophomores, he was redshirted, in effect stored away for a year to work the weights and better learn the system. Then, when he started messin' with the big boys, banging away day after day in practice, the injuries hit, as they always do at this level, stalling his progress. Third string in fall '85, he got hurt (ankle) and slipped back to fourth team. Up to third (injured again), back to fourth. He finished the '86 season on the second team, averaging 5.6 yards on 54 carries. But the pain of '85 lingered. "When they moved me to fourth [string, the scout team] the last time," he said, "I didn't stay intense. I never have handled the pressure of being filmed and graded [every day at practice] very well. Then, when the third-string guy got hurt, they took the fifth-string guy on the traveling squad for two weeks. I remember the week of the Oklahoma game. All the coaches were so intense. I knew I wasn't going to travel. I just wanted the season to end."

"It was so much like a business," recalls tight end Williams. "When I left there, I think I was kinda burnt out psychologically on football because you got so much of it. Ah, it was such a stressful situation. Because you know when you're losing it's stressful because they're always making changes, and when you're winning it's stressful because they want to continue winning. And they've got so much tradition there it's always five, six guys behind you, hungry, waiting to get their shot."

"Sure we put pressure on guys," says Epley. "But isn't that what athletics is all about, being the best?"

"Nobody wanted to believe what happened."
That's what folks said about Brian Hiemer: Wanted to be the best. Never gave up. And at Nebraska his rags-to-riches tale inspired walk-ons and scout teamers, overachievers who dreamed of climbing the ladder. The "Comeback Kid," they called him. A 185-pound walk-on, he was cut outright following his first spring practice. "He was pretty marginal," recalls

Osborne. But Hiemer persuaded Osborne to give him one more chance in 1982, and through nothing more than want-to, he rose rapidly from tenth string to eighth, to sixth, to third. Finally, in 1985, his junior year, he shared starting tight end duties with Todd Frain, catching twelve passes, including a team-leading 4 touchdown receptions. In the '86 spring game the rangy, powerful (6'3", 218) senior-to-be was the star of the show, scoring the game-winning touchdown on a leaping grab between two defenders. In the classroom Hiemer carried a solid B average in mechanized agriculture. In high school he'd been an All-State kicker and tight end on a team that won the Class C state title. He had been yearbook editor and prom king, and had sung in the school choir. His IQ was listed at more than 120. "He was a high achiever," said assistant coach Huey. "He didn't want to fail at anything."

That's why nobody in Nebraska, certainly no one in his hometown, the quiet, sweet-corn community of Shelby, Nebraska (pop. 720), certainly not his parents, Loyola and Willard, or his teammates could understand why on August 13, 1985, the day varsity players were to report for fall practice, Brian Hiemer, just twenty-one years old, walked behind a wooden shed on his parents' 320-acre farm and shot himself one time in the head with a .22-caliber rifle.

"It was a very difficult thing to accept because nobody could understand why," Osborne said at the time.

The Hiemer home, white and wood-framed, looks a little lost, standing as it does near acres and acres of cornfields just off a dirt road outside Shelby, some thirty-five miles from downtown Lincoln. It's a sultry September day in 1985, and a leaden late-afternoon sky is streaked with ribbons of blue. Inside the house, cooled by several shade trees out front, Willard and Loyola Hiemer and a few family members gather around the dining room table, fighting back tears. Proudly displayed on a nearby cabinet is an eight-by-ten photo of Brian in uniform—No. 94—smiling on team picture day; Brian again, in another shot, flashing his high school ring.

The room barely breathes as the family mourns. Willard, in plaid work shirt and jeans, his face leathered from years in the fields, keeps a close watch on his wife, who sniffles and shakes as she tries to speak. "No one knew what went on inside his head," says Loyola Hiemer, her voice a whisper. "Brian wasn't one to talk about it. He kept things . . . to himself." Willard walks outside. As he stands near the fateful spot, tears well in his eyes. Brian, he says, had come home from school on Friday. Over the weekend he mowed the lawn and walked the fields with his dad. By Tuesday, however, Brian seemed unusually quiet and restless. At about 3:30 it started to storm, so Willard hustled the tractor through the north fields and up to the house. It was just after 4:00 when he arrived. As he parked the tractor he noticed his son in a sitting position with his head back against the shed. Odd, thought Willard. Brian's car was all packed; he had a team meeting at 5:00. Why would he be sitting behind the shed?

The emergency call was logged into the local sheriff's office at 4:06. The ambulance arrived at the Hiemer home eight minutes later. In heavy rain Hiemer was transported to Columbus Community Hospital, where he was pronounced dead shortly after arrival. "I wish I knew, I'da done something," says Willard. He glances back at the house long enough to see Loyola staring out the back door. "I hope she's okay," he says softly. "She won't let go.

"You look for something, a warning. . . . Maybe there was a reason, but Brian didn't tell us."

Family and friends could only mourn Hiemer's passing and ask themselves why. "Nobody wants to believe what happened," said Bill Morgan, owner of the A and B Cafe in Shelby. "Everyone wants to know why." Twenty miles away at Aquinas High, basketball coach Dale Kerkman remembered how his starting center enjoyed practice more than games. "Brian's happiest moments were shoving, laughing, playing pickup games with his buddies," says Kerkman. "No. 1 position on the No. 1 team—maybe that's not that big a thing. Maybe this shouldn't shock us so much. We elevate Nebraska football to such a high level, a religion."

"He told us it was no big deal," said Father Robert Roh of Aquinas. "He said people made too much of it—the idolatry associated with Nebraska football."

Back in Lincoln, Kriss King, a classmate who had dated

Hiemer briefly in the spring of '85, says that Hiemer, with an eye on a pro career, was trying unsuccessfully to put on weight. "At lunch one day he told me if he could put on twenty pounds he could be an All-America," says King at her off-campus apartment. "He'd sit down with two entrees, two of everything. He said, 'I'm so sick of stuffing myself all the time.' I think he was a little frustrated." Epley, however, says that Hiemer showed none of the telltale signs of steroid use. "Brian was everything you look for in an athlete," he says, "academically and physically."

Dan Krafka, who once lived with Hiemer, had eaten lunch with his good friend on Thursday. "We talked about girls, football, how hot fall ball had been." For all his talk, Hiemer rarely dated around campus, preferring to work out, ride his bike, or play a round of golf. A big night out for him, away from the rigors of football and his mechanized agriculture major, was bellying up to the bar at the Lucky Lady and pulling on a longneck Pabst. Says King, "I told him, 'Brian, nobody drinks Pabst Blue Ribbon anymore.' He just laughed." King, Krafka, and Husker teammate Gregg Reeves all recall that Hiemer, in the days before his suicide, acting anxious about his future, worried about life back home. "That's the only change I noticed," said Krafka. "He went home a lot more often the last month or two. Almost like clockwork. He never missed a weekend." Says Reeves, a defensive end on the '85 team, "He didn't think that with just him and his dad it [running the farm] was economically feasible."

Whatever the reason for Hiemer's passing, his death left an indelible mark on Husker football. Players chose to wear the numeral 94 on their helmets during the '85 season in tribute to their teammate. Osborne stressed how Hiemer's death placed football in a different light. But still, he told Steve Sinclair of the *World-Herald*, "You just pick up and go on. I'm sure Brian and his family would want it that way.

"I told all the players they are important to us," added Osborne a few days later. "Whether first or fourth string, they are important to us as people. Many times, if young people realized the impact [suicide] has on family and friends, pals, they wouldn't do it. Hopefully it will be a learning experience here."

Back in Shelby, Loyola Hiemer trembles while reading sympathy cards at her kitchen table. The house is deathly still; Willard is out in the fields. "Today is especially tough," she says. "The first day of school."

The only sound now is of her tears. Softly, she begins to speak. "Every day," she says and sighs, "every day is tough."

The third weekend of the 1987 season. Nebraska traveled to Tempe to play 12th-rated Arizona State, a game televised nationally on ABC-TV; the Big Red prevailed, 35–28, thanks to a 3-yard Taylor scamper with 3:37 left. Jones's 62-yard sprint had moved NU to ASU's 8-yard line, setting up Taylor's TD. "Playing in front of a large crowd [71,264] and in this kind of heat (93 degrees), it makes you grow up a lot," said Osborne. "We got a good dose of what it takes to win."

On Saturday, October 3, the Huskers faced some more bad medicine: explosive South Carolina (2–1). The visitors held a 21–13 lead midway through the third quarter, but the Cornhuskers rallied behind reserve quarterback Clete Blakeman, a cagey, twenty-three-year-old senior who had entered the game when Taylor went out with an injured shoulder and severe headache—compliments of the Gamecocks' kamikaze defense. Behind Blakeman the Big Red scored the game's last 17 points and won, 30–21. Jones shared star billing, gaining 61 of his game-high 129 yards in the fourth quarter. He also scored 2 final-period touchdowns. "I was thinking, 'Hey, we can't lose this football game,'" he said after the game. "If we lose this game, we're going to pretty much be out of the goals we set this year. We talked about it in the huddle, and the guys just gave extra effort. That's when the holes started opening." Closing, too. Thanks to the likes of weakside linebacker Steve Forch, whose booming hit with 9:58 remaining and Nebraska trailing 21–19, caused a fumble that senior safety Jeff Tomjack recovered. Four plays later Jones scored from the three to put the Huskers ahead to stay.

Tomjack was one of the special ones, too. Growing up in

tiny Ewing, Nebraska (pop. 550), he listened to Bremser's call on radio. "When I was little, in third grade," he said one day, "I was just like everyone else in this state, listening to the game on the radio. There was one guy in my hometown who had season tickets. I begged and begged and begged, and finally one year my parents took me to a game. I couldn't believe it. We walked around downtown. It was a sea of red."

His twenty-three-member high school class had eighteen boys, so Tomjack was pretty much the entire offensive show in football (2,057 yards rushing, 3,501 yards passing, and 45 touchdowns.) *Sports Illustrated* even chose him as one of its famed "Faces in the Crowd." Now as a 6'1", 210-pound senior, Tomjack had the kind of body—and face—high school girls pine over, oblivious, perhaps, to the stiff price No. 11 had paid to wear the Big Red jersey.

Recruited in '82, he lost the entire year to major reconstructive surgery on his knee that kept him out of school until January '83, when he still ran a 4.7 40 and got off a vertical leap of 34.5 inches. Started at strong safety on the freshman team. Redshirted in '84. Lettered behind starting safety Brian Washington in '85. Played in every game—and started twice—when Washington went down with an injury in '86. This season was much the same song. Play nickelback in passing situations. Hustle down on kickoffs. Don't make mistakes. In your spare time, earn a 3.42 average in premed. Answer a lot of hometown how-comes.

"People see me do these things in football in high school, and it's tough to explain why I'm not able to do the same things here," said Tomjack. "They don't realize, I don't think anyone realizes, what goes on around here. . . . During practice—and during games, maybe—you feel like you're playing not to make plays, but not to screw up because you know they'll find it on the films. We've had people, sports psychologists, come in and talk to us about that."

The Huskers let their talent do the talking for the next three weeks. Kansas fell like phone lines in a tornado, 54–2, as Oz emptied the bench. Oklahoma State was blown away 35–0 as Thomas, the nation's leading rusher at the time, was held to 7

yards rushing. Kansas State crumbled, 56–3. It was only after
Missouri (42–7) that, uncharacteristically, the victors began
to boast—words that would later taste suspiciously like crow.
Iowa State was next. The Cyclones tumbled (42–3) like so
many dominoes. After a week off, it was time to play Game of
the Century II.

1:00 P.M.

The week's first practice is still two hours away. On campus—
a clutch of comfortably aging red-and-white-brick buildings—
students shuttle back and forth between classes. Most wear
the standard midwestern collegiate garb, a grab bag of jeans,
tennis shoes, backpacks, and parkas. The trees are bare, the
sky gray and gloomy. Snow scents the air. In the bright two-
story Nebraska Bookstore, Springsteen's *Tunnel of Love*
blares over the loudspeakers, sending students swaying and
singing as they pick through music posters, swimsuit calendars, school supplies, and—what else would you expect?—
two large main-floor sections devoted exclusively to something called The Big Red Collection. Besides the usual assortment of hats, T-shirts, sweatshirts, and posters, what the well-
dressed Husker fan can buy these days are boxer shorts
($8.95), briefs ($5.95), suspenders ($10.50), car mats
($26.50), bumper stickers (When You Play NEBRASKA SHIT
HAPPENS, $1), even wallpaper (thirty-three square feet for
$21.95) and ice scrapers (69¢). There's even a stack of the
Fellowship of Christian Athletes–sponsored Tom Osborne
videos for coaches and parents wanting to "develop character" in school-age kids.

Back across campus, at the bustling sports information
office (first floor, South Stadium), associate SID Tom Simons
and assistant Chris Bouma prepare for the upcoming media
blitz. Simons, a bearded, affable sort, feels like a cheerleader
at prom time—more requests than he knows what to do with.
More than 500 credentials . . . and counting. And it's only
Monday. "The only people I haven't heard from yet," he quips,
"are the Japanese."

Ten minutes after 1:00 P.M., Tom Banderas takes a seat

outside Simons's office. Banderas, twenty-two, is 6'2", 245, a senior, and an All-Stater from Oak Grove (Missouri) High. Curly-haired with a choirboy face, yet strong enough to bench press 365 pounds, he had alternated at tight end with junior Todd Millikan all season, blocking as Nebraska tight ends are expected to block, that is, like a bull, while snapping up 8 passes—6 for touchdowns, 3 in one game (Missouri), a game after which Banderas bluntly predicted that Nebraska would kick the living shi . . . uh, daylights, out of Oklahoma.

Ironically, considering his earlier boast, he now viewed Oklahoma as little more than a means to a very big end. "We need to win this game as much as any other," he said. "I don't think anything's going to get in the way—the lights, the cameras, anything." He said the team was now competing against itself. "I just don't think the Nebraska Cornhuskers have to play their best ball game of the year to beat Oklahoma. We're a good football team, ever since the preseason games when we had some tough ball games and we had to come from behind in the fourth quarter and jelled as a team. The chemistry came in there somewhere."

Banderas shifted in his seat. "Our goal this year is to win the national championship," he said. "We're not going to let anything distract us this year, because it happened in the past, and we ended up losing a ball game we had total control of."

You mean like last year, against Oklahoma?

"That's right," said Banderas. "We're just tired of seeing that. We're just plum tired. It's not gonna happen anymore."

Last year, it was suggested, was rough around here. The NCAA investigation, Noonan's bar fight, defensive tackle Neil Smith and middle-guard Lawrence Pete nabbed with a bottle of steroids . . . police problems ad infinitum. This year, same thing. Smith and Pete arrested for slashing tires on a police car. Thomas getting tossed in jail after a scuffle with the cops over some unpaid parking tickets. Etienne arrested in early November for breaking a window in the apartment of a former girlfriend—no charges were filed—but a week later, at a team meeting, Osborne laid down the law. "The thing is," said Banderas, "he might have put more heat on us. He kinda put it if you get in trouble with the law and it's your fault, you're off the team. There's no more playing around, no more second chances. We're all 19-, 20-, 21-year-olds, and if you can't stay out of trouble and just dedicate, say, four or five months to win a national championship, something you can only do once in your life, you just don't deserve to be here.

"He was kinda upset. He said, 'It doesn't matter. Nebraska is a good program. If someone gets in trouble—I don't care if it's Steve Taylor—if he's wrong, he's gonna be off the team.'"

Did he say this at a team meeting? "Full team meeting. Downstairs in the meeting room so everybody knew it. I think we're gonna take heed now, and I know me and my buddies, the last three or four weeks, we've stopped even going out to bars to have a good time. We've just really dedicated the season to winning a national championship."

Forch slipped in the interview chair next. His light brown hair, thick neck and shoulders, and toothy grin just the kind of combination that swivels a woman's head—and hips—in a bar. A 6′2″, 240-pound senior, the team's starting weakside linebacker and leading tackler, Forch was another of those bright Lincoln lights. He starred at Lincoln East High only to find himself in limbo behind All–Big Eight performers Marc Munford and Kevin Parsons his first four years at NU. Like Heibel and Tomjack—and so many other Huskers—Forch had overcome frustration, long odds, and injury (mononucleosis in April '87, arthroscopic surgery on his shoulder in the fall of '86) and worn the redshirt for a season. But like few others, he'd blossomed into a true team leader, the kind who stays up all night switching channels on the tube because his mind won't let his body succumb to sleep. "I'm really ready to play," he said. "It's been a long week, we had a week off . . . we're all getting kinda antsy. I think the attitude is this is the game that makes or breaks our season. You know, I'm a senior, and I've seen us lose in '84, '85, and '86. I think last year's game really sticks in a lot of peoples' minds as something that shouldn't have happened.

"I look at this as one of the biggest weekends of my life as far as coming through and doing what I have to do. You know, I've been here five years, and I've had good players in front of me. You know, Marc Munford was in front of me, and he was a great player. I had to redshirt last year with a shoulder injury, so I said to myself, 'I'm gonna come back here next year and start.' This definitely means a lot to me—this is my last chance. My first chance, really, and my last chance really to play against Oklahoma. I want to do my best."

3:30 P.M.

In groups of twos and threes they strut and stroll out of the locker room, fresh from a film session and position meetings where individual and group goals are set. Dozens of cleats clickety-clack across concrete leading from the locker room under the South stands to the bright light, open air, and artificial turf of Memorial Stadium. An oval facility originally built back in 1923, it had undergone a number of facelifts and improvements over the past twenty years, pushing its listed capacity to 73,650, a number exceeded by 3,000 fans each and every Saturday. Great fans, too. Not obnoxious booze-hounds hell-bent on making asses of themselves. No, rather the type that ABC's esteemed college football announcer Keith Jackson once lauded as "the most informed" in college football, the kind of folks who sit on their seat cushions all day, bundled up in red, and root, root, root for the home team, but when an opponent upsets the home-boys—as Florida State did in '85—chances are they'll cheer the visitors, too.

The shrill of a coaching whistle. The team huddles without delay. Practice starts, the cadence crisp and calculated, like clockwork. With Taylor at quarterback, Heibel and Jones behind him, and Hendley Hawkins at wingback replacing an injured Dana Brinson (out with back spasms), the redshirted first offense runs a passel of Power I option plays against the yellow-jerseyed scout team defense. Over and over and over. And over. Bread-and-butter football. The toss sweep. The inside isolations. The power pitch. The sprint-out passes. It's an offense Osborne critics have termed predictable and dull, but actually, like a game of chess, the Nebraska offense is deceptively complex, keyed to split-second reads, moves, and countermoves. The playbook contains as many as 120 different plays, though Osborne tends to read the same pages— again and again. So what? say his supporters, including a coach named Switzer. "Those people [critics] know nothing about football. Nothing," the OU coach once said. "Everyone knows what Nebraska is going to do! The trick is stopping it! You don't win with schemes or playbooks. You win with players. Nebraska uses only six or seven running plays, but they execute them. I mean how many plays can you run off the I-formation?

"Football is a game of repetition," continued Switzer. "Other people run the Nebraska offense, but when they run the ball on first down, it's second-and-eight. When Nebraska runs it, it's second-and-two. Then they run it again, and it's first-and-ten. I like that type of predictability, those down and distance factors. I want to tell you something—you try to stop it."

Wearing grayish sweats and a red wool Nebraska cap, arms clamped tightly to his chest, Osborne patiently patrols practice in silent thought, like a proctor during final exams. Criticism, when it comes—which isn't often—is low-key and instructional in nature. A better blocking base. A sharper cut. *Dadgummit, let's think out here, fellas.* "He only gets upset when kids make the same mistake over and over," says assistant coach John Melton. But nobody screams or yells; Osborne won't permit it. "When it happens," says Melton, "which isn't often, he just points to a spot at his shirt where it says 'Coach.' We know what he means."

Today his assistants are as strong and stable a group as any in the nation. Five full-timers—Melton (linebackers), McBride (defensive coordinator/line), Milt Tenopir (offensive line), George Darlington (secondary), Frank Solich (running backs)—have nine or more years of service with Osborne.

Melton: the bespectacled, mischievous elder statesman. In his twenty-sixth year of service, he remains the lone link between the Devaney and Osborne eras. The former Wyoming fullback looks like your next-door neighbor, chuckling as he points to the office plaque that reads "We Interrupt This Marriage to Bring You the Football Season."

McBride: eleventh season, a prep All-America in two sports in high school (football and baseball), an All–Big Eight end and punter at Colorado, he eventually played in the old AFL for Denver. Fiery, fastidious, well dressed, and the leader of Nebraska's famed "Black Shirt" defense.

Tenopir: Native of Harvard, Nebraska, twelve years of line duty working with the likes of All-Americas Rimington, Steinkuhler, Bonness, and Tom Davis. Former high school coach in Colorado, Nebraska, and Kansas.

Darlington: fifteenth year. Master's degree from Stanford. Mr. Versatility. As a coach, he had moved from secondary to defensive end and back again. Brains behind the development of four Husker All-America defensive ends—George Andrews, Jimmy Williams, Derrie Nelson, and Bob Martin.

Solich: rising star. Handsome Tom Watson looks. Name most often mentioned as heir apparent if Osborne retires and takes over the athletic director job. All–Big Eight fullback and co-captain of undefeated 1965 NU squad. Coach at Lincoln Southeast High from 1968 to 1979. NU freshman coach for four years, rolling up a 19–1 record. In ninth year of coaching varsity stars like Rozier, Jeff Smith, Doug DuBose, Roger Craig, and Tom Rathman (the last two currently the starting backfield for the San Francisco 49ers).

The message Osborne sends to his staff is this: "I'll pay you more than most and won't meddle, but don't let me catch you cutting corners or standing alone on too many when it comes to recruiting." Osborne's greatest demand on these men and the rest of his ten-man staff comes in the vital area of recruiting—perhaps his most obsessive concern. Consider the call Melton says he received in February 1985, right after Osborne's open heart surgery and just twenty-four hours before national letters of intent could be signed.

"I got this call," says Melton, eyes twinkling, "and on the

other line was this squeaky voice asking how the recruiting was going. It was Osborne. I don't know how in the hell he got a phone in the room."

And woe to those who fail to meet his high standards, who, as one ex-assistant recalls, "lose their fire" for recruiting as that assistant did. Osborne isn't very big in the excuse department. That same former assistant who admits he "flopped" in the recruitment of talent-rich Texas saw his territory changed to include dreary North and South Dakota. "That's about as mad as I've ever seen him," said the assistant who left the program shortly thereafter.

4:30 P.M.

Game of the Century II. No. 1 vs. No. 2. National championship on the line. Some coaches would be breathing fire, spitting out quotes like coins from a Vegas slot. Not Osborne. Standing near the goal line of the new facility after his first-ever indoor practice, he puts it on autopilot and starts right in as he always does, calm as can be, droning on with the daily injury report, telling a tight gathering of writers how Brinson strained his lower back tying his shoes and, oh yes, Neil Smith's right ankle is still bothering him and, oh yeah, this new field house sure is nice.

"Tom," interrupts a local writer, "you were just named No. 1 in both polls today. Your reaction?"

"Well, I've got mixed feelings. We're probably as deserving as anyone right now . . . I don't think it makes any difference if we're one or two because it will be settled on the field. So it really doesn't have much effect on the situation here right now."

Writer (the gates have officially opened): "Coach, does the loss of [Sooner quarterback Jamelle] Holieway and [fullback Lydell] Carr [both out with knee injuries] put more pressure on you? Fans expect Nebraska to win now. Do you feel that pressure?"

"Well, I think there's a lot of people here that expect us to win if we were playing the Chicago Bears." Laughs all around. "There's that kind of pressure anyway. I think realistically it's already been beaten to death."

Writer: "Earle Bruce got fired today . . ."

Osborne perks up. "He did?" Pause. "You don't want to follow Woody Hayes or Bob Devaney. It's not easy."

By the time Osborne finishes, remarkably fast for a man whose team has just hit No. 1 in the nation, more than a hundred sweat-stained players have streamed out into the night. All but Thomas. He remains behind, leaning against a cream-colored wall near the entrance, head back, eyes shut tighter than a Pullman shade. Slowly he begins to speak. "Tired of the wait," he whispers. "It's gettin' harder and harder day by day. Thank God tomorrow's another day."

Someone wants to know how he's passing the time. His eyes pop open.

"Listening to the Beastie Boys," he says. "Thinking of big plays. Thinking about a lot of heartache. Last year. The last two years. All the embarrassment. Redeeming myself and helping the team redeem itself as a national power. That's what it's all about."

And just what is B.T. all about? Few in Nebraska would profess to know—including Osborne. From day one the irrepressible 6'3", 235-pound defensive end–linebacker had chattered and shaked and baked like his hero, Ali. Overnight his spontaneous towel waving and emotionally charged outbursts off the field—and his remarkable quickness and penchant for making the big play on it—had endeared him to Husker fans all over the state, made his name a household word. Of course, with Thomas one was never quite sure which word that was. One week he pinned the moniker "The Master of Disaster" on himself; the next he was the "Sandman" because he "put people to sleep" with his aggressive style of play; the next he wore a "1987 Hell Raisin' Tour" T-shirt and dubbed that the motto for the 1987 season; next, his controversial cutting tongue was off and running about how Memorial Stadium was "Our House" and nobody except the

Huskers had the key—despite what Holieway had to say. True to form, plastic house keys became all the rage in Lincoln.

Yes, it was Thomas who unquestionably shattered the mold when it came to the media. "Broderick spoke out and said some things that needed to be said," explained Keith Jones. That he did. For centuries it seemed NU players had signed the same nonaggression pact as their head coach. "We just want to do our best." "Kansas State can be a very dangerous team." "I just got lucky today." Dullsville. Now, thanks to Thomas, the players were talking. And talking. And talking.

Thomas had arrived at NU in the fall of 1985 as a heart-stopping prospect out of Houston's Madison High, where he was named the state's Defensive Player of the Year by the *Houston Post*. Turned off by what he termed the "bullshit" of then–Texas A & M head coach Jackie Sherrill, Thomas turned instead toward Nebraska, in part, he says, "because I got no promises from Osborne . . . the only coach who doesn't shoot you no bull. Talk to him one minute and you know he's not crooked." The nephew of the Chicago Bears' perennial All-Pro middle linebacker Mike Singletary, Thomas was a hit—and a hitter—from the start. Just the kind of ball-hawking, in-your-face defensive stud Osborne needed to slow Oklahoma's speed and deception on the line of scrimmage.

After playing in 8 games as a freshman, Thomas earned All–Big Eight accolades his sophomore year, recording 58 tackles (third best on the team), 4 quarterback sacks, and 6 fumble recoveries (a school record, including 3 against Colorado, a single-game record). Now, in his junior year, opponents were paying him the ultimate athletic compliment—running the other way. A preseason pick by Big Eight writers as '87 Defensive Player of the Year, Thomas had rebounded from a slow start—brought on by ten extra pounds and poor concentration—to lead the Black Shirts with 29 unassisted tackles and 5 sacks.

But being Broderick, he made almost as much news off the field, though some of the more—how shall we say?—judicial matters never made the local papers, especially since, according to Lancaster County court records, Thomas was slyly using the last name Singletary (his mother's maiden name) on police citations. (Better to confuse curious reporters.)

Twice Thomas had found himself with some explaining to do, once for lying to police officers after a car accident involving Taylor in November 1986 (the making-a-false-statement charge was later dismissed) and again in August '87, after what Osborne termed a "misunderstanding" over whether Thomas had paid $46 in fines and court costs for an overdue traffic ticket. Some misunderstanding. After a bench warrant was issued for his arrest in late August—Thomas said he'd paid the ticket; the court disagreed—police officers and Thomas argued over whether he would drive himself to jail to pay his fine or get into a police cruiser. A scuffle ensued. It took four officers, using handcuffs and leg restraints, to subdue Thomas—which probably gave some ideas to several Big Eight offensive line coaches. As it was, Thomas was transported to Lancaster County jail and cited for failure to comply with a court order and resisting arrest. A second resisting-arrest charge was added later that night when Thomas, upset over his inability to reach anyone by phone from the jail, kicked over some chairs. Another melee ensued; this time three correctional officers and two police officers were needed to wrestle Thomas back to his cell. Thomas was back at practice the next day, only this time it was Osborne who was doing the talking.

"We told him to just keep his mouth shut," Osborne said.

To the average fan it appeared to be little more than a youthful indiscretion, a regrettable brush with the law. County court records, however, reveal Thomas had compiled a long and rather reckless list of traffic offenses and displayed a rather dubious regard for the criminal justice system. Since October 30, 1985, two months into his freshman year, Thomas had been cited for negligent driving (charges were dismissed), three speeding tickets (he paid a total of $52 plus court costs), violation of a traffic signal (he paid $25 plus costs), and twice operating a vehicle without a license (one was dismissed, for the other he paid $250 plus costs). In five of the six cases a failure-to-appear (in court) charge had been added to the docket sheet—only to be dismissed later, a relatively common occurrence in cases involving football players.

But so what? Local folks probably would have done the same thing. Just Broderick, they'd say. And he'd keep talking, like he was right now, bubbling away, like a bottle of imported champagne.

"It's show time," said Thomas, opening his eyes. "Somebody, *somebody* has to pay. I don't think the boys in red and white are going to pay. We paid the last two years." His voice rises. "*I'm tired of paying!* That's what this is all about. Going to the Orange Bowl. Enjoying shrimp and lobster."

Building now, the words flowing faster. "I'm gonna be calm until Saturday. On Saturday it's just like a volcano is going to erupt. It'll be like a volcano erupting and an earthquake all at the same time. Measuring 8.9—which is my number. Imagine 8.9 on the Richter scale. I don't think anyone can walk on an 8.9, and that's what I'm waiting on."

Waiting. Slumped against the wall again. He brings up the Beastie Boys once more. How they'd "come up from the bottom." How they were "just T-shirt and jeans."

"I like the Beastie Boys," said Thomas. "You don't hear a white group that can rap. They can rap."

How about you, Broderick? Are you gonna rap?

A sly smile creeps across his face. Gold teeth glitter in the artificial light. "Oh yeah," he says, strutting away. "We gonna rap. We gonna rap . . ."

As witnessed by his postpractice press conference, rapping, particularly to the press, is not one of Tom Osborne's favorite pastimes. For the most part his speech is robotic, passionless. Given the proper moments and mood, though— usually around his assistant coaches—he'll engage in droll and witty repartee. ("He's actually very funny," says Melton.) From the perspective of a player or the media, those moments are few and far between. In fact, in more than fifteen years of halftime talks only three speeches stand out: the Liberty Bowl against North Carolina in 1977 when NU trailed

14–7 at intermission, Auburn '81, and Iowa State '86. Both the Liberty Bowl and Iowa State were shockers in the sense that Osborne lost his composure; got pissed off is what he did. Red-faced. Berated the team a bit. Threw in a fistful of *dadgummits*. What made the Auburn speech perhaps the most memorable—storied enough to be preserved on a plaque in the locker room—was the articulation of a predominant Osborne theme: the Us-Against-the-World message. The plaque reads:

"Even though we have been good in other years, this year holds no guarantee. It does not come automatically. Fans are fans. Some will stick with you, some won't. The only people who really understand, the ones you can count on beyond doubt, who will ultimately be with you whether you are 8–3 or 3–8, are the people in this room."

Osborne is a staunch believer in the "people in this room" theory of coaching. "He is really protective," says one former player. "He just hated to see players get into the papers for the wrong thing." And when they do, Osborne's response is often influenced not only by the need to protect his image and that of his program but also by a vexing and sometimes volatile set of "factors" as well—each and every one applied to protecting the program.

Factor No. 1: Osborne's "naive" and trusting nature.

"If you don't put [wrongdoing] right in front of his nose," says one longtime Osborne observer, "he doesn't see it. He puts his blinders on."

"Trusting almost to a fault," says a former Husker assistant coach. "If I was on trial for murder, I'd want him on the jury. He's going to take you at your word. Even if he's got definite proof, it's still fifty-fifty."

"Osborne likes to believe his players," says Mike Babcock, the well-respected beat writer and columnist for the *Lincoln Journal-Star*. "He's done that ever since J.R. [Rodgers] was here."

"You either believe them or you don't," responds Osborne. "I think I come across that way [too believing] because until I have evidence otherwise I'm always going to be on their side.

I don't want to feel like I can't trust them, I'm not a gestapo type guy. But when the evidence is there, then I'll act." Of course, evidence is in the eye of the beholder.

Factor No. 2: hypersensitivity to criticism.

This one is linked to the stress of Osborne's childhood, the demands of early adulthood, his staunch religious beliefs, the theory that Osborne operates on what might be called the "higher plane" theory, that he lives a life above others. Asked if he felt Osborne was sensitive to criticism, NCAA Enforcement Director David Berst replies, "Yes, I have that feeling. And it runs to the institution too. They do not want to tarnish that image."

Factor No. 3: media mastery.

As state senator Chambers suggested, Osborne excels in the fine art of the "qualified" answer, in talking around an incident. He's mastered phrases such as *to the best of my knowledge, as far as I can tell, almost positive, probably, from what I know,* and *I have no evidence.* And any reporter who persists is stonewalled. "He becomes very political," remembers a player.

Factor No. 4: no stone unturned.

Relentless in his pursuit of information. As resourceful as they come. One day while eating lunch with a reporter, he pulled an index card from his shirt pocket. On it, numbered neatly from 1 to 11, were the names of specific incidents or people the reporter was trying to develop and/or contact. Osborne had never even been questioned about half the list, but he knew exactly whom and what angles the reporter was pursuing.

Also in August 1986 the NCAA Committee on Infractions was forced to postpone a hearing with NU after the school filed a record six-inch response to charges—with just three weeks lead time. "We had a couple of attorneys working day and night, a faculty rep, myself," said Osborne. "I don't know what it was, but it was a ton of time."

"I don't know of any university that was ever better prepared," recalls Berst.

Factor No. 5: a certain self-righteousness.

Start with Osborne's deep religious convictions and his persistent push for perfection. Now toss in this observation from a former player: "Nebraskans just think Tom Osborne is this *god!* And I think, I believe, he has a problem with that. I would talk to people about certain things, and they would always say he was right no matter what it was. If he would spit in someone's face—and he would never do anything like that—they would always say he was right." It adds up to a perception of infallibility.

"He doesn't like his integrity to be questioned," says Osborne's younger brother, Jack, president of an industrial irrigation company in Hastings. "He lives [the image]. It hurts when someone has doubts about it."

Factor No. 6: a suspicious nature.

Even Osborne admits he can get "a little paranoid" about negative news. And when he reads it, or senses it coming, he doesn't sit still. At its most mild level, this anxiety manifests itself in frequent calls and letters to reporters questioning a certain slant of a story or the purpose of the piece. Many times Osborne's argument is based upon the skewed notion that the reporter is out to "get" the program—not to report news but to discredit something or someone. "He's not gonna talk behind your back," says Melton. "You're gonna get a phone call or letter right now."

Factor No. 7: retribution.

Osborne is known to have made unsubstantiated accusations against two out-of-town reporters investigating his program. Once he accused them of trying to distract him from his preparations for an Oklahoma game; another time he claimed they were trying to undermine recruiting. Art Wilkinson, the Philadelphia sports agent with close ties to the school, once accused—in his capacity as Osborne's representative—a reporter of offering a former NU player $30,000 for an interview. When the reporter flatly denied the charge, Wilkinson reportedly responded, "Well, it was either $30,000 or $30." In no case, the reporter insisted, was any money ever offered to any source.

In another incident a former player said he was subtly

pressured by Osborne not to talk about his experiences at Nebraska. At one point the player said Osborne suggested a harassment suit be filed against two reporters investigating the program. "Those guys are trying to do a dirty story," he reportedly said. "They're after Nebraska football." Osborne is then said to have asked the player what he had told the reporters.

"I told them the truth," said the player.

At this point, the player said, Osborne replied, "I didn't know you didn't get your degree. We would welcome you back to the university."

The player was later asked if that comment could be construed as an inducement not to talk to the reporters. He quickly said no. Then he thought for a minute.

"Yes," he said, "I guess it was."

"He's the Supreme Being in the state," says an observer. "If you challenge him, you'd better be prepared for the fallout."

His greatest challenge undoubtedly came when NCAA investigators Hale McMenamin and Dan Calandro arrived on campus in the spring of 1986. Together they spent nearly 400 hours during that spring and summer probing suspected irregularities in the football and women's softball programs at Nebraska. Week after week after week they arrived in Lincoln from their headquarters in Kansas City, conducting interviews, checking records, making a general nuisance of themselves. Yet Osborne was guardedly optimistic about the outcome of their investigation; an exhaustive internal probe had turned up no deliberate cheating or ticket scalping of any kind. So when the university informed the NCAA of its findings in a report delivered in late August, Osborne felt reasonably sure the NCAA gumshoes would get little more than tired feet for their troubles.

Then on Wednesday, September 3, the bomb dropped.

The NCAA's powerful Eligibility Committee announced that it was ordering the suspension of fifty-three Nebraska players for one game and seven for two games, claiming deliberate violations of an NCAA bylaw that states, in part,

"Complimentary admission shall be provided only on a pass list for family members, relatives, and fellow students desig-nated by the student-athlete." The committee members were also said to have been disturbed by the players' unethical conduct and by the "misinformation" presented by the school.

"It's an ethical-conduct thing," one unnamed committee member told the *World-Herald*. "The thing that disturbed us was that players put down 'aunt' or 'uncle' when it was a girlfriend or high school coach." If the violations had been unintentional, the member said, the players would not have given a false relationship for their guests.

The decision—the biggest eligibility case in NCAA his-tory—sent Osborne's defense mechanisms into overdrive. He admitted "guilt" (such as it was), agreeing that sixty play-ers—an estimated 80 percent of his top forty—had unknow-ingly broken the rule by inadvertently placing the names of no-goodniks like girlfriends, neighbors, and family friends on the pass-gate list for complimentary tickets for each of Ne-braska's football games during the 1985 season. Major col-leges all over the country violate this ridiculous rule every weekend—and worse. (In fact, the same week Tennessee suspended ten players for the same reason and a Texas newspaper reported that in 1985 forty-six Longhorns had put unauthorized names on their pass lists.)

But that didn't placate Osborne. Not by a long shot. You could almost hear him thinking: *This is what they found after four months of digging. Drugs, illegal recruiting payoffs, point-shaving, academic fraud, cash, cars, women—all compromising college sport and we get sanc-tioned for pass list violations!* Osborne was about to burst a blood vessel as he angrily denounced the NCAA's timing—three days before No. 8–ranked NU played No. 11–rated Florida State in the Huskers' 1986 season-opener. He openly challenged the association's intentions. In a spirit of "open-ness and honesty," he said he'd advised all his players to tell the two NCAA investigators the whole truth and nothing but. He even charged that McMenamin himself had brushed off the pass rule as "unenforceable."

"He told me not to worry about it," said Osborne.

Feeling duped and cheated, Osborne labeled the entire Tix-Fix a "travesty," taking the NCAA head-on, suggesting at one point that he might forfeit the nationally televised prime-time game in defiance of the decision.

"I'm very angry about the whole thing," he said after the announcement. "It looks like cooperating hasn't resulted in any benefits to anybody that I can see.

"We're going to fight it every way we can."

Locals saw red as well, expressing outrage at being "singled out" by a "nitpicking" NCAA. "No Class At All" and "Nuke the NCAA" T-shirts sprouted like seeds in a spring rain. One fan wore a button showing a chicken sitting on a toilet, labeled "NCAA." Democratic gubernatorial candidate Helen Boosalis dubbed the NCAA the "No-Class Athletic Association" and blithely remarked that when the NCAA was finished with Nebraska it "planned on investigating Santa Claus for breaking and entering."

"I think Nebraska should tell the NCAA to go to hell and go ahead and play Florida State," said a seventy-five-year-old Husker fan, Al Bauer, on September 6, the day of the FSU game. Added another fan, Vernon Dill of Gretna, Nebraska, "They're [the NCAA] looking for publicity. So who do they go after first? The Big Red, that's who."

On Thursday, September 4, Devaney had burned up the phone lines making personal appeals to longtime friend Walter Byers, executive director of the NCAA, to intercede on NU's behalf. Byers agreed to the point of contacting Dave Maggard, athletic director at the University of California, and head of the NCAA Council's Sub-Committee on Eligibility Appeals. Maggard's committee quickly granted the Huskers a stay pending an eligibility ruling.

That decision was due on Tuesday, September 9. So it was on Monday in the third-floor employees' cafeteria of Miller and Paine department store downtown, at the first weekly meeting that season of the Extra Point Club booster group, that hundreds of Husker fans lined up to hear what the coach had to say. As Osborne walked in, broomstick-erect, a record crowd of 500 fans stood and thundered its approval. Two reasons: not only had the man engineered a 34–17 drubbing of FSU, but more importantly he'd spearheaded the school's successful appeal of an NCAA decision.

"This has been a very confusing week," said Osborne as he stood behind the lectern at the head table. "Reminds me of the time I spent at Fort Ord in the army. I didn't understand why I had to do things. . . . We had this post commander who liked to keep his finger on everything. He'd call around to various departments checking up on people. One day he called the motor pool—not saying who he was. He asked the private [the fans are led to believe it was Osborne], 'How many vehicles do we have?' The private said five tanks, four half-tracks, and two jeeps that big fat generals like to drive around in.

"Well, the general bristled. 'Young man,' he said. 'Do you know who you are talking to? This is General Evans, the commander of this post.'

"'General,' said the private, 'do you know who you are talking to?'

"'Well, no,' answered the general.

"'Well, then, so long, fatty.'"

Once the long laughter had subsided, Osborne turned dead serious. He explained how neither the NCAA nor Nebraska had found any record of even a single instance of ticket scalping—or of any other major violation.

"We have not bought players here," said Osborne.

He stopped for a second, shaking his head. "The one thing this whole incident brought home," said Tom Osborne, "is what an awesome responsibility we put on our fans and players. I can control how the players get here. I just don't give alums names and phone numbers and tell them we need this guy or that guy and don't care how we get them. But if you make phone calls, or take a player to lunch, what you do as representative of this university I'm ultimately responsible for. It's a hard line to walk."

How hard was evident from reading today's front page of the *Lincoln Journal Star* and *World-Herald*. Both papers ran stories on how tough this year's NU-OU game ticket was to find. A woman looking for a ticket for her week-old baby.

One man, as part of his company's relocation package, flown home to Lincoln from *Kuwait* to watch the game. Fifty-yard line seats, when available, selling for $200; end zones for $100 or more. Each and every dollar of profit deemed perfectly legal in a state that wisely has no ticket-scalping laws on the books. Instead a capitalistic system is left open to react to the forces of nature. Supply and demand . . . demand . . . demand!

It's simple math, really. Memorial Stadium, no matter how you pack it, won't seat many more than 76,600. Now subtract some 40,000 season tickets allocated to the general public, 10,000 for faculty members, 12,000 to 14,000 for students, and 2,000 to 4,000 for fans traveling from the visiting school. Take away a few thousand more for university and athletic department needs. So that leaves us about 6,000 "single-game" seats each week. Great. Now divide that by the remaining 1.5 million fans living in the state, most of whom would give up breathing for a week for the chance to see a live show. And don't forget all those out-of-state booster clubs and fans living in nearby Kansas and Iowa who'd cross the state line to see the Huskers play as sure as look at ya. Maybe that's why 8,000 red-clad rooters regularly travel to Colorado to watch their Huskers play and another 4,000 have been known to motor over to Illinois and South Carolina. And twenty-five thousand show up for the Red-White scrimmage each spring, and 10,000 fans congregate on a weekday afternoon just to watch the *freshman* team play.

Yes, good neighbors, it's no coincidence that Memorial Stadium has been sold out each and every Saturday home game since November 3, 1962—156 games stretched over twenty-five straight seasons, the longest consecutive sellout streak in NCAA history.

Which is pretty much what both McMenamin and Calandro were thinking when they launched their investigation. Yet when all was said and done, they found nothing. Bupkus. Not one verifiable incident of ticket selling by any player; no history of ticket scalping or abuse.

"The problem from our point of view," said Berst, explaining the goose egg, "is not only do we have to come up with the questions, we have to come up with the answers. With Nebraska, no firsthand knowledge was our problem."

One December morning former NU fullback Andra Franklin politely orders eggs ("Over easy, please") and a glass of milk from a young, honey-haired waitress at the Howard Johnson's restaurant in Coconut Grove, Florida. Franklin, in his late twenties, had recently returned to the Sunshine State to finish school and rehabilitate his knee from a serious injury that ended a productive four-year career with the Miami Dolphins. Before getting selected in the second round of the 1981 NFL draft, Franklin, a quiet country kid from Anniston, Alabama, with a bouncer's body (5'10", 225), had lettered four years at NU (1977–80), earning All–Big Eight honors his senior year. A year, he now says, a gray-haired businessman from Omaha paid him between $4,000 and $5,000 for his season tickets. "This guy . . . we worked out a deal," says Franklin while waiting for his eggs. "He just paid me all the money up front, and I just turned my tickets over to him. So at the beginning [of the season] he just gave me a check and I just gave him the tickets. The check was for about $4,000 to $5,000, something like that."

Franklin came to Nebraska dirt-poor and wide-eyed. In high school he'd played everything from nose guard to tight end to linebacker before starring as a running back during his senior year. He'd signed a Southeastern Conference letter to attend Alabama but chose Nebraska after a February recruiting visit where he was escorted around by I-back Curtis Craig, brother of Roger. "The last thing I said to Curtis when he dropped me off," recalls Franklin, "was 'See you next year.' I don't know if he believed me."

See him Franklin did, especially after getting promoted to varsity late in his freshman year. A year in which Franklin says he sold his game tickets "a couple of times" to Curtis Craig. "For good seats, 40-yard line, it was like $200, $250," says Franklin.

In his sophomore and junior years Franklin roomed with a high-steppin' I-back by the name of Isiah Moses "I. M." Hipp.

Franklin said Hipp routinely sold game tickets—as many as a total of twenty per week—to that Omaha businessman during this period. "Isiah knew the guy that bought the tickets," says Franklin, still working on his eggs. "So I sold [mine] to him. We sold together for about two years. . . . For good seats, on the 40-yard line, I'd sell those for $200, $250. And the end zones you'd get anywhere from $75 to $125, depending on who you sold them to."

During his senior year Franklin said he began to deal directly with the Omaha buyer. In a preseason arrangement, Franklin says he was given the $4,000 to $5,000 check in exchange for a weekly delivery of tickets. For a poor kid from Alabama it proved a saving grace. "It helped pay for my apartment," says Franklin. "It was money I depended on."

Nattily dressed in designer jeans and a pea-green raincoat to weather the winter chill outside, tight end Jamie Williams relaxes in the players' lounge at the Houston Oilers' practice facility not far from the world-famous Astrodome. A black and white "Houston Police" cap is perched atop Williams's head, barely covering the sea of soft curly hair that flows over his ears, touching his shoulders in spots. Since the spring of 1983, after the New York Giants tabbed him in the third round of the draft, Williams had kept that head up and those broad shoulders square and blocked as well as any tight end in the NFL. And with looks not unlike another Williams (actor Billy Dee), Jamie was already looking at life after football—talking about movies and modeling and maybe some singing, too.

At Nebraska Williams sure played a pretty tune. A rare four-year letterman (1979–82), he was a two-time All-Conference selection and was voted an All-America by several organizations by the end of his college career. After his senior season, he played in the prestigious Hula and Japan bowls, hanging out and swapping stories with stars like Eric Dickerson, Dan Marino, Curt Warner, Willie Gault, and Anthony Carter. "You hear those guys talk about their schools," said Williams. "Things that were going on. You're out having a good time in Hawaii, you're going to talk about it. Those guys, they'd say shit like 'If I was coming to Nebraska, it's so cold up there, they'd have to pay me this.' Guys would ask me, "Why'd you go to Nebraska? Man, they had to pay you a lot of money, it's so cold up there." And I'd say, 'Man, they didn't pay me shit.'

"They'd tell me things that were happenin' at their school. Like cars, cash, alumni. It was like, wow, dang! I guess we're not doing anything that bad at Nebraska. I was thinking to myself, 'Nebraska has a little room to work with.'"

Where Nebraska kept up with the Joneses of college football, said Williams, was in ticket selling.

"You know," he said, "I really don't see any way of stopping it. . . . All I know is at Nebraska things weren't done flagrant. And the biggest thing at Nebraska were the tickets. . . . I made a lot of money on my tickets, a whole lot of money. That's flagrant. That's why it didn't surprise me when they [the NCAA] questioned them on it. . . . But they [the school] really didn't pay much attention to it; nobody thought that much about it. It was part of the thing. They didn't push it or condone it. It was kinda like they didn't say anything about it."

Williams said that during a season he would generally receive "at least $100" per ticket, often receiving between $400 and $500 per home game for four or five tickets. "I had a couple of friends who would buy my tickets, you know, ah, businessmen, sometimes Lincoln, sometimes Omaha," he said. "I had people wanting my tickets all the time."

Was Osborne aware of the ticket selling?

"He was pretty much a stickler on keeping things straight," said Williams. "I really can't say that about his assistant coaches. A few of them might have known things and didn't say nothing."

Nine other former Huskers, who all asked not to be identified, described as "common" or "very common" the sale of their complimentary tickets to boosters or fellow students. The sale amounts, they said, ranged from $25 per ticket per game to $100. Another player—Rozier—while denying he peddled his tickets for cash, admitted to occasionally trading them for merchandise. "I might take one, once in a while, downtown to trade for a radio, stereo, something like that," he said.

"The whole time I was there," said one player who played in 1981–82, "the going rate was $50 [per ticket]."

"I don't want to lie or anything," said another. "Some guys were making a real killing. Varsity guys [in 1983] would come down to the freshman team and offer to buy tickets for $25. Some freshmen said they were getting $100 a ticket. I don't know if they were bragging or making it up."

Sources say this varsity-freshmen connection dated back to the late 1960s. During most seasons prominent players—or an enterprising offensive lineman or two—would act as a clearinghouse for tickets. Each week they would purchase blocks of tickets (often twenty or more) from varsity team-mates or freshmen for anywhere from $15 to $25 apiece. Then those tickets were brokered to boosters at double or triple face value. Several former players and other sources identified those players who collected and who occasionally sold groups of ducats as Rodgers (1970–72), running backs Tony Davis (1973–75), Monte Anthony (1974–77), Curtis Craig (1975–77), Hipp (1977–79), and quarterback Mauer (1980–81).

Said Franklin, "What they did is, ah, you know, they'd have about five guys collect the tickets, and those guys would take them and give them to just one guy."

Both Davis and Curtis Craig denied selling tickets. "I gave mine to my family," said Davis. Said Craig, "I never sold tickets to anyone." Anthony could not be reached for comment. Hipp declined comment. Mauer denied brokering tickets. Rodgers would not speak on the record regarding ticket sales.

As a precaution against such ticket selling, the athletic department instituted the pass list system in 1985. Instead of receiving "hard" tickets, the players were instructed to rec-ord the names of people using their tickets on a list. In an interview that ran over the UPI wire after the ticket mess broke at NU, 49er fullback Tom Rathman, who started on the Huskers' '85 team, called the system "weird" and unsupervised. "[Nebraska] had a weird way of getting tickets to players," he said. "They [those listed on the sheet] could pick up the tickets a few days before the game or right before the game. They never checked out the people who were getting the tickets."

One member of the '85 freshman team said he still sold his ticket allotment despite the pass list system, "You still had to work at it, but everybody sells tickets."

So who was buying? Former players and other sources describe a vast and eager network of buyers consisting of businessmen, corporations, and visiting booster clubs. One individual name, however, surfaced more often than any other—that of Omaha businessman Everett Alger.

"A serious fan," said Williams.

Serious enough that sources say Alger bought several thousand dollars' worth of tickets from players like Rodgers, Curtis Craig, and Fryar. Williams also said on "a couple of occasions" Alger had purchased his tickets for "a hundred, hundred and fifty dollars." But Williams stressed that other players knew Alger far better. "Turner [Gill] knew him real well," said Williams. "Lots of those guys. Mike [Rozier], Roger [Craig] knew him. Roger introduced me to him, so he had to show me some respect. [But] his boys were the guys who were handling the ball. It was Turner and Mike and Irving and Roger."

Williams and Roger Craig had attended the same high school in Davenport, Iowa. They eventually roomed together at NU. "Me and Roger were tight," he said. "I know a lot about Roger, and he knows a lot about me. Roger was the type of guy who never wanted to get into trouble. But, ah, Roger was also one of those guys looking to the future. And, you know, if he could make a buck he was going to do it. . . . He was worried about his family. His father had died when he was in high school. And he had, ah, a little girl. He was always talking to me about how [he] had to take care of them [his daughter and future wife] and make sure they had a future.

"[Alger] took care of Roger because he had compassion for Roger. Because he was sympathetic to his needs and not because he was playing football for the University of Nebraska. Well, maybe it had something to do with it. Roger was pretty much a part of their family. They kinda adopted him in a sense."

On a sun-kissed Sunday morning, Everett Alger answers the knock on the front door of his $400,000 white brick mansion high atop a hill in northwest Omaha. It's a magnificent home set on 37.25 tree-filled acres, the house well off the street at the end of a long, languorous drive bordered by dozens of weeping willows. A series of columns stretch across the front, giving the house a southern look straight out of *Gone with the Wind* or "Dallas." Inside are expensive shotguns, large-screen TVs, even a downstairs disco. "Everything is big," remembers one visitor. "Big bathrooms, big beds, sunken tub."

On this day Alger's dress is decidedly casual: blue double-knit pants, blue shirt, gray Hush Puppies—a far cry from the French-cut suits and flashy jewelry he's said to favor. He looks to be in his early sixties, although his hair, by far his most distinguishing feature, isn't gray but auburn, almost red, and is combed up in a pompadour style like Elvis Presley's. It affords Alger the look of a country-western singer or that of *Nashville* actor Henry Gibson.

Alger is asked about buying player tickets. "I never bought players' tickets in my life," he says. "Players would give me tickets."

Considering his rags-to-riches story, Clement Everett Alger, Sr., could easily answer to the first name Horatio. Over the years, records show, he's grossed millions of dollars in the supply, poultry, and trucking business. A former Kansas state highway patrol officer, Alger once told a reporter he spent time in Dodge City and recruited for former Jayhawks coach John Hadl. He described Devaney as "a close personal friend," adding, "I remember I could sit in the stands and tell what play they were going to run." A fan of Nebraska football since "long before Rodgers," he reportedly missed only one scheduled Husker football game—home or away—in the eighteen years prior to 1984.

A frequent guest at his Omaha home remembers how Alger would rap to black players about his hardscrabble youth, the times he slept with eight brothers and sisters in a shack. "He told them he could understand where they were coming from, how hard it was," remembers the guest. (Alger denied having made any such statement, saying he enjoyed a normal childhood with just one brother and sister.)

Records filed in relation to Alger's companies show he was born in 1923 and served a stint in the armed forces from 1941–1945. Later he owned and operated a trailer court in Kansas City before becoming a partner for sixteen years in a company called Alger Industrial Specialties Corp. According to company records, Alger then formed the Alger Corporation, which in 1986 consisted of, according to a Dun & Bradstreet report, two wholesale supply companies—Mid-West Supply, and Poultry Produce of Nebraska. Alger is listed as chief executive officer and president of both companies. His son, Kevin, is listed as vice president and Alger's wife, Joyce, now in her mid-fifties, as secretary. The companies reportedly employed some forty people, including officers.

According to another 1986 D & B report, Alger is also CEO and president of K & K Transportation Corp., a long-distance trucking company he founded in 1971. Clients include Goodyear Tires and the Safeway stores. K & K covers two square blocks at 23rd Street and Ames in a seedy section of Omaha, and records indicate that it leases thirty-six tractors and fifty trailers and employs some sixty-five people. A December 31, 1985, financial statement for the company listed 1985 gross sales of $3,386,075.

Two years earlier, according to a story in the *World-Herald*, Alger organized a testimonial dinner for Turner Gill at Mister C's, one of Omaha's finest restaurants. The paper reported about 170 people attended, with Osborne, the

Omaha mayor, city council president, and legal counsel to Governor Kerrey among them.

During his long association with Husker football, in which he said he helped recruit for both Devaney and Osborne (a statement Osborne denied) and provided dozens of summer jobs, Alger was considered such a big-shot booster that he was evidently allowed access to both the practice field and post-game locker room—the latter the rarest of privileges at a school where the players' locker room is strictly off-limits to the media and interviews are conducted in the players' lounge at South. "I saw him [Alger] in the locker room more than I saw anyone else," remembers former Nebraska lineman Stephen Thomas.

Alger says he quit going to the locker room because "there were so many people I couldn't talk to the one I had worked with in recruiting."

Osborne says that during one such locker-room visit, in 1984, one of his "sports information people" overheard Alger making "a general statement" about how he was "buying" at Tony & Luigi's, considered Lincoln's premier Italian restaurant. Shortly thereafter, on May 21, 1984, Osborne wrote Alger a letter. In it, however, there's no mention of any locker-room boast; rather Osborne seems to be sending a subtle but clear message to Alger while soliciting his support "in eliminating such abuses you might be aware of." The letter:

Dear Everett:

Some of the remarks attributed to Mike Rozier last January have led me to be somewhat concerned about the role of our fans and alumni in relation to our players.

I have repeatedly warned the players about the consequences of scalping tickets or receiving any type of illegal aid. Sometimes such warnings are sufficient and sometimes not. I am hoping you will support me in eliminating such abuses you might be aware of.

I have no direct evidence as to who might be involved in such activities, I'm simply contacting those individuals who know some of the players and might possibly be asked to buy tickets. If you have any questions about this matter or any information you feel I should know, let me know.

    We greatly appreciate your help in getting summer jobs for players in the past, and we appreciate your great interest in our football program. Best wishes.

Alger said his eighteen-year game attendance streak ended the following fall and he no longer was stopping in the locker room. His reasoning? "I have to work Saturdays," said the trucking magnate. "I miss some games. I have no choice." Later he added, "Now I can't even go talk to these people. I can't have anything to do with those people."

Osborne declined to divulge why Alger, whom he calls "a friend," was no longer allowed in the locker room. But, in a broader vein, he did acknowledge, "He's stayed away the last couple of years," and that "I've had to disassociate four or five people from the program in the past because of tickets."

"I've never done anything illegal," says Everett Alger.

Tickets were not the NCAA's prime investigative target in 1986. It was cars. Actually, *a car.* The $19,000 cherry-red 1985 Nissan 300ZX driven by Heisman Trophy hopeful Doug DuBose, a senior I-back from Connecticut. Berst says his staff began making inquiries about the car in April 1986 after learning that a local sportswriter was checking out the lease. Berst also acknowledges the NCAA received "an anonymous call" pertaining to the automobile.

In mid-summer 1986 the university had received an official letter of inquiry from the NCAA listing eighteen separate suspected violations. One item on the list mentioned the lease of DuBose's car. (Other alleged problem areas included game tickets, improper reimbursement of airline tickets from the 1986 Fiesta Bowl, and possible abuses in the Lincoln Parent Program, in which athletes were "adopted" by local families.) NCAA investigators were interested in not only whether a "representative of the university's athletic interests," that is, a booster, was illegally—at least by NCAA standards—paying the lease, but also what, if any, involvement an assistant academic counselor by the name of Marsha Shada may have had in (a) making the lease payments or (b) acting as a possible conduit for booster money. In her mid-thirties, with appealing features and coal-black hair, Shada had joined the athletic department in 1983 after working at a series of teaching and counseling jobs with the state.

And as a matter of policy NCAA officials declined to discuss an ongoing investigation, so public information about the investigation generally came from one source—the head coach.

"Every dime that Doug got, as far as we know, came from his parents," Osborne said at one point. "We know that Doug did not receive any money from anybody [else]. We don't believe the cosigning ever occurred, and the person that was accused of the cosigning we don't believe was a representative of the university." He declined to name that nonrepresentative and repeatedly said financing for the car came from DuBose's parents, Charles, a truck driver, and Sandra, a mail carrier and the owner of a women's clothing boutique in rural Uncasville, Connecticut. Osborne said DuBose's parents had been interviewed by the NCAA on at least three separate occasions and were irritated by all the questioning. So, it appeared, was Osborne. "Let me tell you this," he told reporters. "His brother had two cars that his folks bought him, an everyday car and a sports car. His dad has two cars, a sports car and an everyday car. They have a swimming pool at their home. Both parents work. They're not wealthy people, but they believe in spending money on their kids."

According to sources close to the investigation and court records and interviews, the background on the case was this:

▶ The car was originally leased on August 28, 1985, in the names of Dave Martin and Doug DuBose—the two names that appeared on the original car title. Martin, Osborne later said, was an "old farmer" out near Denton, Nebraska.

(It was Martin whom Osborne would not immediately identify to local reporters.) Osborne said Martin's name appeared on the registration only "as a local credit reference."

▶ Sandra DuBose had told the NCAA on several occasions she sent her son his $350 lease payment in cash or money order every month.

▶ Osborne said, "We found out right away that Doug had a cosigner on the lease. By right away I mean November. I called the Big Eight office. They said it sounded okay, but we'd better get his name off the lease." However, according to Department of Motor Vehicles records, it wasn't until five months later, on April 17, 1986—during the initial stages of the NCAA investigation—that the names on the title of the 300ZX were changed from Martin-DuBose to GMAC, the leasing company, and the title reissued four days later to Sandra and Charles DuBose, P.O. Box 30227, Lincoln, Nebraska 68503.

With less than thirty days to mobilize their forces before an August 17 Committee on Infractions hearing in Colorado Springs, Osborne and Company went to work. Two university attorneys, a faculty rep, and the coach himself "broke their necks" to prepare for the hearing. At the last minute the NCAA postponed the meeting, two days in advance of the hearing; the association wasn't quite ready. Berst later said the NCAA needed more time to develop additional information. "At that point," he said, "the university didn't think it [the delay] was appropriate. They didn't appreciate we didn't agree [on the need for a postponement]."

On Saturday, September 27, Osborne and six other university officials, including Shada, traveled to Portland, Maine, to meet the following day with the members of the Infractions Committee. The only missing member of the NU delegation was DuBose. "He didn't make the plane" was the coach's cryptic reply.

"The [NCAA] staff was reasonable and accommodating,"

said Osborne after a three-hour session on Sunday. "Everything went smoothly."

Not that smoothly. On October 20, the NCCA announced its decision: the football team would be placed on a maximum one-year probation, a sanction that did not affect postseason play, TV appearances, or scholarships. The football program was cited for three "extra benefit" violations: (1) illegal use of summer work transportation by a student-athlete (2) the "inadvertent and unintentional" reimbursement of the price of commercial airline tickets to two student-athletes (Thomas and DuBose), and (3) a staff member's involvement in assisting a student-athlete in obtaining an automobile lease.

[The NCAA had determined that a staff member (Shada) had assisted a student-athlete "in obtaining an automobile lease" and later "again assisted the student-athlete in delivering a delinquent payment on the vehicle."]

"The university is pleased that these matters have now finally been resolved," said school chancellor Martin Massengale in a prepared statement. "As we have in the past, we intend to work diligently in providing the necessary reports to the NCAA and in assuring all Nebraska sports fans that we intend to comply with and abide by all NCAA rules and regulations."

Although the decision consisted of little more than a public reprimand, Osborne was shocked and saddened by the news. "As low as I've ever been in coaching," he insisted once again. He almost choked when he saw the word *probation*—indignant at the thought that *his* program was being lumped in with outlaw schools like Florida and SMU. It disgusted him that after the NCAA had invested all that time and found "no recruiting violations, no allegations of players receiving money, no players being bought," his program still ended up on *probation*.

To combat negative news and to counteract rival recruiters who would be, no doubt, warming up their "You know, they're on probation" lines, Osborne's staff within hours of the announcement had already begun to crank out 800 letters to recruits across the country. "We just wanted them to know exactly what happened," he later explained. "So many kids never read it in the paper. So many times other coaches—not all, but some—will say, 'Well, you know, Nebraska is on probation,' and give the inference that we really did some bad stuff. I wanted people to know what we had done. So many times people associate the word *probation* with sanctions."

Berst, for his part, staunchly defended the NCAA action. He repeated the fact that "extra benefits were provided to student-athletes," a reference to senior offensive guard Mike Hoefler's living with his Lincoln parents for two weeks in the summer of 1983 and using their van, despite the fact that, as Osborne argued, Hoefler's mother paid the Lincoln family $100 for food and lodging and that Hoefler filled up the van with gas twice. "He also cleaned the van, waxed it and washed it," said the coach.

But Berst wasn't budging. In some ways he felt the university had gotten off easy. "The issues were significant and serious," he said, adding that the investigation was "heightened" by his belief that the NCAA had been provided "false information" by the school, that DuBose and Shada had "adjusted" their stories "at least twice" during interviews with NCAA investigators, and that "other aspects of their story changed along the way.

"We were not told the truth by the individuals involved," said Berst. "We didn't know what the final answers were going to be with the automobile. Certainly we have no apologies for looking as hard as we did."

Doug DuBose leans back into a couch in his smartly furnished apartment, a ten-minute walk from the edge of campus. On this day in 1986 he cuts a cool figure in a red and white "Ft. Lauderdale" T-shirt and designer jeans. In the background VH-1 is playing softly on the large-screen TV, Stevie Nicks's sultry voice blowing softly through expensive-looking speakers. The phone never rests. Friends. Girlfriends.

Teammates. Checking in, checking up. "Catch you later, man," DuBose says time and time again.

Ah, the active social life of a Husker running back. DuBose smiles. "There's a lot of girls," he says. "You wear No. 22 on Saturday, yeah, they want to say 'I was with Doug DuBose.' It gets old after a while . . . but"—sly smile—"it takes a lot of girls before it does. I used to have a girlfriend, but so many girls were calling up we had to break up. You don't have to chase them; they pretty much call you."

A thick gold chain hangs loosely around his neck. Written in a ribbon of gold is the word *Secretariat*, announcing to all concerned just how talented this 5'11", 190-pound halfback felt himself to be. And he might have been right. The slashing DuBose was the first Husker to have amassed back-to-back 1,000-yard seasons as an underclassman. He led the Big Eight in rushing as a sophomore (1,040 yards) in 1984 and followed with another mega-season in 1985 (1,161), finishing second in the conference and ninth in the nation in rushing.

Born at New London, Connecticut, on March 14, 1964, DuBose and his older brother, Gary, tore up one football league after another before making their marks at Montville High. At Montville Doug DuBose was All-State in three sports (football, basketball, and baseball), rushing for more than 3,200 yards and 40 TDs during his career. In his senior year he averaged 10.8 yards per carry, gained 1,702 yards, and scored 25 times. Yet, like so many other high school superstars, he found the early going quite treacherous at Nebraska, especially after competing against seven other I-backs on the freshman team. "You never think you can do it," says DuBose.

But he did: in 1982 he led the freshman team in rushing, scored 6 TDs, and averaged 35.7 yards on kickoff returns. Redshirted in 1983, he hit the big time in '84 and '85. Despite arthroscopic surgery, which kept him out of spring practice in '86, DuBose entered the fall campaign full of Heisman hope—and needing only 610 yards to move into second place on NU's career rushing chart. But now, the season almost over, he was still 610 short. The crutches at his side told why. On the fourth carry of a game-type scrimmage on August 23, 1986, DuBose had torn both the cartilage and anterior cruciate ligament in his left knee. Ironically nobody had touched him; the fifth-year senior had been making a cut when he crumbled to the ground. Extensive surgery followed three days later. His college career was over.

None of which kept the dashing DuBose from remaining the poster boy of the NCAA investigation. Or being intimidated by McMenamin and Calandro, who had sat him down in Osborne's office one day and—not untypically—brandished an NCAA manual and threatened him with loss of his eligibility. "They told me they could take it [eligibility] away if I didn't tell the truth," says DuBose. "They asked a lot of questions. I felt like I was on the witness stand."

Certainly on this day in his apartment, DuBose has taken no oath and is under no such compulsion to talk. But between telephone calls he makes it perfectly clear that he is innocent of all charges—"The dealership didn't give me anything. I wanted to play it straight"—and had nothing whatsoever to do with making his lease payments. "My parents pay," said DuBose. "They've got canceled checks and receipts from the dealer . . . I don't even know the payment."

Later, one week before the NCAA's decision is announced, DuBose will get angry and demand a public apology from the collegiate organization. "I want them to tell me they're sorry for all the things they put me through," he will say.

"Doug has been greatly maligned in this case," said Osborne before the NCAA decision was announced.

The mother insists to the NCAA and a reporter that her son pays the lease payment in cash. The son tells the same reporter that his parents pay and that they have the canceled checks and receipts to prove it. *I don't even know the payment.* Osborne says his injured star has been "maligned" and, when pressed, says the parents mailed or wired cash because "evidently, they don't have a bank account themselves."

No bank account? A family of five, all those cars, their own business, a home, and no bank account?

"I don't think so," said Osborne. "I don't know."

"We wanted to look at [their] bank records," recalls Berst. "The university didn't think it was appropriate." The NCAA, it should be noted, has no subpoena powers.

When bank records are checked, through two separate credit rating services, they showed Charles and Sandra Du-Bose of 90 Forest Drive, Uncasville, Connecticut, as having an account at New England Savings Bank for more than ten years. The couple carried Visa and MasterCard credit cards issued through Chase Manhattan and Union Trust banks, and since 1984 had borrowed money from Connecticut Bank and Trust on three different occasions. They also carried a car loan with GMAC and a mortgage on their home.

And yet another twist to the mystery of who pays: Both the mailman who delivered to 1237 C Street, Apt. 2 (DuBose's residence from the beginning of the investigation until October 1986) and DuBose's former neighbor, Bill Callen, said the lock on DuBose's mailbox was broken from August '85 through October '86. Sending cash in envelopes would have posed an unusual risk. "The door never even shut," said Callen, who lived across the hall.

Then there's the matter of license number 2-P1699, the plate on the suspicious 300ZX. According to Mamie Haggan, a clerk at the Lincoln Department of Motor Vehicles office, the plate number had not been registered as of November 1986 to anyone in the state of Nebraska for at least four years. "Either it's an expired plate put on the car," said Haggan, "or the plate's not issued, which it has to be if it's on the car. Speaking logically, it shouldn't be on the car. That's a violation of Nebraska law." Also, according to DMV records, the car wasn't properly registered under plate number 2-P1699 until January 13, 1987—well after the NCAA investigation had ended.

On the subject of Martin, Osborne said he talked to the farmer: "I tried to find out if he was a rep of the university."

The upshot was, according to the coach, that he and Martin had met one time at practice; neither was Martin an alum nor had he recruited for the school.

But if DuBose needed a local "credit reference," why not someone from the university? Why someone from Denton? Why not ask his former Lincoln parents? Why not Osborne or backfield coach Solich? Why would he need a credit reference anyway if *his parents* were making the payments?

The M/B Ranch stands at the crest of a long, steep hill on West Denton Road, which bisects the fertile farmland of tiny (pop. 160) Denton, Nebraska, some twelve miles southwest of downtown Lincoln. The silhouette of the 400-acre spread— the silos, stables, and heavy machinery—shimmers in the mid-morning sun. Out back, behind a two-story house, its white paint eaten away by the elements, Dave Martin sits behind the wheel of his dusty, trusty Cadillac Fleetwood. Speaking in a raspy voice, Martin relives some of the forty-seven years he has spent on the farm—raising cattle, training three world champion cutting horses, growing acres of corn, wheat, oats, and hay. "It's been a lot of fun," says Martin.

What wasn't fun, he says, was when he discovered, back in the summer of 1986, that his name was on both the title and registration of a cherry-red 1985 Nissan 300ZX being driven by DuBose. "I knew nothing about it," says Martin. "It kinda perturbed me. I told Doug, 'I want that son of a bitch taken care of right now. I want no part of this.'"

How Martin became a part of it evidently dates back to the days of Bill Janssen, a member of NU's national championship teams of the early seventies. It was through Janssen, says Martin, that he got "acquainted with a bunch of the boys," and offered them jobs hauling hay on the farm. That association with NU football players "carried over" right through the DuBose era, as DuBose, Neil Smith, Lawrence Pete, former Husker quarterback Travis Turner, and others—about a dozen players from the 1985 and '86 teams—hauled hay for Martin. Not that he paid much. "I'm a poor man," he says. "They'd always bitch that I only wanted to pay four bucks an hour."

But there were fringe benefits. Martin says he often let DuBose and other players ride his horses. "I let them ride for free," he says. "I never charged them."

It was in the summer of '86, with DuBose still stopping by to ride or just say hi, and, as Martin remembers, "quite a little bit before the Infractions Committee hearing on August 17th," that two separate incidents, three days apart, set off alarms in Martin's head. The first alarm rang the moment he opened his mail and found a parking ticket for a 300ZX he didn't own—and had never even seen. The second and more serious ring was a phone call from an insurance company in New Jersey inquiring about coverage on the car. "I got scared," Martin remembers. "It was time to do something. I went to checking. It would have been bad for me if he got in a fucking wreck."

Martin says he discussed the ticket and phone call with DuBose and Osborne. The problem was discussed and re-solved; Martin's name was to come off the lease. So why had it appeared on the title and registration in the first place? The old farmer, dressed in jeans and a faded work shirt, squints from beneath his cowboy hat, white cigarette smoke filling the front seat of his Caddy.

"It turned out he [DuBose] forged my name," says Martin.

Was Osborne told of the forgery?

"Yep, yep," says Martin. "I told him."

And his reaction?

"He never said nothing much," Martin says. "He was con-cerned about the fact I had some of these kids work when they were not eligible to work. He was concerned about the four bucks an hour hauling hay."

Martin, who claimed he was unaware such employment violated NCAA rules that prohibit scholarship athletes from working except during specific time periods in the summer, added that he informed the NCAA of the forgery. "They knew it," he said. "They knew he [DuBose] forged my name." He said he was quizzed some ten different times by two NCAA investigators and insisted—as he did on this day—that he never paid a dime on the car. Not even the parking ticket. "They [the state] tried to get me to pay that son of a bitch," he smiles, "but then I'd have been guilty. I never paid it."

Of the NCAA, Martin says, "That's one tough son of a bitch. They questioned me and questioned me. They looked at my bank statements, my checks. If there had been one damn thing wrong, I guarantee you they'd have found it."

It was Martin's theory that DuBose, at the urging of a local car salesman, put the farmer's name on the leasing documents in order to secure in-state financing on the vehicle—an act that took their casual friendship one giant step too far. "Doug was like a little kid who got carried away," says Martin, lighting up another smoke. "He apologized, but I noticed he never came around much afterward. That kinda put things to an end."

Martin takes another long, deep drag on his cigarette. He says he has since solved all the employment problems with the university; henceforth no Husker will haul any hay without Coach Osborne's approval. "One thing about Coach Osborne," says Martin. "He wouldn't lie to nobody. If Doug had been guilty, he would have burned him."

The old farmer laughs and punches a visitor in the knee. Three years after the fact, he has found some humor in his ordeal. "You know," he says, a twinkle in his eye, "I never even got a ride in 'my' automobile."

In another aspect of the investigation, rumors flew around town that Shada was up to her eyeballs in this mess. And, indeed, sources close to DuBose say the running back and assistant academic counselor were sharing far more than the car keys; those same sources indicate that Shada had a history of forming such personal relationships with star Huskers, to the point of buying them gifts such as jewelry and bicycles. "When one graduates, she picks up another," said one source. In a brief interview, Shada said she had "no comment" on any aspect of the NCAA investigation. Asked about her relationship with DuBose, she replied, "Talk to Coach Osborne."

Publicly Osborne admitted that Shada had helped DuBose "check the car out," pick up some lease papers, pay a lien,

and pick up the car after a local dealer had repossessed it for
back payments. (Where had the lien money, which was paid
in June 1986, come from? Why a lien at all if DuBose's
parents were paying?) Such actions, said Osborne, were
"beyond the scope" of Shada's job description. Privately,
when asked about a possible personal relationship, he said, "I
heard rumors about it. And I talked to both Doug and Marsha
about it. I confronted her and confronted Doug. Both denied
it. There were all kinds of rumors going around. Marsha's
bank records were looked at by the NCAA. Her bank statements from several months back were looked at. She has no
money. There's a lot of things about the [car] deal that led
one to wonder, led us to wonder, led the NCAA to wonder.
Everybody's checked it out. . . . There's some players who take
quite a bit of her time, and we talked to her about that. I think
four, five guys occupied about 50 percent of her time. And I
would say that Doug was one of those, certainly. I couldn't
swear one way or another on it [about their relationship], but
all I know is I have no evidence."

Late one night in Lincoln in the spring of 1986, as patrons
of P. O. Pears, a popular downtown bar, began spilling into
the street, a sports car roared up in front of the bar at around
12:45 one Thursday morning. Wednesday night is 89-cent
beer night at Pears, making it a must on many students'
social calendars, so the sidewalk outside the bar was
swamped. One eyewitness says the car in question was a
bright-red 300ZX, DuBose's car, and that Shada was driving.
    "Doug," she was heard to say, "get in the car."
    DuBose declined the offer.
    "Get your ass in here, Doug," the eyewitness said Shada
shouted. "If you don't, there's going to be some shit." Again
DuBose refused. He and some friends left for his apartment
only to find Shada waiting outside. At this point, remembers
a friend, DuBose politely asked his buddies to leave.
    Shada was eventually reprimanded for her role in the car
caper, put on university probation, and moved into under-

graduate advising. She subsequently left the university.

7:30 P.M.

I. M. Hipp had arrived near the end of the day's practice to volunteer his services. The very same I.M. who ranked second in the school's career rushing records (2,814 yards and a 5.68 average) and was drafted in the fourth round by the Atlanta Falcons in 1980. Hipp had recently returned to Lincoln from his native South Carolina, where he'd struggled a bit after leaving pro ball. With Osborne's consent, he had been holding individual postpractice counseling sessions with members of the first offense and defense and some key freshmen. The purpose: to "fulfill the dream" and to help unlock potential. Hipp said the counseling concept was based on his experiences as a pro. "As a player, you tend to rely on the system," he explained. "If a person can come in and give you an extra step, maybe one word, a couple of words to help you accelerate your brain power—I call it creativity imagination—then it's going to help. Create and imagine everything a No. 1 All-America would do. . . . It's all within themselves. I try to find things to pull it out."

A year earlier the price for those interested in pulling any information out of Hipp was said to be rather steep. For what a reputed Hipp representative by the name of Wade White called the story of "the rewards he [Hipp] had received while a running back at Nebraska" the price tag was $50,000. Reward money. Fifty grand. "He'll have to move out of town," said White. The request was denied.

12:23 A.M.

The tenth floor of The Cornhusker Hotel affords a clear view of the FirsTier Bank building, and at this hour the bank's combination clock-thermometer blinks out 36 degrees. Rain slashes down in sheets. It desperately wants to snow. Game of the Century II and better weather are still 110 hours away.

TUESDAY

7:53 A.M.

Around here Bruce Melichar is considered the Carnac of college football. Unlike "Tonight" show host Johnny Carson, a native Nebraskan, Melichar, in his early thirties, doesn't do late-night television or wrap a towel around his temples to make wacky predictions. No, he's just your basic gas station owner, friendly to a fault, but still just ol' Bruce down at Melichar's 66, corner of 9th and P, across the street from the *Journal-Star*. But as the king-sized "Go Big Red" sign on his property attests, Melichar is Husker through and through.

Melichar, you see, has a nose for numbers. Football scores. Nebraska scores, to be precise. What's more, he's brave enough to post them on a sign above his pumps for all the world—friend and foe—to see as they enter downtown on 9th. A year earlier that sign had read "Bruce-Craig say NU 24, FSU 16." The Huskers took that one, 34–17. This morning Bruce says he's going with the Huskers—surprise!—but he's fuzzy on the final score. "I don't know," he says while wiping down a window. "We've been playing awfully well, but you know how hard it's been for us to beat Oklahoma. I'm think-

ing maybe we're gonna blow them away, especially with
Holieway and Carr out. But I don't know. I need to do some
more thinking. Come back tomorrow."

It's a five-minute walk over to the red-canopied Nebraska
Stadium Shop, but a biting wind angry enough to glue your
lips together makes every step count. Inside the shop, right
across the street from the west side of the stadium, Loraine
Livingston is warmed by the thoughts of another big day. And
Loraine has seen some doozies.

During a typical Saturday afternoon home game more
than 3,000 rooters from around the state pour into the
privately owned shop, a slice of Husker Heaven where every
imaginable icon is up for sale: license plates (lighted or not),
megaphones, clocks, wristbands, hats, T-shirts, sweatshirts,
sweatpants, lighters, towels, combs, golf balls, flags, mirrored
sunglasses that flash "Go Big Red," buttons, stickers, red and
white shoestrings, fly swatters, cups, glasses . . . and the
season's hottest item, a genuine set of cardboard "Our
House" keys. Though lately, says Loraine, there's been a real
run on these phony referee flags. "You throw these down if
you disagree with the ref," she says, picking one up. "In your
home, though. We don't recommend you do it on the field."

After nine years Loraine is pretty good at this recom-
mending business herself, acting as adviser and counsel to
countless shoppers seeking that "perfect something" for the
Husker fan in their life. Christmas, birthday, Father's Day,
anniversary, housewarming, baby shower, bar mitzvah—you
name it. Of course, if you press her on the issue, she'll admit
to a few personal favorites, going so far as to dig around a
table near the cash register and pull out a dusty cassette tape.
"Not too many of these left," she says with a smile. It's "I'd
Rather Be a Husker Than an Okie," by Bill Hogan and the
Sons of the Huskers. "Came out one of the years we beat
Oklahoma," beams Loraine, popping the tape into the
cassette player.

I'd rather be a Husker than an Okie
Huskers always have a lot more fun
We come to play college football
Nebraska showed 'em all how it's done.

"A good omen," says Loraine, edging up the volume just a bit. In seconds she's doing a respectable Loretta Lynn impression. *We come to play college football/Nebraska showed 'em all how it's done.* The doorbell jangles. Another customer? No, just another pad and pencil. The pace is picking up.

"Can I help you?" asks Loraine.

"Well," says the visitor, "I've got a couple of questions for ya if you've got a minute."

"Come on in," says Loraine.

Ten minutes later, over at South, Devaney is pondering a few questions. "Tom, as far as I'm concerned, has no fault as a person or a coach," he says. "He's just a great football coach—the best in the business—and I don't think anyone tries harder than Tom to do it right." Devaney views the upcoming game as a "big hurdle" for the team, but one it's infinitely capable of jumping. "This is a very, very fine football team," he says. "They opened up and played three pretty good teams, teams I don't think they realized how good they were at the time we played. Right now I think this is a tremendous football team."

An hour later the head coach of the "tremendous" team settles back in the high-backed swivel chair in his warm, spacious office. In one corner of his large wooden desk are twelve copies of *More Than Winning* stacked the way a school librarian would arrange them. Mounted on the wall directly behind the coach is the three-foot-long, thirty-one-pound, eleven-ounce king salmon he pulled out of Lake Michigan back in July 1978, a constant reminder of one of the true anchors in T.O.'s life (with family, football, running, and religion completing the list). "Fishing is my dad's escape," explains Osborne's only son, Mike. "It's a place he can put everything else aside and forget about football."

Tom's brother, Jack, agrees. He says that mentally and physically Tom "empties himself" while on the water, swimming free and clear of all the other goldfish in the bowl. "We've been in a boat together, and we'll go a half hour or more without saying one word to each other," says Jack.

Yet Osborne, according to Jack and others, brings the same competitive fire to a rod and reel that he brings to everything else in his life. "Tom doesn't fish like anyone else," says Jack. "Most people work a line for three hours, take a break, grab a bite to eat. Tom stays from sunrise to sunset."

Unfortunately there will be no escapes this week, no time to reflect. From dawn to dusk it is Oklahoma, Oklahoma, and more Oklahoma. "I think they'll be ready," says Osborne of his opponent. "What we have to do is not play the best game of our lives, but to play like we've been playing. Because I think sometimes players can get so caught up in the mood, you know, Nebraskans get so fired up about this game, the players get the feeling it's a different level of football than they've been playing. I don't think that's healthy myself."

He looks healthier himself today, alert and crisply dressed in a white shirt, red print tie, and tweed coat. In less than twenty minutes he'll meet the media in his weekly press conference, so questions about OU are right up his alley. The game, he predicts, won't turn on the loss of Holieway and Carr or even on their respective replacements, Charles Thompson and Rotnei Anderson. And it won't be a Steve Taylor or a Broderick Thomas or an End Zone Jones that decides it. No, this will be a Battle of the Bulge, a war waged, as most memorable ones are, in the trenches, in hand-to-hand combat along the offensive and defensive lines. "It's not anything that's revolutionary," Osborne says, "but a lot of the focus has been on the quarterbacks and Rotnei Anderson and whether he'll hang on to the ball, those kinds of things. But I think the game will essentially be decided up front. It's never 100 percent, like one team starts knocking the other team off the line every play, but whoever starts winning the majority of the matchups, who starts changing the line of scrimmage as the game goes along, eventually that will tell the story."

A few moments later, at exactly 12:05 P.M., he walks briskly into the players' lounge, his eyes widening as he scans the crowd, a record-breaker by local standards: four rows of twenty chairs occupied by an army of print reporters and TV newsmen from Lincoln, Omaha, and beyond. As he sits down at a long table, he's dwarfed by the huge red and white banner on the wall behind his shoulder, the white block *N*, and signature red-and-white helmet with the magic word *Huskers* written in script below.

"Good afternoon, Mr. President," quips a local beat writer.

Osborne smiles faintly and says, "The stock market must have crashed again. I can't really believe we've got this many people interested in something on a Tuesday."

The assembled group of sportswriters is impressive—Herschel Nissenson, the national football writer for the Associated Press; Ian Thomsen of the *Boston Globe*; Sally Jenkins of the *Washington Post*; Ivan Maisel, late of *Sports Illustrated* and now with the *Dallas Morning News*; and other writers from Atlanta, Miami, and New York. All except Nissenson are young, in their late twenties and early thirties, and therefore are getting their first good look at Osborne and his deliberate style. A few shake their heads and roll their eyes as his early answers sound like he's reading roll: the team is reasonably healthy. Brinson and his back may pose a problem. The same with Neil Smith and his ankle. The week-long layoff has helped. Oklahoma's secondary is the best we've seen. Not a comma or catchy quote in sight.

Then, surprisingly, Osborne perks up, as he's quite capable of doing when the subject matter suits him or he has a point to make. Today he does, and he tackles a controversial subject head-on—the firing of Earle Bruce despite an 81–26–1 record for Ohio State in nine years. "Normally I wouldn't say much about it," he begins, "but I know Earle pretty well." He goes on to describe Bruce as competent, honest, intense—a far cry from what local beat writers recall Osborne's saying during Bruce's tenure as head coach at Iowa State when the two weren't exactly kissin' cousins, but no matter. A national audience is listening, and Osborne wants to send a personal message about unrealistic expectations—the win-or-else syndrome that's eating up college coaches all over the country.

"It's kind of a commentary on the coaching profession that

may not be very good when you see someone like that, with that kind of track record, get released because he's about .500 in a season." He tosses out a striking statistic: there have been twenty-three coaching changes in Big Eight football in the last fifteen years at six schools (only Nebraska and Oklahoma have remained stable). "That's one change every three or four years," he says. "I don't think maybe that's really the way to build your program. I think if you have a competent coach who works hard and is honest, you stay with him. You usually come out ahead rather than changing coaches every three years. I'm just not sure what we're doing is right when you look at the track record in the Big Eight."

The questions roll on, and Osborne rambles on, with so many *mights* and *probablys* mixed into his answers that when he makes some snappy statement it gets stuck in the muck. Finally, near the end of the session, someone pops The Question:

"Coach, what about the fact you haven't won a national championship?"

No soft shoe here. Instead Osborne speaks wisely and from the heart, in a manner that might not endear him to every Husker fan but with a mien that the coach would do well to bottle and have Loraine Livingston sell at the Stadium Shop, right along with the towels and T-shirts.

"I never felt at any time that I wouldn't want to win it," he says. "But sometimes, because we've never won a national championship since I've been head coach, people feel that somehow I'm like Captain Ahab chasing Moby Dick—that I'm obsessed.

"But it's not that way with me. I feel the most important thing is to play well. National championships happen. They're not like Big Eight championships, where you go out and play every team, and if you beat every team you win it. You've got to be voted the national championship. And you've got to have a lot of things conspire—you need to stay healthy, and if you have an easy schedule it helps. . . .

"It's not going to drive me crazy if I finish coaching in

three years, four years, five years, ten years and have never won a national championship. If I don't do it, I might end my career more quickly because somebody might get me out of here. But it's not something I have to have happen. . . . It's the pursuit of it that's more important than the winning of it. It's always the process that's more fun than the end results."

The "president" then departs and is replaced in short order by sophomore noseguard Mike Murray, senior wide receiver–punt return specialist Rod Smith, and defensive coordinator McBride. Murray looks more like a fireplug than a middle guard. At 5′9″ and 240 pounds he's the current version of the "classic" walk-on success story, a South Sider from Chicago who overcame the odds to make All-Catholic League as a guard and linebacker at Mount Carmel High, proving to be the best player on a high school team that included fellow Huskers-to-be Mark Antonietti (second-team offensive guard) and freshman and *Parade* magazine *All-America* Nate Turner (a split end). Yet Murray never got so much as a "sniff"—McBride's word—from the major colleges. "So I wrote [NU freshman] Coach [Scott] Downing a letter," says Murray. "I think he was pretty impressed with my letter. I just told him, I'm short, you know, but my head overcomes my body." Downing asked for some film. Murray sent it himself. Nebraska invited him for a visit. In 1986 he started at middle guard for the freshmen and finished as their second-leading tackler. "He's a tough, smart kid who learns quick," said McBride. "A real scrapper!"

By spring '87, Murray was bench pressing more than 400 pounds and running a close second behind Lawrence Pete at nose. In '87, he'd already started twice—against UCLA and Kansas State—and recorded a game-high 7 tackles against Iowa State. He would literally be a man in the middle against OU. "This game could really turn on the play of our nose-guards, Pete and Murray," says McBride, a South Sider him-self. "Every war is won up front."

In another corner Smith stands chatting amiably with some reporters, answering questions with an air of confi-dence, a kind of (Thornton) Colorado cool that mixed well with his blonde hair, cherubic face, and 6'0", 190-pound frame. But he wasn't cocky—confident, yes; cocky, no. And unusually articulate. Like so many Huskers, he has earned his moment in the sun. He had played four sports in high school and was All-State (football) and led the state of Colorado in punt return yardage as a junior. He struggled during his first couple of years at NU and talked of transferring during a redshirt year, a time when Smith once said he felt "nonexistent."

"It's kind of hard to adjust," he said. "It's a long road."

By his junior year, however, he had made his move, his shifty moves and sure hands earning him playing time at wide receiver and punt returner—at the latter position performing well enough to lead the NCAA that year, averaging a school-record 18.9 yards per return (breaking a mark set by Rodgers in 1971). Now all the buoyant Smith wanted to do was win one for Tom Osborne.

"I think it would be a great honor to be one of the players that played on Tom Osborne's first national championship team," said Smith. "You know, Coach Osborne is a sincere individual, and he's had a lot of bad luck as far as that [a national championship] is concerned. In the back of our mind, we want to win it for ourselves, but I think we'd all like to win it for Coach Osborne."

Smith viewed the Oklahoma game much as Banderas did— as a means to an end, one of three stones left to turn over. He said he hadn't slept much the last week. "I just lay awake at night thinking [about] what I can do to make a difference. I envision myself making the catches we need to keep a drive going. I envision myself making the leaping catch in the end zone. I envision myself returning a punt to break the game up.

"You're sitting there [in bed], and you get these little bursts, where your body moves in anticipation of making a play. You're sitting there thinking about it, and all of a sudden you're so worked up making these moves you want to go work out, do something, lift weights, whatever it takes."

Rod Smith looks a reporter straight in the eye. Then he

says, "I'd love to be one of the guys who makes a difference in this game."

KFRX-FM (103) in Lincoln had a smash hit on its hands. A rap song written by Erik Johnson, Don Sander, and Chip Thompson, NU fraternity brothers and members of the rap group Tone Def, was suddenly KFRX's No. 1 request record. Seems the group wanted to do some-thin' for the team/so they rented a drum and a re-verb machine/took along a tape deck and mi-cro-phone/and used San-der's basement to re-cord their song/KFRX mixed the tune and added some sound/and now, plain and simple, it was the hottest song around:

> Come the 21st of November we'll give those Sooners a day to remember
> When they come to Lincoln town the red and white will take them down. . . .

KFRX Operations Manager J. J. Cook flipped over the response—ten to fifteen requests an hour for the song, which, by the way, FM-103 would be playing at least once every 60 minutes until Saturday. Cook was new to town, having arrived just two weeks earlier from Springfield, Missouri. "I've never seen people go this nuts over football in my life," he said.

1:45 P.M.

Tom Simons is under siege. Well, not Simons, 37, as much as his desk. Yellow phone message slips are stacking up like 747s at snowbound O'Hare. CBS Sports called. So did Craig Sager at Turner Broadcasting, Channel 6 in Tulsa, and Bob Lipper of the *Richmond Times-Dispatch*. There's also a stack of official scoring summaries from the ill-fated '86 game, showing nice and neatly how the Sooners had rallied with 13 points in the last 10:39 to pile another year of misery on the Huskers. All of this paper shares space with assorted Game of the Century II paraphernalia—media guides, newspaper clippings, photographs, notepads. And a battered Rolodex opened to the most famous name in the history of Cornhusker football: Johnny Rodgers.

> Wylie stands at his own 24 and waits for the snap. Rodgers deep for Nebraska. Here's Wylie's kick—it's high, it holds up there. Rodgers takes the ball at the 30 . . . he's hit and got away . . . back upfield to the 35 . . . the 40, to the 45. He's to the 50 to the 45 to the 40—*to the 35!* To the 30! To the 10! . . . He's all the way home !!
> Holy Moly! Man, woman, and child, did that put them in the aisles!! Johnny the Jet Rodgers just tore them loose from their shoes!

That he did. In one shining moment, regardless of all his other accomplishments—and they were stunning—Johnny "J. R. Superstar" Rodgers earned athletic immortality in Nebraska. The wingback went on to win the Heisman Trophy in 1972 and All-America honors in both his junior and senior seasons, and in three years (1970–72) he gained more than 6,100 all-purpose yards and scored 50 touchdowns. In his final performance as a Husker—in the 1973 Orange Bowl against Notre Dame—he played I-back for the first time and scored 4 touchdowns and passed for another as the Huskers routed the Fighting Irish, 40–6, on New Year's Day.

After being drafted No. 1 by the San Diego Chargers, Rodgers and his agent, a bright, brash-talking USC student by the name of Mike Trope, thumbed their noses at the NFL and instead signed a three-year mega-deal with the Montreal Alouettes of the Canadian Football League. Rodgers went on to play for four years in the CFL and two more with the Chargers before bad knees forced his retirement in 1979.

Afterward, however, the transition to the Game of Life proved sad and vexing for Rodgers. "Johnny," says a friend, "was always looking for the hustle." Sixteen years after the Game of the Century, the kid who "tore them loose from their shoes," whose autograph often included the phrase "Dare to Be Different," was, at times, lost in a different world—that of a bankrupt convicted felon fighting drug and alcohol dependence and, it seems, fighting for self-respect. Left now with little more than faded memories and the hope that a talented son, Terry, a budding star at Nebraska, could learn from his father's mistakes.

"One thing about Johnny is he can take care of himself," Terry Rodgers once told the *Los Angeles Times*. "He'll find a way to get back on top."

Certainly he found a way to touch bottom.

It's hard to pinpoint when all the serious trouble began. Not long after retiring from pro football, Rodgers was reportedly the subject of a Bureau of Alcohol, Tobacco and Firearms investigation involving automatic weapons. In the early eighties he was publisher of a weekly entertainment-TV guide called *Tuned In*. The magazine made an impact in San Diego and kept Rodgers in the limelight, but it eventually went under in 1985—not a kind year for Johnny Rodgers.

In August 1985 Rodgers was reportedly stopped by U.S. Customs agents at the San Ysidro Port of Entry at the Mexican border. A minuscule amount of crystal amphetamine was found in plastic baggies in his possession, and Rodgers was fined administratively for this offense. He later had to pay a huge fine to retrieve a European luxury car confiscated in the arrest.

During this period Rodgers was seen palling around with one Douglas "Dutch" Schultz, better known in law enforcement circles as the San Diego chapter president of the Hell's Angels. Schultz was also president of a limousine company that was trading service for advertisements in *Tuned In*. "My problems with the police started with Doug Schultz," said Rodgers.

The biggest problem materialized in October 1985, when a cable TV technician by the name of Jaime P. Rojas arrived at Rodgers's $250,000 suburban home to disconnect Rodgers's cable service for failure to pay the account. According to court papers and attorneys close to the case, after first requesting payment on a bad check and getting an unsatisfactory answer from a woman answering the door, Rojas climbed a telephone pole in the backyard and was in the process of shutting off service when, according to San Diego deputy district attorney Stephen Anear, who prosecuted the case, Rojas peered down and saw Rodgers pointing a gun at him. (Rodgers, while not disputing he was carrying a gun, said he kept it in his pocket.)

"What are you doing?" said Johnny Rodgers.

Rojas told him.

"Do that," said Rodgers, according to Anear, "and I'll shoot you off that pole."

Rojas ignored Rodgers and reached for his wire cutter. Rodgers again made a threat. Rojas climbed down the pole without cutting the cable.

Rojas showed Rodgers the work order. Rojas used this moment to scramble to his truck and get away, an attorney in the case said. When the police arrived, Rodgers consented to a house search, which turned up a gun in the bedroom closet, according to Anear. Rodgers was eventually charged with assault with a deadly weapon, possession of a concealed firearm by a felon, and brandishing a firearm.

This was not Rodgers's first felony charge. In a much-publicized incident during the summer before his junior year at Nebraska, Rodgers was charged with grand larceny in connection with the attempted robbery of a gas station in nearby Lancaster County he had committed two years earlier. Rodgers later deemed this little episode a "college prank" brought on by too many vodka and orange juices. Only got $90, he said. The local courts saw it differently, and Rodgers was convicted and sentenced to three years probation. Later in life Rodgers would inform friends he was pardoned for the offense, but a record check showed that no such pardon was ever approved. According to Anear, "What Johnny had was a document which essentially restored his civil rights, meaning he had completed probation. It did not mean he had been pardoned. He argued long and loud—and unsuccessfully—about this." So in 1985, as an ex-felon in possession of a gun, J.R. Superstar had a major problem; he was facing five years in federal prison.

By early 1986, as pretrial proceedings unwound, another Rodgers was moving into the national spotlight: young Terry. During his senior year at Sweetwater High School in San

Diego, the 5'7", 156-pound scatback, whom one admiring coach had called a "little ball of dynamite," had set the all-time rushing record in San Diego County (3,764 yards), breaking Marcus Allen's old mark, and established new single-season county records for touchdowns (32) and points scored (202). He was voted San Diego County Player of the Year and Prep All-America. Major colleges all over the country coveted his 4.4 speed, agility, and tackle-breaking ability.

But on May 1, 1986, national-letter-of-intent day passed without a formal announcement. What was the family waiting for? The assumption all along was that T.R. would follow J.R. to Lincoln; Nebraska had been Terry's first recruiting trip, and as he once admitted, "I was more impressed with Nebraska than any other school."

As recruiters and coaches puzzled over the delay, Johnny Rodgers went back to court. The cable TV case continued. In pretrial motions and local interviews Rodgers described himself as "indigent," telling Superior Court judge Earl Maas at one point, "I have zero money—no income, my savings are depleted." Yet true to his image, Rodgers was seen arriving for court dates in a chauffeured limo and wearing expensive jewelry.

During this time Rodgers also testified in Schultz's drug detention hearing. The Hell's Angels leader faced thirty-four years in prison on drug charges when Rodgers labeled him a respectable member of the San Diego business community. "This boy has got integrity," he said. A month later, Doug Schultz was sentenced to five years in federal prison for drug trafficking.

June spilled into July, and still no official announcement on Terry Rodgers. The trial date in the cable TV case was set for July 14. The rumor mill around Lincoln and San Diego was working overtime, with the intriguing scuttlebutt being that Johnny Rodgers was trying to cut a deal, holding his talented son out as a carrot, putting pressure on both Devaney and Osborne to produce a governor's pardon for the 1971 robbery conviction. (Rodgers needed the pardon, or he faced time in federal prison as a two-time felon.) When the pardon came through, so the story went, Terry Rodgers would commit to NU.

Osborne denied that any such scenario existed. "There are no deals at all," he said. "I haven't promised anything. I'm just a football coach. We can't manipulate the courts to get Terry."

Devaney seemed to indicate at one point that the school had contemplated interceding on Rodgers's behalf. "I found out the governor could not do that [authorize a pardon]," said the athletic director, "so there was no use calling. We told Johnny there were no strings attached to Terry coming to school."

The trial was postponed once more. The pardon never arrived. Summer vacation ended. Rodgers still refused to sign the standard national letter of intent that would authorize his son's commitment to Nebraska. Instead J.R. had another idea, which, if it worked, would not only ease the family financial burden but teach the antiquated NCAA a righteous lesson. So it was that Rodgers announced his son would forsake an athletic scholarship and walk on at Nebraska, thereby, he figured, skirting NCAA rules that prohibit scholarship athletes from taking outside employment. Terry, a budding communications major, would pay the bills by writing a "unique" syndicated weekly newspaper column, the "inside" story of Nebraska football. Rodgers had it all figured out! Out-of-state scholarships at Nebraska are worth about $6,200 a year. If just twenty-five Nebraska papers, mostly weeklies, paid $20 a week per column six months out of the year, Terry could take in $12,000. And J.R., being a "big picture" guy, was visualizing 200 papers signing on. "Sixteen grand a month," said Rodgers. "That's good enough for me."

It never happened. The NCAA, it turns out, had the power to deny young Rodgers the right to author such a column. So in early September 1986 Terry Rodgers accepted a full scholarship from the school. By then he already registered the highest "athletic index" mark for freshmen—which included a vertical jump of 34½ inches—and was one of just three pure freshmen to make the varsity. He wore his father's once-retired number—20—although Terry later told the *New York Times* the decision to ask for his father's jersey had little to do with sentiment; it was just the closest thing available to 21, his high school number. "Comparisons are going to come whether I had No. 115 or No. 20," said the soft-spoken freshman who was born in Omaha but grew up in San Diego. "The number doesn't make for comparisons; the individual makes for comparisons. . . . My dad was a great ballplayer, but that was him. I'm Terry Rodgers. I have to make a name for myself."

And he did. Playing behind Jones and Tyreese Knox at I-back that season, he averaged 5 yards per carry (27 for 135) and drew cheers from the Memorial Stadium crowd for his daring and dazzling moves while returning kicks. He led all rushers in the 1987 spring game, picking up 105 yards on 25 carries, before a knee injury forced him to redshirt.

Meanwhile his father's personal and legal woes mounted. He ran through attorneys like sand through a strainer as he feverishly fought the gun charges. The case became a tragicomedy played out in public. One star-struck attorney said he took Rodgers's case in exchange for having Rodgers work out with him twice a week. Another attorney ended up keeping Rodgers's Heisman Trophy in lieu of an unpaid legal tab.

In February 1987 that trophy sat on the defense table before Superior Court judge Jack Levitt, who stared out at Rodgers and the rest of a hushed courtroom. Rodgers had finally represented himself at a jury trial and lost. He was convicted on the charge of assault with a firearm, a felon in possession of a concealed firearm, and two counts of contempt of court, for what Anear termed Rodgers's "obstructional" behavior during the trial. (Rodgers was found not guilty of the charge of brandishing a firearm.) At sentencing time Levitt looked first at the trophy and then at Rodgers before he addressed Rodgers and the courtroom. "You've ridden that horse far too long," he said. "Mr. Rodgers expects to be treated differently. As a society maybe we're somewhat to blame. We give respect and adulation to athletes, then all of a sudden there is a big fall, and they're treated like everyone else." When Levitt had finished speaking, Rodgers had been sentenced to two years in state prison, an order that Levitt agreed to stay if Rodgers spent 180 days in the county jail (plus three years probation) and submitted to both a psychiatric evaluation and drug and alcohol treatment. His fine was $1,000. Rodgers eventually served about a month in jail before being released on $35,000 bond while his case went before the 4th District Court of Appeals. In early June, Rodgers's assault charge was thrown out by the appeals court, which stated that Levitt had improperly defined assault as "an unlawful threat coupled with the present ability to commit a violent injury on a person." The appeals judge defined assault as an unlawful *attempt*—not a threat. Rodgers's weapon possession charge was upheld.

A sad story, indeed, for a man whose sentencing papers had included forty-seven letters from community leaders, each and every one praising his character. Testimonies had arrived from Osborne, Melton, and even Everett Alger.

The Rodgers and Alger friendship went way back. Back to the early seventies and those autumn afternoons at Memorial Stadium and other locales. Back to a long—and, it appears, quite prosperous—relationship, one not confined to the more mundane matters of the buying and selling of game-day tickets, because sources close to Rodgers and the football program have linked the former Heisman Trophy winner and at least three of the most famous names in Husker history—Rozier, Fryar, and Gill—to Alger in a pay-for-play performance scheme in which Alger is said to have rewarded game-day performance—yards gained, passes caught, and touchdowns—in cash.

Rodgers, sources say, contends he received thousands and thousands of dollars in performance money from Alger during his Nebraska career. The incentives, when applied, are said to have ranged from $2 to $5 a yard for rushing and receiving to $200 to $500 per touchdown.

"I'm the one who started it," Rodgers once told a source about the pay-for-play setup. "It never changed. I had some $1,000 days. I didn't get paid for wins or losses. I got paid for individual performances."

Sources say Rodgers also admitted he was responsible for funneling performance money to other players on the team. "I had to add up yards and tackles," Rodgers told a source. "There had to be some paper involved. I'll tell you one thing—guys couldn't wait to see that stat sheet."

And the purpose of pay for play? "It was a way of controlling different players at different times," Rodgers told the same source. "[It was] a way to pump up guys."

When contacted about the reputed payoff plan, Rodgers declined public comment. Devaney denied any knowledge of a pay-for-play scheme. "If Rodgers was paid, he was paid by someone I knew nothing about," he said. "That's the one thing we have tried to stop. I can't say someway, somehow, someone might not give a kid something like that. I would say if Rodgers said it, it might be true, it might be true. I don't know who would have paid him."

Everett Alger? A thousand dollars or more per game?

"That's very significant," said Devaney. "I know nothing of this. It's the first I've heard of it. I believe I would have known or heard of it."

Former NU players recall that Alger enjoyed befriending black backfield stars such as Rodgers, Curtis and Roger Craig, Rozier, Fryar, and Gill.

An ex-Husker star who says he "hung out" at Alger's house on days off, playing pool and watching TV, said Alger "always had certain guys he was closer to."

What guys?

"His boys were the guys who were handling the ball. It was Turner and Mike and Irving and Roger."

Another former Husker, who spoke on the condition he not be identified, says he witnessed Alger discussing what the player described as a pay-for-play arrangement with Rozier and Fryar and Gill in 1983. "I remember him making out that little deal for them," said the player. "Certain touchdowns. I remember him saying that. Mine, mine wasn't like that. . . . He gave them all a sheet of paper. He wrote down on a sheet of paper and told them if they did this and this, they would get that."

The player also said that he had seen Rozier, Fryar, and Gill each accept an envelope from Alger in the Booster's home in 1983. The player said there was money in the envelope he received from Alger.

Another time, during a dinner one night at an Omaha restaurant, the same player said he felt "this little tap under my leg." Reaching down, he was handed what he thought was a piece of paper by Alger. The player deftly slipped the "paper" in his sock. Later he discovered Alger had passed him $300 "for stickin' it out. Being a good guy." The player also told of making visits to Alger's home in the first few weeks of the '83 season. Always on Wednesday nights. "Wednesday was always payday," said the former player. After "three or four weeks," the player said, he stopped attending.

"I got tired of feeling like I was one of his boys," he said.

On the doorstep of his hilltop home, Alger denied ever paying players. "I never had any involvement in that stuff," he said. "Summer jobs is all I've ever done."

You never paid anyone for touchdowns or yards?

"No."

You never paid players on Wednesday nights?

"On Wednesday? No, I never paid them. They worked for us. We didn't pay the full amount in the summer. We'd pay them on a weekly basis through the year."

Who worked for you?

"Mike, Turner, J.R., Roger."

What kind of jobs?

"I don't know what kinda work they did, where they worked," said Alger. "I know they didn't drive a truck."

Pressed on which other players worked for him, Alger said, "Hell, I don't know who worked for me," before adding, "I didn't do anything illegal. I've never paid a player to perform on the field. I helped recruit players. I told them the advantages and value of playing for the university."

Interviewed in Houston, Rozier said he never worked for Alger: "Turner did; I never worked for him." He described Alger as "a good man, good people to be around. I went up there and ate dinner a couple of times. We were just real close."

Had Alger paid him for yardage or touchdowns? "Nah," said Rozier. "I'd go up [to Omaha] on Wednesday nights to see a young woman named Gail. I'd stop at his house. . . . Me, Irving, Turner, Jamie [Williams], and Roger on Wednesday [would] go up and party."

Through a spokesman for the New England Patriots, Fryar declined to comment on any subject relating to that team or his playing years at Nebraska. (When contacted, Fryar's Dallas-based agent Sherwood Blount said, "I have no intention of listening to that trash, no interest in answering your questions. I don't give a shit what you put in your book, and I tell you Irving won't have anything to say either.")

A former girlfriend of Fryar's said he told her he had received "several hundred" dollars from Alger in 1983 and regularly drove to Omaha to pick up the cash. At one point, during a conversation in Fryar's apartment, the source said the wingback mentioned he had to go pick up $1,500.

"For what?" asked the visitor.

"For play, baby," said Fryar. "What do you think?"

Asked if she could identify the house where Fryar sometimes collected the money, the source drove to Omaha and independently identified Alger's home.

Gill declined any comment on a friendship with Alger. "I'd rather not talk about it," he said. "I don't want to get into stories about Nebraska football. My football career is over."

Had he been paid by Alger during his senior year? "I have no comment on it," said Gill. "Sorry about that, but there are too many things going on here; I want to stay out of the news. I've always been that way. Nothing's changed. No comment."

One of the many photos in Alger's sprawling home is said to show him dressed in a salmon-colored leisure suit with open collar, a birthday smile on his face. Also pictured are Rodgers, former NU quarterback David Humm (1972–74), and a football player Alger could not immediately place. The imprint on the back of the photo said it had been taken at the MGM Grand in Las Vegas. A casino source at that hotel said Alger had "good credit"—Vegas vernacular for being able to sign for a minimum of $10,000 in chips at the hotel. Alger admitted to a reporter to making frequent trips to Vegas and said he enjoyed playing blackjack. " I know a lot of people in Las Vegas," he said. "I go there a lot."

Asked if he had ever bet on a Nebraska game, Alger answered, "I don't bet football. Oh hell, I met a $1 bet in a pool."

3:30 P.M.

One sure thing about the '87 team was that Mark Blazek and Steve Taylor would have finished at the top of local popularity polls. Mark Blazek has the kind of rugged, be-all-you-can-be kind of face found in armed forces recruiting posters, which in Blazek's case wasn't far from the truth, since in his off-hours NU's starting safety had been making some big hits off the field driving M-60 tanks for the Nebraska National Guard.

More often than not, the roar of the crowd still ringing in his ear, the junior would rise by 7:00 A.M. on Sunday and drive thirty miles north to a National Guard post in nearby Wahoo. There Blazek would don a green helmet and change to Tank Gunner Blazek for search-and-destroy missions of a nonathletic order. "You go through stages," said Blazek. "There's four men in a tank. You have a driver, loaders who load the main rounds, your gunner, and then your tank commander. I've been a driver up until about two months ago. I've loaded, and now I'm a gunner. Basically all we fire are training rounds—they're not near as powerful as regular rounds. It's kinda fun, though."

Raised in rural Valparaiso, Nebraska, just north of Lincoln, the rangy Blazek was a local hero at Raymond Central High School, where he made All-State as a running back and wingback, picked up second-team All-State honors in basketball, and lettered four years in track. On the academic side he was listed in *Who's Who Among American High School Students* and *Distinguished American High School Students* three years running.

He walked on at NU in 1984 but barely played because of

the sheer number of players and a bum ankle. He missed the
'85 spring game with a broken wrist, then lost the subsequent
season to Army National Guard training. "The first couple of
years," he said, "you ask yourself, 'What am I doing here?'"
In the spring of '86 he began to find out. Listed seventh on
the ten-deeps when drills started, he was alternating with
starter Bryan Seibler when they finished. That fall he had 27
tackles and 2 interceptions and stuck his nose in places
where it hurt, all the while, off the field, keeping it pressed
deep into a book. By the OU game Blazek's brain (his 3.957
GPA in social science education was tops among Big Eight
defensive players) and brawn (6'2", 200 pounds, key interception and tackles against ASU and South Carolina) had
established him as one of the team's defensive leaders. Now
he was hell-bent on beating the Sooners. "Last year, everyone
was uptight," he said. "This year we feel we can go out and
play like we have all year and win this game."

But just like tanks, football teams can have only one
commander. One leader. And without question the leader of
the 1987 team was quarterback Taylor.

Here was no surprise package. No walk-on who hustled his
way up the depth chart. No, here was instead just the kind of
Taylor-made talent Osborne needed if Nebraska was going to
compete against the bewildering and ever-increasing size
and speed ratios of schools like Miami, Oklahoma, and Florida State.

To meet the challenge Osborne realized Husker football, as
most fans stereotypically view it today—a slow, grind-it-out
offense—needed to be updated and streamlined. Speed was

now the name of the game. So whomever Osborne chose to
succeed Gill as the field general had to be special—instinctive, creative, strong-armed, and nimble. But most of all,
calm and collected *and* fast and smart enough to execute
Osborne's complicated offensive schemes.

Enter Taylor, the fastest quarterback in NU's history. Born
in Fresno, California, on January 7, 1967, he'd grown up in a
rough neighborhood before moving to sunny San Diego

during his senior year in high school after his legal guardian and coach at Fresno's Edison High, Ray Hooper, was hired at Lincoln High.

Resentment surfaced immediately. "I was an outsider," Taylor once said of his early days at Lincoln High. "I wasn't a city boy. I really didn't try to be one. They thought I was different because I had my hair cut short. I was from up north, where wearing short hair was the thing.

"I knew I was different, and I knew I was going to be somebody. So it didn't bother me. I felt good about myself . . . but some players were mean to me. They didn't want to respect my talents."

Oh, but in the end they did. Especially after Taylor broke the school's total offense record held by the gifted Marcus Allen, now a star with the Los Angeles Raiders. Taylor rang up 3,211 total yards in his senior year, averaging a school-record 11.2 yards per carry. Dozens of Division I schools courted him, including NU. "I graded the high school quarterbacks myself, and I rated him the highest one I saw," Osborne once told the *Los Angeles Times*. "I liked the way he threw, and although they didn't run many options at Lincoln, I could see he could run the ball. I figured running the option was something he could pick up here."

Ironically, in high school Taylor had patterned himself after the classy, bookish-looking Gill, the "ideal" athlete in Osborne's mind, a player whose dignity and grace under pressure—both on and off the field—made the transition for all black athletes easier in Lincoln. Washington, California, Colorado, and Minnesota had all courted Taylor, but the QB said he liked Osborne's "realism."

"Some head coaches were cocky," he recalled. "They thought they were too good to talk to the athlete directly. He [Osborne] didn't make any promises he couldn't keep."

And when Gill took time out to meet with Taylor on his recruiting visit—the day before Gill was to be married—it was game, set, and match, Nebraska. "He wanted to know about the black and white situation on campus," Gill told the

Times. "How it felt being away from home. If this was the right place and the right coach for him. Steve wondered about being a black quarterback, but at Nebraska it doesn't matter what you are—black, white, Mexican. Football is No. 1. The Nebraska football team is in the spotlight."

Soon, so was Taylor.

As a freshman in 1985, he went from starting quarterback on the freshman team to backup on the varsity in four games. He sparkled in a fourth-quarter relief role against Michigan in the 1986 Fiesta Bowl, bringing the scarlet and cream to within 4 points of the Wolverines after trailing 27–14. In his first start the following fall, in the midst of the "Passgate" scandal, he completed 10 of 16 passes for 130 yards and 2 scores and rushed 12 times for 139 yards and 2 more TDs in crushing Florida State. Nebraska went 10–2 that year, and Taylor capped a strong personal season by being named MVP in the Sugar Bowl.

Celebrity was his—all of it, any way he wanted it—but knowing how deep that double-edged sword can cut in Lincoln, Taylor purposely kept a low profile, like his mentor Gill. Let Broderick and others rap. He would lead by example. Stay out of trouble. Out of the press.

And he did, until November 4, 1986, a dry, clear night in Lincoln.

According to the police report, Taylor was driving his white 1986 Honda Civic east at 30 to 35 mph on Vine Street near the corner of 17th at 6:35 P.M. when, according to the report, he "swerved" over the center line, missing one person but striking another pedestrian crossing Vine. That pedestrian, coincidentally, turned out to be I-back Ken Clark, who was redshirting that season. Clark hit the windshield with such force that he cracked it. Clark said at first he was all right and walked away. He was later treated at a local hospital for abrasions and bruises on his left leg and shoulder and was released. Taylor and two passengers in his car—teammate and roommate Thomas and Taylor's girlfriend at the time, Kelly Bell—at first denied there had been an accident or that

Taylor's car had struck anyone. The first local newspaper coverage of the accident did not appear until Thursday morning, some thirty-six hours after the incident. On Friday, Taylor, Thomas, and Bell were all cited for giving false information to the police and Taylor for negligent driving and improper lane change. In providing an account of the accident to the local papers, Osborne made it clear he felt the coverage overblown. But, he said, "I don't condone not telling the truth."

Taylor was upset, too. He told the *World-Herald* that he "didn't appreciate" the extensive coverage of the accident. "Why should you [cover it]? There are thousands of people out there having accidents every day."

But there are not thousands of starting quarterbacks in Lincoln. And though the papers didn't mention it, it wasn't Taylor's first brush with the local law. According to court records, he had been cited for failure to yield right-of-way in March and fined $25, and on July 22 he had been charged with leaving the scene of what was presumably an accident; the court records provided no other information. That case was dismissed one week later.

Within a week the pedestrian accident was old news, off the sports pages altogether. The three eyewitnesses whose names appeared on the police report were never mentioned publicly. When contacted, one eyewitness described how she and two other law-student friends had been behind the Taylor car at the time Clark was hit. After reading Osborne's account in the local papers, she said they had "marched down" to the police station. Asked if she noticed anything unusual about the report, she said, "Yes, them marking 'normal' under 'condition of the driver.'"

The eyewitness wouldn't explain what she meant by that remark, saying only that she and her friends were angry at the fellow students "for not telling the truth" and "that as law students we are very indignant."

She would say no more, preferring to let the legal system run its course, to wait and hear from a police officer or the city attorney's office. A week passed. Still nobody called. In January Taylor pleaded no contest to a reduced charge of driving left of center and giving a false statement. He was found guilty and fined $100 plus court costs.

After practice, as Taylor walks away from the indoor field, thoughts of court costs and negative publicity are far, far away. As he enters Memorial Stadium on his way back to the locker room, a lone spotlight shines down from the press box roof, illuminating a large red N at midfield. How fitting, for the normally low-key Taylor would be in a similar spotlight all week. OU coaches have already targeted him as the player they must contain to beat Nebraska. "Stop him, control him, neutralize him," said OU linebacker Dante Jones, "because he makes their offense go. Getting to Taylor is the key."

It won't be easy. The junior QB would enter the game having completed 50 percent of his passes (50 out of 100 for 841 yards) and 13 TDs, while rushing for 551 yards and 7 more scores on 129 carries. For Taylor this game will provide a fitting showcase, a welcome opportunity, despite the absence of Holieway, to step out of the shadow of the Sooners and establish once and for all who's the best QB in the conference. "I don't like to be second to anyone," Taylor says. "It bothers me. I held a lot of things in while I established myself." Not anymore.

Uncharacteristically Taylor had indulged in some explosive postgame Sooner-bashing following the 42–7 Missouri massacre in which he threw 4 touchdown passes. "The flat-out truth," said Steve Taylor, "is Oklahoma can't play with us. They are not good enough. Let me tell you, it might not even be close, and I mean that."

Oklahoma players ate that up like it was USDA choice Omaha sirloin. Faster than you can say "incentive," Taylor's quote was plastered to lockers, walls, windows—probably even a shower stall or two. Some OU players even started some "death threat" nonsense, woofing how Taylor was in for a "rude awakening" and how they planned to "deck him whether he's got the ball or not."

Like the spotlight, Taylor just shined it all on. "If all eleven

[Oklahoma] players are out to get me, then obviously ten of our guys are going to be free," he says. "We have a team where you really can't concentrate on one player. We've got other players who can hurt you. So I think it might work to our advantage.

"I'm a big-game person. I like to play in big games. I think that's the difference in our team this year. We've been improving against weaker teams and playing better against stronger ones. We've got a great team, and we're looking forward to playing Oklahoma."

Taylor is past midfield now, moving slowly down the sideline. A cool wind whips around the stadium. Night has fallen. Taylor doesn't even seem to notice, says how much he felt "at home" in Nebraska now, no second thoughts whatsoever about his decision to follow Gill. "I couldn't have made a better choice. I think the offense, the city, is suited to me. . . . I feel I'm one of the better quarterbacks around the nation, I think people are starting to recognize me." He scuffs a toe across the turf. "You know," he says, "there's no better feeling than being out here and playing well.

". . . I think they embarrassed us our freshman year; Jamelle made his debut, whatever. Nebraska hasn't been Nebraska the last three or four years. When I came here, I was under the impression they won Big Eight championships all the time. I'm kinda glad now the tide is turning and things are on our side."

Steve Taylor is off the field now, about to enter the red double doors that lead down a wide hall to the locker room. But before he does, he stops and says: "I think it's time for Nebraska to be Nebraska again. To be on top for a while."

7:15 P.M.

Darkness settles over Lincoln. Icy gusts blow through downtown streets. The windchill dips toward zero. The Dow Jones is dropping, too, down nearly twenty-seven points today.

Weather and stocks, an ebb and flow not unlike that of athletic emotion. Game day is still seventy-six hours away. In his second-floor office Tom Osborne continues to play his chess match with Oklahoma.

Making tracks: a farmer tends his fields in Nebraska.

Omaha state senator Ernie Chambers has questioned the Huskers' holy image.

Reporters from across the country converged on Lincoln for Game of the Century II against Oklahoma in 1987.

The last five years haven't been easy for NU coach Dr. Tom Osborne.

At Hastings College, a young Osborne starred in football, basketball, and track.

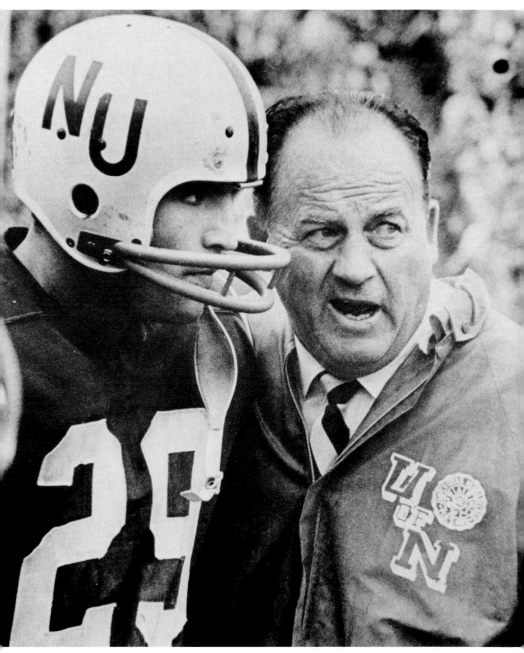

Dynamic Bob Devaney coached NU to two national championships before he handpicked Osborne to succeed him.

I-back Doug DuBose and his leased sports car became the focal point of a lengthy NCAA investigation in 1986.

Former Huskers tight end Jamie Williams (below) and fullback Andra Franklin (above) were two of the many Huskers who sold game tickets for profit.

Quarterback Steve Taylor (9) drew everyone's attention during OU week.

Wingback Dana Brinson (front) and defensive
tackle Neil Smith were two of many black
athletes who had some difficulty adjusting to
life in Lincoln.

Raw emotion, spectacular plays . . . and a motor
mouth made Broderick Thomas (89) a big hit with
the fans and the media.

Wide receiver Rod Smith was No. 1 in punt returns—and in the heart of many female fans.

In their own ways, I-back Mike Rozier (left), wingback Irving Fryar (27), and quarterback Turner Gill (below left) left an indelible mark—good and bad—on the football program.

Hard times have hit former Heisman Trophy winner Johnny Rodgers (left), but his son, Terry (inset), an I-back, hopes to make a name for himself at Nebraska.

For NU strength coach Boyd Epley (kneeling), they're never too young to pump a little iron.

Superstar lineman Dean Steinkuhler admitted to using steroids during his junior and senior years.

In Game of the Century II, Sooner QB Charles Thompson put the moves on Thomas (89).

Taylor (9) attempts to engineer a late rally against OU. The Sooners eventually won 17-7.

Priorities intact, the future of Cornhusker football enjoys a fatherly ride.

WEDNESDAY

6:15 A.M.
The morning *World-Herald* has already been dropped off
outside the hotel door. This week's collection of letters to the
sports editor, entitled "The Voice from the Grandstand,"
proves particularly biting.

> Husker fans, get ready for a Taylor-made Husker vic-
> tory as Sandman & Co. bury Switzer and his Sooners in
> our house. Orange Bowl, here we come!
>
> Mike Vlach, Lincoln

> Tick . . . tick . . . tick . . . tick. Do you hear that, Barry?
> It's the time running down on the Sooners' reign as Big
> Eight champs. And you can't rewind the clock because
> we've got that key, too.
>
> Dave Sjutz, York

> Arrogance—a fitting description of Oklahoma foot-
> ball. Intimidation—the single most utilized ingredient
> Barry Switzer employs to win. We need to follow Broder-

121

ick's lead and put the monkey on Barry's back—intimidate him.

Go, Big Red! Git 'em, git 'em, git 'em.

John E. Chestnut, Omaha

If you are a gambling person, you should bet on the coach that is 11–4 and count on the choking trend to continue.

Ed Hengemuehler, Sioux City, Iowa

I don't care if the ball boy has to play quarterback for the Sooners. Nebraska always finds a way to snatch defeat from the jaws of victory in the big games, especially Oklahoma.

M. A. Chaney, Chicago

12:00 P.M.

One by one they parade into the players' lounge at South Stadium, like beauty queens, to face an ever-growing gathering of broadcasters and writers. Taylor speaks first, followed by Thomas, Neil Smith, and "End Zone" Jones. When all is said and done, the press conference proves a catharsis of sorts, a chance for players long stifled for geographic and psychological reasons to voice their emotions. For years, given this very same forum, Husker players routinely talked in clichés ("We're just happy to have the opportunity . . ."), but now the new and improved—that is, laid back—Osborne has allowed a whole new breed of ballplayer to show up—more open and honest—and emotional—than ever before. "This is my twentieth year of covering Nebraska," says Virgil Parker, sports editor of the *Journal-Star*, after the press conference, "and I've never seen them like this. They never did this at any stage under Devaney."

Taylor as he had the day before, comes off cool and confident, a *GQ* kind of guy who shows up looking smooth, dressed in baggy turquoise sweatpants and gray and white windbreaker. He doesn't equivocate when asked about his

"Oklahoma can't play with us" statement. "That's the way I feel," he says. "I don't want people to take it out of context, think I'm cocky or arrogant. But I feel we're a much better team than Oklahoma this year."

Taylor went on to applaud Thomas for injecting some pure passion into the program, for building the fire that has thawed a glacial image and drawn an entire team together. "Broderick is Broderick," said Taylor. "He says what he feels. What he says comes strictly from the heart."

Thomas follows with one such heartfelt interview. Or should we say performance? Either way, it captivates the crowd and leaves assistant sports information director Bouma gently shaking her head and whispering "Oh, Jesus" at some of his answers. Dressed in his Hell-Raisin' tour T-shirt, white Nebraska cap, and enough neckware to challenge Mr. T, Thomas approaches the audience warily at first, like a bomb-squad member eyeing a suspicious package.

At first he just sits down and smiles, licking his lips over and over, taking shallow breaths in between. You can almost hear the ticking inside his chest.

Seconds pass.

Someone coughs.

Finally:

"Jamelle says he has a spare key to your house."

Thomas leans back in a folding chair and shuts his eyes. His breath is rapid, distressed. "Is that right?" he says, opening his eyes. "I think our scout team will give us a little better game than what we might see Saturday."

"Oh, Jesus," says Bouma.

And off he goes on what turns out to be one wild thirty-minute "Heeeeere's Broderick" scat-alogue. Some highlights:

Q: "Keith Jackson, Oklahoma's tight end, says you have a big mouth."

A: "I don't like to hear him tell me to shut up, so I'll put it like this. He'll be here Saturday, and we'll see who does the shutting up. No problem. We will have contact, me and him."

Q: [Oklahoma reserve quarterback] Eric Mitchel said ear-

lier this week the Oklahoma defense would hit Steve
Taylor even when he didn't have the ball."

A: "Jamelle's not there to talk. I noticed his buddies on the
defensive side of the ball, they're pretty quiet. The only
guys that are talking are the guys on offense, the guys
not playing. Eric Mitchel. They're sending death threats
to Steve. It's going to be fun. We're going to see who's a
man and who's not."

Q: "The Sooners' Lydell Carr also will miss the game with a
knee injury."

A: "I'd rather have Jamelle and Carr back. That way we
won't hear any excuses why we beat Oklahoma."

Q: "The Sooners say 'Your house' has become their 'winter
home.'"

A: "Is that right? Well, tell them to try and come on in their
winter home and take a vacation."

Q: "Switzer talks about his fourth-quarter magic when he
plays the Cornhuskers."

A: "Houdini is not allowed in our house, so there's not
going to be any fourth-quarter magic around here,
unless we're doing it."

Q: "Banderas said in a TV interview that Oklahoma would
leave with a 42–10 loss."

A: "I like the 42, but I can't vouch for the 10."

Q: "What score do you pick?"

A: "No prediction. Just be there or have your TV set on."

Unfortunately, Smith and Jones have to follow this act, and
they pale in comparison, causing about as big a stir as their
two last names. Smith, at least, *looks* interesting. He shows
up wearing a diamond stud in his left ear, the metalworked
words *Twisted* and *Steel* pinned on his shirt collar. An
homage, one suspects, to either a heavy-metal group or
Smith's style of play. Still reporters are nonplussed; chatter-
box Thomas has already stolen the show.

The one issue not raised during the press conference is less
obvious than all this newfound freedom, even though it's right
there in, uh, black and white: that all the interviewed players

are black and that their very presence behind a microphone heralds a significant change in Husker football.

How significant was revealed in these numbers: a record ten of Nebraska's twenty-two starters for the OU game are black. All the black starters but Jones, the 5'10", 180-pound streakster (4.3 in the 40) out of Omaha Central High, are from out of state, another Nebraska record. And thirty-five of the top ninety-five players are black—another milestone.

Yes, the disparate roads Taylor, Thomas, and Smith had traveled to Lincoln—from California, Texas, and Louisiana, respectively—reveal a major social change, a socioathletic revolution or evolution, really, in Husker football, one that isn't generally discussed in the local press or, certainly, on downtown streets or at booster luncheons. It is clear that in its stated desire to infuse more "speed" into both its offensive and defensive teams, Nebraska is following a widespread practice employed by college athletic programs and reaching out to the inner cities for help.

Ironically, the first major college black football player, running back George "G. A." Flippin, who was viewed as something of a gridiron mercenary, played—and lettered—at Nebraska in 1892-94, his very presence causing such a stir that Missouri actually forfeited a game, 1–0, to the Huskers in 1892. After his career ended, Flippin remained in the state and became a successful doctor.

It wasn't until more than seventy years later, however, during a progressive period under Devaney, that Nebraska had its first black consensus All-America, an offensive lineman by the name of Bob Brown, from Cleveland, Ohio, who went on to become a first-round draft choice of the Philadelphia Eagles in 1964. Tight end Tony Jeter and split end Freeman White, from Steubenville, Ohio, and Montgomery, Alabama, respectively, were similarly honored in 1965. Nebraska's next black stars were stalwarts of the national championship teams—Omaha's Rodgers, noseguard Rich Glover from Jersey City, New Jersey, defensive end Willie Harper from Toledo, Ohio, and offensive tackle Daryl White of Newark, New Jersey. But in the next eight years, while schools such as Oklahoma, Texas, Ohio State, Michigan, Michigan State, Pittsburgh, USC, and UCLA, embraced the black athlete, Nebraska, like so many other midwestern and southern schools, lagged behind, primarily because, as Osborne saw it, recruiting problems related to "population, distance, and weather." Five blacks gained All-America honors at NU from 1973 to 1980. Yet during this period two-deeps on both sides of the ball, especially in the lines, were stocked by what today is still considered the predominant image of Cornhusker football—the beefy farm boy.

In 1974, however, integration hit college football harder than Jimmy Brown hit cornerbacks. Witness the string of eight straight black Heisman Trophy winners: Archie Griffin (1974–75), Tony Dorsett (1976), Earl Campbell (1977), Billy Sims (1978), Charles White (1979), George Rogers (1980), Marcus Allen (1981), and Herschel Walker (1982). Prior to that, since the award was instituted in 1935, only three nonwhites had won the trophy. But now, in the late 1970s and early 1980s, the times were obviously a-changin', and Osborne—very competitive—was moving right along with them.

"I'd say the conscious decision was made from about 1977 on," he says. "We've tried to recruit speed for years. You have guys visit campus, and you just don't get them. There are just not a lot of real fast kids in the vicinity. Most of the them are coming in from a distance—and those are harder guys to get because you've got to get them past Ohio State and Michigan and USC and Texas and Oklahoma to get 'em here."

Osborne's initial attempts to recruit black players had been largely regional in nature, with forays into New Jersey, Ohio, and California or small towns in the South (I. M. Hipp came from Chapin, South Carolina, Andra Franklin from Anniston, Alabama). As the 1980s began and NU stars like Russell Gray (drafted by New Orleans), Jarvis Redwine (selected by Minnesota), Jimmy Williams (Detroit), and Rodney Lewis (New Orleans) were chosen early by the NFL, Nebraska caught a break. Three breaks, actually. Big ones. They came in the form of Rozier, Fryar, and Gill, the so-called "triplets," three truly remarkable athletes.

"We got lucky with Rozier," recalls Osborne. "He was a wishbone fullback in high school, and the teachers at his school were on strike. It was hard to get films, so he wasn't seen by a lot of other schools. And we discovered Irving by accident. We saw him catch one pass [on film]; we never saw him run the ball. I told Coach [Gene] Huey, 'If you think he's a good player, go ahead [and give him a scholarship].' Turner was heavily recruited, but for some reason Texas backed off and he picked us over Oklahoma."

In 1980–81, as Gill and company paid their dues, the entire NU football complex—the players, coaches, and community—was still adjusting to the arrival of increasing numbers of black football players. "It was a culture clash," recalls one who played on the team during that period. "Lots of white players from small towns, cities with all-white schools, never associated with black athletes. I'm not saying it was a racial problem. Everybody just learned and grew."

For some black athletes the transition process, the adjustment to the tone and tenor of life in Lincoln, was easy. For others it proved particularly daunting. Both Thomas and Taylor recall problems; Thomas said he was stunned when he realized Lincoln had so few black residents.

"I came here, and it was culture shock," he said. "I had a problem getting dates. Houston was ten beats ahead."

"Black people party differently," added Taylor one afternoon. "White people get drunk or whatever. Black people like to go out and dance. There [were] only two black fraternities on campus, but they don't have a house." Consequently both Taylor and Thomas said during their early months at NU in the fall of 1985 they spent a lot of time at the black cultural center on campus.

Rozier and Fryar, however, were of a slightly different state of mind. They were real city boys. Rozier grew up on the mean streets of Camden, New Jersey. Fryar spent his youth in the rugged neighborhoods of Mount Holly, New Jersey. They came to campus with a more aggressive—some said almost defiant—demeanor. Rozier arrived in 1981, a year after Fryar, having spent his freshman year at Coffeyville (Kansas) Community College raising his grades. The homesickness that drove him to ride buses for hours on the interstate to get back to Camden had not abated. "I hated it [Lincoln]," he once said. "It was too slow. I couldn't wait to get the hell out." Fryar wasn't much happier. So it was after their sensational junior seasons, when the hype and hysteria of Husker football were beginning to build to their highest pitch, that the so-called "New Jersey Jets," fueled by what one friend described as an "above the law" attitude, effectively turned Lincoln into their own private playground.

"Things got way out of hand that season," remembers a close friend of both athletes. "The sky was the limit. You know how people party all night and leave a house in shambles. When they left Nebraska, the program was in shambles. . . . Irving and Mike tried to run Lincoln the way they would New Jersey. Lincoln was a drag. The city boys came to the country to teach folks a lesson."

Fryar had arrived on campus in a junky old car, but by the time his senior season ended he was seen styling around town in three late-model cars—a yellow Corvette, a blue Datsun 200SX, and a brown Maxima. "I didn't even know," said Osborne when informed of Fryar's car collection. Rozier, meantime, was cruising around in a black late-model Cadillac. Osborne remembers checking on that car. "I called him in and asked [Mike] where he got the car," says the coach. "He said he leased it. I had Frank Solich check with the company. Yes, he was leasing it and paying $200, $300 a month. I asked him where he got the money. Said he got it from back home. It's kinda hard to push too hard."

Many of the players' cars—including all of Fryar's—sources say, were obtained from the same place—an Omaha leasing company managed by a young, enthusiastic Husker booster. Recalls one of Fryar's and Rozier's former teammates who also leased a car from the same company: "The owner was just one of those guys who just wanted to be around, [to] go out and have a beer with you. That kind of guy. A good guy."

Rozier, who recalled his lease payment being $116 per month, said the lease money came from two sources: "I was working for a doctor," he said. "Cleaning up his yard, raking leaves. And my mom would send me money."

Fryar was said to have paid little or no money per month to drive at least one of his cars. "He'd just send in the [$125] payment slip without the money," said a source close to Fryar. "Irving never sent in a dime."

Fryar, it appears, didn't stop at free transportation. Sources say his off-campus house was furnished (sofa, lamps, end tables, chairs, TV) with the help of his "Lincoln parents."

The Lincoln Parent Program (LPP) had been established in 1974 by Louis L. Roper, now a vice president for FirsTier Bank, Dave Meyers, a printing executive, and Mike McNair, an insurance broker, shortly after a high school All-America linebacker from Lawrence, Kansas, left school homesick just one week after classes began. In principle, the program provided an innocent "home away from home," a place where a player could do his laundry on Sunday night, get an occasional home-cooked meal, watch a little TV, have a quiet place to study. At its peak the program included some eighty Lincoln families—one family for every scholarship player and valued in- and out-of-state walk-ons.

Those applying for membership were said to be screened carefully. Potential "parents" had to apply to the program and submit to questioning. The various families' backgrounds, said Roper, spanned the economic spectrum, and sponsors attempted to find a "commonality" between athlete and surrogate parents, but it was common knowledge around town that star players were routinely matched with the more prosperous "parents"—doctors, lawyers, bankers—to the point where the program was known by another name, "The Adopt the I-back Program." To his credit, Osborne lectured both players and "parents" each and every season about possible NCAA abuses. He even went so far as to have "parents" sign an agreement clearly outlining activities as "permissible" and "not permissible."

"We don't support them financially," said Roper. "In no way is anything illegal done. The real value of the program is it helps provide support and lets the kids get degrees."

Over the years the program enjoyed varying degrees of social success. Some players saw their "parents" once, maybe twice a year. Others embraced their newfound families with open arms and ended up making lasting friendships with the families and their children, benefitting all involved. "I never would have made it at Nebraska if it wasn't for my Lincoln parents," said Thomas, who was paired with Mike McGowan, the manager of a grain elevator company in Lincoln, and his wife, Maggie. The McGowans had also served as Rozier's second family.

"I went to [my Lincoln parents] a lot on Sundays," recalled Tomjack. "I'd have supper and sit around and read the paper and eat all of [the wife's] great desserts."

"My Lincoln parents treated me like a son," remembers running back Albert Lewis, who went to high school in Las Vegas. "I would go over on Sunday to eat dinner and do laundry, but I never got any money."

A change in NCAA policy in 1986 forced schools such as Nebraska to cancel family programs which afforded athletes a "home-away-from-home" environment. The association was said to be anxious about potential abuses and what competitive advantages such schools enjoyed with the sponsorship programs. The "extra benefits" presumably being, in the NCAA's perspective, TV watching, family dinners, and the use of a permanent press cycle. Roper was crushed by the decision. "A big mistake," he said one day, adding the NCAA had "missed the point" of Lincoln's largesse. "Frankly," he said, "I'm sick. It helped a lot of people get an education they may not have otherwise got because of this support. I have a real problem thinking what was done was illegal."

Well, then, Roper would have had a real problem thinking about what Gary and Cindy Meyer, Fryar's "parents," allegedly did. Because, sources say, when they weren't dropping by with secondhand furniture, Gary, a vice president of Dean Witter at the time, was "loaning" Fryar small amounts of cash—$20 or so at a pop—and taking him out to dinner and the racetrack, suspicious activities by NCAA standards. After being informed of these alleged transgressions, Osborne contacted both Gary Meyer and Fryar. "Gary denied it, and so did Irving," said Osborne. "I don't know what else I can do."

(Attempts to obtain a comment from Meyer were unsuccessful. In a brief office interview one morning he described himself as "too busy" to talk. Told the visitor would come back at Meyer's convenience, Meyer said it wasn't necessary; he had nothing else to say.)

Fryar clearly was not the only Husker to enjoy the less-publicized benefits of the program. A close friend of DuBose remembers the I-back's Lincoln parents repeatedly stopping by DuBose's apartment offering food, use of their blue Lincoln Town Car, and dinners at Tony & Luigi's. "It was a revolving door with his [Lincoln] parents," says the friend. "They were coming over a lot, asking, 'Doug, can we get you this? Doug, can we get you that?'"

It now appears that the one thing several Husker players had no trouble getting, when the need arose, was drugs.

It was the summer of 1983 when one of Rozier's teammates struck up an acquaintance with a sexy blonde by the name of Ann at a party. "She liked athletes," recalled the teammate. "Later I saw her at a party, [but] Mike went up and talked to her. She was with him from then on. I had a conversation with her a couple of times, but she was with Mike." At the time, however, Ann Waldron was also with someone else—her husband, Chuck Waldron, a local realtor—and court records show that the two were living in Lincoln and had been married in Aspen, Colorado, in 1977. They had a son born on November 1, 1982.

On April 26, 1984, according to court records, Chuck Waldron filed for divorce. In the divorce papers he would accuse his wife of "consorting with single men," adding that she had had "single men stay in her home on numerous occasions in the presence of said minor child." On December 4, 1984, the marriage was dissolved.

Shortly thereafter, on January 14, 1985, Chuck Waldron took some rather unusual and dramatic legal action. According to U.S. District Court records, he filed a rare "alienation of affection" suit against Rozier and requested a jury trial. Rozier responded by arguing in court papers that Ann Waldron was estranged from her husband when he met her, although in the papers he admits to having sexual relations with her on at least four different occasions in January, June, and September 1984.

Exhibits filed in the lawsuit underscored the depth of the Waldron-Rozier relationship, one that continued well into 1984, when Rozier was a member of the USFL Pittsburgh Maulers. The exhibits: A valentine postmarked (February 11, 1984) from Rozier to Waldron. A card with a poem by Laine Parsons signed, "Love Always, Mike." A poem by Linda Gatto: "You mean the world to me" signed A.W. A card: "Can't you get this through your thick hide? Love you always, Mike." A letter from Ann asking Rozier to quit football and return to Lincoln.

The Waldron vs. Rozier suit was subsequently settled out of court in early 1986. The Lincoln attorney who represented Chuck Waldron said the suit was brought after his client discovered a calendar kept by Ann Waldron that included references to her relationships with Rozier and other NU players.

It was during pretrial proceedings in this case that the word *cocaine* reportedly first surfaced in connection with Rozier. The attorney said he questioned Ann Waldron during her deposition about cocaine use by herself and Rozier, and Waldron, while admitting to using cocaine on one occasion, denied ever seeing Rozier use the drug. Yet the attorney charged there was a "clear indication" of cocaine use by Rozier, contending that a key reason the alienation suit was settled was the specter of Rozier's drug use being aired in open court.

"You don't have to be a rocket scientist to know the minute a jury in this area heard about those parties and stuffing that powder in their nose, they [Rozier et al.] were done," said the attorney. "I was aiming for that in deposition. . . . They just didn't need the bad publicity."

In the fall of 1986 Ann Waldron was working in an accounting department and, in her words, "putting my life back together." In an interview she continued to deny any involvement with cocaine but said that in 1984—while Rozier was with the Maulers—she witnessed him freebase cocaine on one occasion in her apartment. "He brought his own pipe," said Waldron. "I knew he was using it [coke] in 1984."

According to those who either sold to or did drugs with Rozier and Fryar or witnessed their drug use, Rozier and Fryar began to dabble with the drug during the summer of 1983. "Before they were just smoking [dope]," said a dealer who said he regularly sold coke to both players, "but after they got turned on to coke they went crazy, crazy. . . . They started using it after games, on Wednesday nights. But they kept it quiet. They didn't want to be out in the [public] eye."

At first, sources say, both players just snorted the drug, often at impromptu postpractice parties at Rozier's apartment or Fryar's rented house, parties deemed "a status deal" to attend. A close friend of Fryar's during this period said she saw him use cocaine "at least eight or nine times" at these parties.

The same sources identify, in addition to Rozier and Fryar, other NU players who were present at the parties as Guy Rozier (Mike's brother), Ricky Simmons, Kevin Biggers, Anthony Thomas, and Todd Frain. (Simmons denied using coke, and despite repeated attempts, the other players could not be reached for comment.)

Sometime that fall a starter on the NU basketball team joined the party crowd. He remembers snorting coke with Fryar, [Mike] Rozier, Biggers, Thomas, and Simmons "a couple of times" while watching Monday Night Football games at Simmons's apartment. "Mostly it was drinking," says the player, who spoke on the condition he not be identified, "but a couple of times coke happened to be there."

The player also said that free cars and booster payoffs were not limited to football players. He said that during his recruiting visit to Lincoln former Nebraska basketball coach Joe

Cipriano, who died of cancer two years later, introduced him to a booster by the name of Dan Hergert Sr., who told him he would receive $500 upon signing with the Huskers and $100 a month thereafter. "Every month I'd go over to Hergert's office and pick up an envelope," recalls the ex-player. "It was in twenties, and he'd ask me how practice was going—that's about it." Hergert, who owns Hergert Oil and is on the board of directors of the Touchdown Club, failed to respond to numerous phone calls and messages left in person at his office.

The starter also said players were allowed free access to rental cars parked at Lincoln's airport. This was also arranged by Cipriano. "The coach set it up," he said. "We used to go to the airport and pick them up. Sometimes I went by myself, sometimes [others] took me to the airport. We never filled out any forms."

As the 1983 season wore on, sources said Rozier and Fryar spent increasing amounts of time and money on cocaine, sometimes freebasing the drug for a richer high. Sources who both supplied the coke and did the drugs with them said the pair routinely purchased "eight-balls" (an eighth of an ounce of cocaine) for $300 during the season, driving to Omaha to make a connection or buying the coke locally.

One night in Omaha, Rozier, Fryar, Simmons, and others met up and reportedly snorted coke until 5:00 A.M. "They went through a quarter ounce [$600 worth] like it was nothing," said one who participated in the drug use. "Then they bought two more eight-balls."

Other times the two stars were said to have sneaked out of Kellogg Center, where the team was lodged on Friday nights before home games, and slipped over to a friend's house to party. "The first thing we did was get on the rock [coke]," said one who participated in the drug use.

Money apparently never proved a problem for Rozier or Fryar. "Mike would flash some cash," said one supplier. "He had long dollars at will." As they got high, the two stars were heard talking about selling tickets, getting paid to play, agent money . . . and other sources of income.

Sitting behind the wheel of a customized red 500 SEC Mercedes, as he waits in the parking lot at the Houston Oilers' practice facility, Mike Rozier says, "I don't want to talk about anything negative. It's history, man; that's '83. I'm not saying anything." In the running back's left ear a diamond sparkles. "That's all I'm going to say," he announces. "Talk to me tomorrow, man." He speeds away.

Tomorrow comes, and Rozier is asked if he used cocaine during his senior year at Nebraska. "I never did coke in college," he says. Pressed on the subject, however, he admits experimenting with the drug briefly—and liking it—in 1985. "I tried coke [in '85]," said Rozier. "It was okay, but it was too expensive.

"I smoked reefer [at Nebraska], but I never did cocaine. I talk a lot of shit here [in Houston]. I talk about drugs here every day. It keeps me motivated. So, the press, the coaches, the fans—that shit don't bother me. I like to keep talking. I don't let that shit bother me."

Asked about Rozier and Fryar and cocaine Osborne said he was "not particularly" worried despite hearing persistent rumors linking his two New Jersey jets to drug use. "You always hear rumors," he said, "and I guess I heard a couple or three. But that was the year we started drug testing. We didn't have any of those guys turn up positive."

Told that his star players had been heard boasting about skipping drug tests, Osborne replied, "They [Rozier and Fryar] tested. . . . They were tested, oh, three, four times prior to the bowl game. Marijuana. Cocaine. We usually sent them right in off the practice field. They were tested every three or four weeks, random, backs one week, line the next. We were concerned in general. But we really didn't hear anything in particular about those guys [Rozier and Fryar]. But cocaine is only detectable forty-eight, seventy-two hours, so a guy might not get caught."

Rozier offers a radically different view on drug testing. He says he never took a drug test in his senior season at Nebraska. "No," he said when asked about the tests, "I didn't need to. I wasn't on drugs. . . . I never took a drug test except for beginning-of-the-year physicals. They could tell I wasn't on drugs. I performed well. I acted the same every day. Why would I have a drug test?"

(By March of 1985 cocaine use at Nebraska had escalated to the point where, according to a well-placed law enforcement source, one of the team's offensive starters was said to be under investigation by both a Lancaster County grand jury and local and federal authorities [DEA] for cocaine possession and trafficking in what was described as "fair size" amounts of cocaine—up to four ounces at a time. Asked about such an investigation, County Attorney Mike Heavican answered, "There is nothing filed in that case. No record.")

In a letter to a reporter, Osborne explained his team had just one positive result for cocaine from 1983–86—and just 7 percent for marijuana. "This [cocaine use] is entirely possible," he wrote, "although we did not have any of the players you seem to have questions about . . . ever test positive."

The fact that Nebraska was playing for a national championship in January 1984 evidently failed to slow the use of cocaine among team members; purportedly it actually increased during the days preceding the Miami game. One Husker remembered that during the team's stay at the Fountainbleau Hotel in Miami, the hotel for the Big Eight representative, local street dealers made frequent visits to players' rooms to peddle small amounts of cocaine and other drugs. Said the player, "I was in the room once when a guy came with . . . cocaine. He was selling to people who didn't even know anything about cocaine."

When was that?

"It was like the first week before the Orange Bowl; then it kinda tapered off."

How many guys were buying?

"It was a lot of guys, a lot. [The dealer] was selling it in capsules, like a pill capsule, stuffed with cocaine. Or basically whatever you wanted."

Who were the main buyers?

"The main people were Ricky, Mike, Irving, and Anthony Thomas."

Fryar's performance in the bowl game was disappointing, when compared to his season statistics. The gifted wingback had averaged 11.6 yards per carry in his career and 17.9 yards on 67 catches. But in Miami, to the eternal grief of Husker fans everywhere, he dropped a wide-open touchdown pass from Gill with time ticking away and Nebraska trailing the Hurricanes by just seven points.

In retrospect, it appears no one was more dismayed and confused by the drop than the Huskers' assistant coach, Huey. He told one longtime acquaintance he ran the film of Fryar's dropped pass "over and over again," searching for some clue or answer. And only after hours of agonizing study did Huey dare suggest, according to someone who heard him say it, that either Rozier or Fryar or both might have "thrown" the Orange Bowl game against Miami.

Rozier played valiantly in the contest, running for 147 yards before a leg injury forced him out of action in the third quarter. Fryar, by comparison, seemed out of sync, despite catching 5 passes for 61 yards. There was Fryar, slotted right, posting over the middle past two defenders, wide open as he streaked toward the goal line. At the one-yard line, he twisted slightly to his left to gather in a tight pass aimed at his left hip. But the ball hits Fryar right in the hands and bounces away. Seconds later, in the back end of the end zone, Fryar—on his knees now—slams the turf in disgust.

In a lunch meeting at Grandmother's restaurant with a former girlfriend of Fryar's, Huey was said to have turned the conversation toward that exact play. As the friend remembered it, the lunch conversation went like this:

"Do you think they [Irving and Mike] played loaded during the [Miami] game?" said Huey.

"I wouldn't put it past them," said Fryar's friend.

"Do you think they'd do that?" responded Huey. "I don't want to think they'd do that. Do you really think they might have thrown the game?"

According to the girlfriend, Huey added, "We've looked over the films over and over. I just can't believe it. I don't see how he dropped that ball." He said, "I understand from some of the guys that [Irving] was involved with gambling."

Yes, said the guest, to the best of her knowledge, Irving did like to gamble, and she remembered hearing him, during his senior year, make calls on Sunday mornings to a contact at a campus frat house. "He would tell whoever it was [on the other end] to put the usual on the games," remembered the woman.

At first Osborne denied any knowledge of Fryar's suspected gambling. "This would be the first I've heard anything about it, to be honest with you," he said when the subject was raised. Told an assistant coach had raised this exact subject at a lunch just a few days earlier, Osborne then said he had "heard some rumors about gambling." He just wasn't clear on the source. "Maybe when Coach Huey talked to her that was the first time I heard that," he said. "The NFL had investigated. He did not play well in the Orange Bowl."

And Huey's remark about the possibility that Fryar and Rozier had "thrown" the Miami game?

"He [Huey] might have been [concerned], but I was certainly not," said Osborne. "That's coming from left field. I would *really* take a dim view of that [being printed]. . . . It's always a possibility. I think Irving felt terrible. He didn't play well that night. I think when all is said and done, he and Mike were under a lot of pressure down there. The agent thing was really heavy on their mind."

In an interview Huey angrily denied asking directly about Fryar and gambling or ever saying he'd run the film "over and over."

"I never did," he said. "She said something that the NFL had come and talked to her. I don't know exactly what the questioning was."

So you didn't ask anything about Fryar and gambling?

"Nothing more than I read in the papers [about] Irving's activities in Boston."

In 1987, Huey left the Husker program after ten years to take an assistant position at Arizona State after working briefly at Wyoming. (He now coaches at Ohio State.)

On May 29, 1986, *Boston Globe* sports columnist Will McDonough reported that the NFL was investigating allegations that Fryar and possibly some of his New England Patriot teammates had been involved in betting on NFL games during the 1985 season. McDonough's sources described a scenario in which New England Patriots coach Raymond Berry had forwarded gambling information—what team owner Patrick Sullivan described as "an unsubstantiated rumor"—to NFL security director Warren Welch. Welch later confirmed to the *Globe* that an investigation was under way but offered no further comment.

For Fryar the gambling investigation marked the third time that year the then-twenty-three-year-old former No. 1 draft choice had made headlines for his off-field activities. In January, just before the AFC championship game against Miami, he had suffered a deep cut on the little finger of his hand as a result of what he first termed nothing more than a kitchen accident. But when it was learned his wife, Jackie, was also treated at a suburban Boston hospital for bruises, Fryar admitted he had been cut during a "domestic situation" at home.

In February, in another *Globe* story, Fryar was named as one of six players who Sullivan confirmed had admitted drug usage to management. Fryar denied that story, saying, "They can test me anytime they want." When the gambling allegations surfaced, he took an equally aggressive stance in the local press. "The whole truth is I don't know anything about all this," he told the *Boston Herald* the next day. "That's the whole truth and nothing but the truth. I never, ever, never gambled on games. This is straight out of left field, totally. I'm going to take a lie detector test to prove it."

The test was done in Dallas, arranged by Fryar's agent, Blount. Eric Holden, the test administrator, told the Boston papers that since turning pro Fryar "had never himself gambled or bet on any NFL games or had ever allowed or let anyone use his name or his money to gamble on NFL games."

One of the Nebraska fraternities Fryar was said by a law enforcement source to be betting with while still in college was Phi Delta Theta—information, the source said, he passed along to the NFL back in June 1986. Earlier that year university police had busted a large on-campus bookmaking operation at the Phi Delta Theta house. The leader of that ring, sitting in the living room of his parents' home in Omaha one afternoon, admitted he began taking bets during the 1983 season and said he had grossed $500,000 in a ten-week period during the 1984 football season, clearing some $22,000. He denied taking any bets from Fryar. So did the "runner" who handled the Phi Delt betting in 1983. Another source who said he had supplied Fryar with cocaine, said he and Fryar had, in the past, discussed college and pro selections on parlay cards. "Parlays, he did that," said the source. "Every week, college and pro games. [Once] he asked me if I had my sheet. We talked about the football games."

The NFL investigation into Fryar's alleged gambling activities was handled by ex–FBI agent William N. Ouseley, an NFL security representative from Kansas City. Ouseley interviewed a number of people around the university, including an ex-girlfriend of Fryar's, a member of the local police department, a campus bookmaker, and Gary Meyer. Welch later admitted Ouseley's investigation indicated that Fryar had a "propensity for certain activities" while at Nebraska.

Was the activity gambling?

"People indicated that," said Welch.

Fryar, however, was never found guilty by the NFL of any gambling-related activities. Ouseley later said although he was unable to completely substantiate claims that Fryar had gambled while in college, "I wouldn't doubt anything said about him."

Whatever their off-field activities, the 24–2 record the Roger Craig–Rozier–Fryar–Gill squads rang up in 1982–83 had a powerful effect on recruiting, elevating Lincoln to the big league of Los Angeles, Dallas, and Miami. Thanks to the attendant press and television exposure, high school stars who didn't know Lincoln, Nebraska, from a Lincoln Continental accepted recruiting visits to the Star City, resulting, beginning with the 1982 recruiting class, in an unprecedented number of great black athletes arriving in Lincoln. Among them:

▶ Quarterback Taylor from San Diego
▶ All-America running back Knox, who broke the state rushing record during his career at Jefferson High in Daly City, California
▶ All-America split end Jason Gamble of Santa Barbara
▶ Wingback Brinson, an explosive but free-spirited wideout who became NU's first Georgia recruit since the mid-1950s; the Big Red beat out Florida, Iowa State, and Florida State for his services
▶ Brian Washington, a prep All-America safety from suburban Virginia, who would become a starter by his sophomore season
▶ Middle guard Lawrence Pete (6'2", 280) of Wichita, Kansas, who chose Nebraska over Arkansas, Tennessee, Minnesota, Kansas, and Kansas State
▶ Cornerback Charles Fryar, All-State and All-America tailback and safety at Burlington City (New Jersey) High School. Cousin of Irving
▶ Defensive tackle Neil Smith

In its 1985 recruiting class, rated the best in the nation by one prominent service, Nebraska signed a spectacular group of prospects—seventeen of twenty-four were from outside the state—Taylor, Thomas, Etienne, kicker Chris Drennan, wingback Richard Bell, and fullback Bryan Carpenter among the biggest names. In 1986–87, twenty-three of thirty-nine freshman scholarship recruits were from outside Nebraska, including nine from Texas.

But there were problems.

Maybe it was the turbulent times themselves, the enigmatic eighties. Or perhaps the aftershocks of the wild ride engineered by Rozier and Fryar and Rimington and Steinkuhler rubbed off on their impressionable teammates. Or maybe the out-of-state athletes discovered that they, quite naturally, had far less loyalty and personal attachment to the school and the city, or little understanding of Osborne (and vice versa) and the true meaning of Big Red football to the fans. That lack of loyalty and deep-seated pride certainly contributed to the rash of discipline problems that plagued the program, becoming, in effect, the precursors of the "distracting and difficult" time Osborne experienced.

"Those guys who came in later," said tight end Jamie Williams, discussing the trend, "they hadn't proved anything and started to do like Mike and Irving. . . . I think that's what really brought a lot of exposure to Nebraska's program.

"My senior year we were 12-1," he continued. "The year after that ['83] they only lost one game. Nebraska was just dominating at the time. We had all these studs going off to the pros. I think a lot of young guys were trying to follow us. You know, Rimington and Steinkuhler won back-to-back Outland trophies, and [they] were on steroids. The younger guys said, 'Shit, I want to do what these other guys are doing. These guys are going in the first round' and all this stuff. Mike Rozier and Irving Fryar, those guys were outstanding players. A lot of those young guys were trying to emulate them.

"I know even Mike told me, I think it must have been [in '85]. He said, 'Have you been back to Nebraska lately?' I said, man, no. He said, 'You should see these guys; they're just trippin', the players were. They walk around with all this gold, think they're so good. They don't seem to be payin' the price like we did.' "

So it seemed. Life in the "goldfish bowl" got considerably hotter after '84. Unlike Devaney's reign, when player problems were quietly and efficiently handled and the press wasn't so interested in exposing errant behavior, every time Osborne turned around he was answering questions about somebody's arrest or steroids or dishing out suspensions or discipline. Some highlights or, if you will, lowlights:

▶ The Neil Smith–Lawrence Pete steroid arrest in March 1986 following a series of break-ins at Harper Hall, a campus dorm. Court papers showed the dorm floor monitor had loaned the two athletes his master key so they could "store personal items" in the monitor's room. A flurry of six or seven burglaries (no forced entries) followed on the dorm floor. One Harper resident reported being awakened near midnight by the sound of knocking on his door. He later reported hearing a key inserted into the lock, seeing the door opened, and the lights turned on. The resident identified both Pete and Smith as the two people who entered the room. Both left, the resident said, when they saw it was occupied.

According to a Lincoln law enforcement source, Pete and Smith's dorm room was eventually searched, and a few of the missing items were found. Police also seized a bottle of steroids (a hundred five-milligram tablets of methyl testosterone). Osborne later told the police that Pete had used the steroids because he was "trying to break the school bench-press record [500 pounds]. He just needed a little extra one day." (The day before, Noonan had set the bench-press record with a lift of 485 pounds.) Pete and Smith were both subsequently charged with one count of misdemeanor theft and put into a pretrial diversion pro-gram to clear their record.

Asked about the incident, Osborne said, "It bothers you. It really bothers you. The police said there were six or seven items they were looking for. All the items they took from the players were returned, which to me is an indication they were satisfied. They maintained they didn't take any-thing, but maybe I'm naive. They said they were going to Broderick's room [but] they got the wrong room. Maybe I'm naive . . . I felt bad when it all came out and [the media] made them out to be thieves and using steroids. Pete told me, and again maybe it's my naive nature, that he barely missed 500 pounds the week before. He had just bought steroids for this. [He] had taken a couple. That he was going to break that record. I treated it as a first drug offense and put him on probation. He was tested every week. I notified his parents. A second time, [he] would be suspended."

▶ In October 1987 Smith and Pete were arrested again—this time for puncturing the tires of two Lincoln police cars outside a downtown bar. Smith and Pete were allegedly out celebrating the birthday of teammate Lee Jones when, at about 9:00 P.M., an eyewitness saw a passenger door of a 1977 Pontiac open and someone reach out with a knife to slash the left front tire on each of the cars. Both players were later charged with two counts of misdemeanor vandalism. Smith eventually pleaded guilty (the charges against Pete were dropped) and paid a fine of $161. Smith was also suspended for one game.

▶ Court records show Brinson had several brushes with the law, including traffic citations (speeding, no driver's license) coupled with several failure-to-appear charges.

▶ Gamble was fined more than $170 on October 26, 1986, for petty larceny and assault in connection with a shoplifting incident at a local store. According to Lancaster County court records, since April 1985 Gamble had been fined about $350 in four cases involving the shoplifting charge, speeding, disturbing the peace, and failure to appear.

▶ Noonan's nasty bar fight at a downtown disco in March 1986. In July he pleaded no contest to charges of disturbing the peace and hindering an arrest in the brawl, one in which it took six officers using nightsticks to subdue the 6'4", 280-pound senior, but not before he reportedly had kicked out the steel cage in the back of a cop car. He was fined $400 plus court costs.

▶ Keith Jones spending 3½ hours in an Omaha jail on September 2, 1986, for failure to pay three traffic tickets. He was fined $22.

▶ At the Sugar Bowl around Christmastime 1987, in New Orleans, eight players and two graduate assistant coaches received national publicity for their arrest for disturbing the peace in the famed French Quarter. The players—who contended the New Orleans police overreacted and they had done nothing wrong—were quickly released by a traffic-court judge, and no disciplinary action was taken.

Even Osborne's perspicuous character came under attack. In August 1987, after a two-month investigation, the *Phila-*

delphia Inquirer questioned the relationship between controversial Philadelphia sports agent Art Wilkinson and Osborne and the Nebraska athletic department. The *Inquirer* story charged, among other things, that Wilkinson had built his business largely through his "unusual association" with the University of Nebraska, several former players (Rozier, Rathman, and former Husker defensive back Brian Davis), and Osborne himself.

The article, headlined "The Sports Agent Who Walked Nebraska's Sidelines," ran almost two full pages. It reported that Wilkinson had a field pass giving him the freedom to roam the Nebraska sideline at home games—something Wilkinson did on at least four occasions during the 1985 and 1986 seasons when he was, in fact, the only agent in the country with such unlimited access. The article contended that Wilkinson had conducted business with DuBose while the injured I-back was on crutches and in street clothes on the sideline during a game in October 1986—an NCAA violation; that Wilkinson was in fact Osborne's agent, a charge Osborne disputed; and that Wilkinson's firm had paid two University of Arizona players—quarterback Alfred Jenkins and wide receiver Jon Horton—during their college careers, a direct violation of NCAA rules that could have cost both athletes their eligibility and scholarships.

"I know what the skeletons are in my closet, and, in all honesty, they're nothing," Wilkinson told the Philadelphia paper. "They're nowhere near the skeletons in other closets."

The article detailed how Wilkinson, after years of representing nondescript athletes, broke into the big time when he took over the business interests of Rozier in 1984, negotiating his departure from the foundering United States Football League in favor of a four-year $1.38 million agreement with the Oilers. Wilkinson told the newspaper this impressed Osborne and his staff. Osborne and Wilkinson formed a business relationship in the summer of 1985, and Wilkinson later counseled the school on a series of legal matters—including the NCAA ticket scandal and investigation. Wilkinson's plush Philadelphia office, the article explained, was

peppered with Nebraska posters on the walls and team year-
books on coffee tables. A Bible was on his desk, a symbol of
Wilkinson's Christian relationship with Osborne. Conversations with the coach, said Wilkinson, were "often couched in
biblical terms."

Osborne's answers to some of the *Inquirer*'s charges were
muddled. The coach insisted Wilkinson had never been his
agent. Yet Wilkinson showed Philadelphia reporters a 1985
letter signed by Osborne that seemed to support Wilkinson's
version of the relationship. The letter read in part: "Please be
advised that Art Wilkinson, Esquire, is my agent," adding,
"Mr. Wilkinson and/or his associates are the only persons
authorized by me to solicit for and negotiate a football
contract on behalf of me, my entire staff and the players in
our program."

Osborne's response: "I didn't even remember signing it,
but he has it, so I guess I did."

He then admitted he'd asked Wilkinson to represent him
and the school in some marketing deals, primarily to find the
football staff a shoe contract, and the letter was intended
solely to ensure the agent would be paid a commission for his
efforts, adding, "He is not my agent, and I have never specified he do anything else for me." Yet Osborne also admitted
that Wilkinson sat in on some meetings with the Houston
Oilers' management in December 1985 when the Oilers
made Osborne a $600,000 multiyear coaching offer. "Art
was present during the meetings," said Osborne.

Osborne also denied having any direct involvement in
getting Wilkinson the restricted sideline passes for Nebraska
games. "I never knew he was there," said Osborne, adding, "If
he's out there, that's against the rules." Told by the *Inquirer*
that Osborne knew nothing about the field pass, SID Bryant,
who said he'd seen Wilkinson on the sidelines at games and at
practice for years, replied: "Well, okay, I guess he didn't then.
In that case, I don't know how Wilkinson got there. I never
gave him a pass. I would never give a pass to an agent. . . .
There are only two places where it would come [from]—the
football office or my office. And it didn't come from my

office." Devaney also acknowledged Osborne had the final say on all such passes. (The next day Osborne explained the passes came from an assistant coach, a photographer, a player, and one time Wilkinson had "just walked in" with university officials.)

Osborne responded to the controversy by implying one *Inquirer* reporter had preconceived ideas about the article. "He had it in his mind what he wanted to write about when he called me. He didn't seem interested in finding out what happened. . . . He was looking to nail Art."

If any one imbroglio serves to illustrate the troubled times and Osborne's sensitivity to criticism and the lengths he will go to protect his image, it's the bitter, running feud he's had with another sports agent—Mike Trope.

"One of the greatest pissing matches of all time," recalls Rick Panneton, a former Trope vice president, who lettered as a tight end on the 1974–75 teams under Osborne.

"Negative and nasty," admitted Osborne.

The feud was touched off back in 1971 when Trope, a cocky nineteen-year-old history major, a junior at USC and the son of a wealthy Los Angeles divorce lawyer, was watching—what else?—the Game of the Century on TV. "I was with a bunch of friends, and we saw Johnny Rodgers return an Oklahoma punt for a touchdown," Trope once said. "It was one of the most spectacular runs I'd ever seen, and I told my friends, 'Boy, I'd sure like to be his agent.' My friends laughed. They said, 'Right. Sure.' That got me motivated. And the following summer I decided to pay Rodgers a visit."

He flew student standby to Lincoln—his father had cut him off financially because he wanted his son to be an attorney, not an agent—and met Rodgers one afternoon at the practice field. As Trope recalled it, the conversation went like this:

"Excuse me, are you Johnny Rodgers?"

"Yeah."

"Look, I don't want your autograph—my name is Mike Trope, and I flew out here from L.A. to talk to you."

"So? What about?"

"I want to talk to you about being your agent."

Rodgers stared at the visitor. Then he said, "Meet me outside the locker room after I take a shower."

Five months later, shortly after Rodgers had starred in that 40–6 Orange Bowl rout of Notre Dame—and after countless phone calls and personal visits from Trope—Rodgers told him: "You're my agent." Over the next five years this disheveled-looking whiz kid revolutionized the sports agent business. Eschewing the old-boy network of coaches who routinely steered players to agents in return for cash and other favors, Trope began mining the sport's most treasured lode— the athletes themselves—and quickly struck it rich. By 1977 Trope had some seventy-five clients, including four Heisman Trophy winners—Rodgers, Griffin, Dorsett, and Campbell. The *Los Angeles Times* dubbed him a "Boy Wonder." At his peak he represented 200 players, including Charles White (another Heisman winner) and All-Americas Johnny (Lam) Jones, Ricky Bell, Anthony Davis, Chuck Muncie, Marvin Powell, and Lawrence Taylor. He owned a $2 million mansion in the exclusive Brentwood section of L.A., was a multimillionaire by the age of thirty, drove a $50,000 Mercedes, and regularly angered general managers, coaches, and critics with deals top-heavy with bonuses and deferred money. He also admitted to repeatedly "loaning" thousands of dollars in cash to student-athletes before their eligibility had expired—a flagrant violation of NCAA rules, rules of which Trope was clearly contemptuous.

Panneton, who worked for Trope from early 1976 through January 1978, remembers it all so well. "I must have spent $145,000 on recruiting in 1977," he said one afternoon in an Atlanta hotel. "It was all limousines, airplanes, and fine hotels. Whatever it took—a Rolls—it was all flash and cash."

Osborne said Trope or one of his emissaries reappeared on NU's campus in 1977 and "approached a couple of guys here and got them obligated" before, Osborne says, "we took a pretty strong stand and got them out." At that point, said the coach, "I got pretty uptight about the name Mike Trope." Shortly thereafter, bored and tired of the intense infighting in

the agent business and the persistent—but unfounded—
rumors linking him to supplying drugs to his clients, Trope
scaled back on his business, enrolled in law school, started a
family, and began investing in Arabian horses. He also
funded and shot two documentaries—one on illegal college
recruiting, another on the sports policies of South Africa. In
1983, however, Trope wanted back in. And the key, according to Panneton, was Mike Rozier—the odds-on favorite to
win the Heisman Trophy.

Trope admitted that a former associate, Bruce Marks,
loaned Rozier at least $2,400 during the 1983 season, al-
though he said Marks had the authority to sign checks and
acted independently. Rozier admitted taking the money but
denied knowing Marks worked for Trope. "The amount was
up to me," he told Bill Brubaker, then a *Sports Illustrated*
investigative reporter, in October 1984. "I wouldn't have to
pay it back. I didn't want to get in anything above my head. I
said, 'Maybe something like $600 every month.'

"Nobody ever offered me anything in my life, so [I thought]
I might as well take it. Guys want to live comfortable. They
don't want to live in no shack. They want a nice car."

"The bottom line is, and I'm telling this to you with a
straight face," Trope says, "I had no knowledge Rozier was
ever loaned money during the year. Until I went and looked at
company records at the end of the football season, I couldn't
tell you if Rozier got $10 or $10,000." Two weeks after Trope
had negotiated a three-year $3 million deal for Rozier with
the Pittsburgh Maulers, Rozier dismissed the agent and
signed with Wilkinson. Panneton says that happened after
Trope traveled to Rozier's New Jersey home and one of the
running back's brothers threatened Trope. "If I hadn't gone
to the house with an associate, I might be in a hospital room
with a plastic band on my wrist," Trope later told the *New
York Times*. (Trope did keep a $300,000 fee for making the
Maulers deal.)

In February 1984, after the news broke that Rozier had
indeed signed early, one of the networks conducted an interview with Trope and reformist agent Leigh Steinberg. The

segment opened with an Osborne interview in which the coach expressed surprise at the Rozier news and stated his desire for players to "stay away from" Trope.

The show host then turned to Trope and said, "Well, you've just heard from the coach. How do you respond?"

Trope later described his response: "I told him if they could package hypocrisy, and it could be bottled and sold, then Coach Osborne would be a multimillionaire."

"It set him off," said Osborne.

Osborne had no idea what kind of fire he was playing with.

What Osborne later called "The Booker Brown Affair" in his book followed shortly thereafter.

"Very unpleasant," he says.

It all began in late December 1984, after Trope had met Brown and several other ex-clients at former USC and Tampa Bay running back Ricky Bell's funeral. Trope said a lunch was arranged with Brown, a former USC lineman, who eventually agreed to be interviewed for Trope's college recruiting documentary. "He talked about some of his funny experiences," said Trope. "What UCLA offered him. Texas Tech. 'But you know what school did me the worst?' he said. 'The University of Nebraska.' Well, when he said that, my eyes lit up like saucers. That's the one thing I'll never forget, because Booker said it divided himself and his mother. . . . [He said] one day Osborne comes and visits his mother. He [Osborne] offered his mother free trips and lodging. Well, that really [blanked] Booker up. He said he and his mother got into an argument because Nebraska was the only school to offer that."

Some coaches would have just issued a flat denial and been done with it. Not Osborne.

The day after the news broke at the end of the month, Osborne sat for a sixty-minute polygraph test, answering "no" to Brown's charges that Osborne had promised to arrange for the sale of the player's game tickets; given Brown $300 when he visited the school in 1972; promised a car as an inducement; promised to provide free transportation to the athlete or his relatives as a method of inducing Brown to attend NU. (He passed.) All during Sugar Bowl week in New

Orleans he repeatedly and painstakingly answered any and all questions. He weighed the possibility of legal action. "I didn't give him [Brown] anything," he said at the time. "I don't know what he's [Trope] talking about. I've never promised a player cash. I've never promised a player a car, an annuity, clothes."

In a further effort to clear his name Osborne tried calling Brown. No dice. Then one night at 9:00 the phone rang; Brown was on the line. In *More Than Winning* Osborne recalls the conversation:

> Booker told me he had taken a polygraph test that day too, and had passed it. He also mentioned he had seen a television show in which I had claimed to be ethical and had made negative comments about his former agent. He said, "I know you're not an ethical person! That's why I've come forward with these charges after twelve years. You drove a wedge between me and my mother. I wanted to go to USC, but my mother wanted me to go to Nebraska because of the trips you promised her."

At this point in the conversation, Osborne suggested that Brown's agent might be orchestrating this (soap) opera. Brown said, funny, the agent is right here. That's when, Osborne says, Trope got on the line, demanding "the key to the front door" at Nebraska to recruit any player he wanted.

"After all that's happened," the head coach said, "you want me to allow you access to our players in the summer?"

"Yes," said Trope. "That's what I'm asking."

Osborne told Trope, in so many words, to take a flying leap.

Meanwhile the press was boring in. If Trope's mission was to make Osborne's life miserable, to frustrate, the agent was succeeding. "I don't know how many times I've got to say it," Osborne told the 1987 Sugar Bowl media. "Do I have to do this every day? You guys keep calling Mike Trope, and he's going to come up with something new every day."

At this time, Panneton, who was living in Dallas and running a Toyota dealership, got a phone call from Osborne.

"He talked about the Booker Brown incident and how Trope was all over him again," said Panneton, who believed Trope provided Brown with an "incentive" to talk. Panneton later arrived in Lincoln to conduct a previously scheduled agent seminar with Nebraska players. While he was on campus, Panneton says, assistant coach Solich sought him out. "He phoned and asked if I would mind speaking to the FBI about Trope—particularly if Trope had ever offered drugs to players," recalled Panneton. "He said, 'If there's anything you could tell the FBI, we'd appreciate it.' I told him, 'Sure, whatever I can do.'"

Panneton said he spoke to both the FBI and Devaney—the latter anxious over Osborne's growing preoccupation with Trope. Panneton said, "Devaney told me, 'I told Tom to leave it alone, you're up against too much. All Trope has to do is [blank] with you. Tom, you've got to run a program. Take your lumps and leave it alone.'"

According to Trope, in December 1985, he received a certified letter from the phone company. It stated pursuant to public law it was notifying him the U.S. District Court in Omaha had subpoenaed his phone records from the period March 24, 1982, through June 5, 1985. Trope was stunned; he immediately suspected Osborne. Says the agent: "I think the man thought, 'Let's find some dirt on Mike Trope. He's bound to have calls to drug dealers, bookies; then we'll decide what to do with it.' Well, they didn't find anything because I've never done drugs, never been around drug dealers, never sold drugs."

Trope's lawyer phoned the U.S. Attorney's office in Omaha. He was told it was a "routine" subpoena issued in a "routine" FBI investigation into drug trafficking and extortion by agents. Later neither the U.S. Attorney in Omaha nor his assistant would confirm or deny any aspect of the investigation.

"Do I think the subpoena was used to intimidate me? Absolutely, of course it was," says Trope. "The reason they can't intimidate me is because I'm clean. . . . I'm not intimidated. I'm infuriated they invaded my privacy to that extent."

So infuriated that he phoned Osborne and raised hell. Said Osborne, "He called me and wanted to know what I had to do with that. He said, 'What are you trying to do?' He was holding me responsible. I told him, 'I can't get the FBI to do anything.' We talked to Rick when he was here to talk to our players about agents. . . .

"At that time, Trope said, 'What would you do if I told you I have names of hotels and agents with present players?' Well, I'd have to turn it in to the NCAA. I wouldn't want to do it, but I'd have to. He just kinda left it at that."

Yet a year later, in June 1987, long after Trope said his attorney had found out the investigation was in "the dead file," news of the FBI inquiry became public—thanks to Trope, who evidently leaked the telephone records story to the *Washington Post*. When contacted by the *Post*, Osborne denied any member of his staff had initiated any contact with the FBI. He made only an oblique reference to Panneton's role—and no mention whatsoever of Solich's soliciting Panneton to speak to the bureau. "I don't know where he's coming from," Osborne told the *Washington Post* at the time. "A couple of FBI agents did talk to me about agents in general and Mike Trope in particular. They came down to see us. But after I talked to them and some other people talked to them, we didn't hear any more about it. . . . We can't call the FBI. They're not our personal representatives, where we can call them up and say 'We want you to investigate somebody.'"

But the feud wasn't over. Not long after Trope discovered the FBI probe, the NCAA started its investigation of Nebraska, following a scent, some felt, left by a petulant agent. "I had a feeling he [Trope] talked to them," said Osborne. "They had been here thirty to forty hours, and it seems to me that after you've been here that long, you'd get an idea of whether a place is totally corrupt or people are trying to do the right thing. I told them, 'I can't see why again and again you keep coming back.' They said, 'Well, you have a good reputation, but there are some people who say you are a phony—in so many words, you are a phony.'"

Trope acknowledged he spoke to NCAA investigators but

dismissed the idea of his having any involvement in the 400-hour inquiry. "That's bullshit," he said. "The NCAA called and left a number, and I called back. They asked if I knew anything about Doug DuBose signing with an agent early and taking trips. They asked if I could provide any information. I declined. I figured, why bother talking to the NCAA about these people? The next thing Nebraska will do is bug my telephone."

But Trope still wasn't finished with Osborne. Not by a long shot. Trope is as stubborn and self-righteous as any man, as obsessive about his reputation as Osborne. So it was that in October 1985 Green Bay Packer running back Kenneth Davis, who was suspended from school for receiving illegal payments while at Texas Christian University, went public—via Trope—with this story: illegal offers had been made to him while he was on recruiting visits to Oklahoma and Nebraska.

At Nebraska, so the story went, Davis was introduced to Bill Wright, a Lincoln attorney and the "parent" of Turner Gill. Davis, according to Trope, said Wright told him he would be "treated like a son" and offered him a lavish lifestyle said to include putting an entire wing of the Wright "mansion" at his disposal, access to a well-stocked refrigerator, and use of a fleet of five late-model automobiles. According to the NCAA, offers of this nature are prohibited.

Osborne quickly denied the Davis allegations, and the NCAA and Berst declined to investigate. "I don't consider information from that source to be credible," said Berst. Trope took some lumps in public. (Later he would say, "All I know is Davis signed an affidavit under penalty of perjury in his application for the supplemental draft [to the NFL], and in it he made those statements.") At the time Davis did not return repeated calls to the Green Bay Packers' public relations office requesting comment.

Postscript: At the beginning of the '87 season, Trope's autobiography, *Necessary Roughness*, was published. In a prepublication interview Trope promised to "lay three people out dead." One of those three would be Osborne. In the book he devoted an entire chapter ("The School That Doesn't Cheat") to the coach and his program. Trope brought up the Davis and Brown charges anew and the FBI operation, arguing that "considering our history, the chain of events, I couldn't help envisioning an extremely powerful football coach manipulating the judicial system to try and take revenge on one of his enemies."

Once again, Osborne issued a denial. And in the end, he may have enjoyed the last laugh on Mr. Trope. The much-ballyhooed book was a bust in Lincoln.

3:30 P.M.

The only person not smiling at Wednesday's practice session turns out to be junior I-back Knox. At the press conference both Jones and Thomas had playfully spilled the beans about how Knox and third-string junior defensive tackle Willie Griffin, another Californian, had been snookered by a smooth-talking "VCR salesman" outside a downtown disco the previous Saturday night. Seems Knox and Griffin were escorting two young ladies home from a club, Celebration, when a man carrying a large brown box wrapped in plastic strolled up, celebrating the big deal of the day.

"Know anybody who wants to buy a top-of-the-line VCR?" asked the man. On the outside of the box was a snazzy photo of a VCR and its remote control accessory.

"Does it work?" asked Knox.

"Does it work? said the salesman, indignant as can be. "Does it work? I already got rid of four of them, man. Only $85."

"It's nice, it's new," whispered Griffin. "Let's get it."

"We'll give you sixty bucks," said Knox.

"Sold," said the salesman.

Knox and Griffin rushed back to their apartment and ripped off the wrapping. Lo and behold, a VCR picture had been taped over a top-of-the-line Bartles & Jaymes wine cooler box. And inside were two—count 'em, two—high-quality . . . bricks.

"Hey, Tyreese," comes the constant cackle from his team-mates, "those bricks come in VHS or Beta?"

5:58 P.M.

The KFOR-AM (1240) radio lines are humming like a chorus of backup singers. In two minutes the "Talk to Tom" Osborne show ("Triple T" to station insiders) will hit the air, just as it does every Wednesday night between 6:00 and 7:00 P.M. during football season. Some seventeen stations of the vast thirty-seven-station Nebraska football network carry "Triple T," and the audience is even larger this week, since in the spirit of goodwill—and better ratings—several stations (including KTOK in Oklahoma City and WWLS in Norman) from SoonerLand have joined in a reciprocal agreement that had Switzer's "Talk to Barry" show on earlier in the week in Lincoln. To a close listener, "TTT" offers little in the way of fresh game information, but it does score heavily in psychological insight into both the coach and the people he must please every year. Time and time again the listeners hear his humble "appreciate it" in response to compliments; or the subtle, sarcastic taunt of an Omaha caller who criticizes Osborne for not passing with a lead down the stretch against OU in '86; the second-guessers who challenge him; the devoted young boys and housewives speaking from the heart . . .

"Welcome to KFOR's 'Talk to Tom' Osborne show," says a honey-tongued announcer. "For the next hour we'll be taking your phone calls with comments or questions in Lincoln at four-eight-nine-twelve-forty. Or outside call our exchange toll-free at 1-800-742-2308. Join us as you talk Husker football with University of Nebraska head football coach Tom Osborne and his assistants. Now here's KFOR's sports director, Chuck Stevens, on the 'Talk to Tom' Osborne show on KFOR twelve-forty."

"Good evening and hi again, everybody; this is Chuck Stevens, and this is the 'Talk to Tom' show. Tonight Coach Tom Osborne joins us for Oklahoma week. And in addition to the phone calls from fans, we'll have a scouting report on the Sooners; and another Cornhusker flashback. And in the final half-hour, another Husker trivia question with a chance to win a Nebraska jacket from Prairie Maid [Meats of Lincoln].

"And now let's welcome Coach Tom Osborne. Tom, it's been a hectic week for you and the players. But this is the week the fans really love."

Osborne: "Well they seem to. And it hasn't been all that bad. We've had a few more writers around. You know, you have people come in from out of town for a game like this. Surprisingly, some of them come in on Sunday and Monday. I don't know what they do all week long. So, ah, I think the game has pretty much been beat to death right now in terms of everything that could be analyzed, and everybody's just kinda waiting to play it now."

"I know at your press conference on Tuesday with that battery of media it looked like somebody'd declared war."

"It was the largest group of media people I had ever been in front of before a Nebraska-Oklahoma game. Again it seems like the game has attracted a lot of national attention. A No. 1- and No. 2-ranked team. Same conference, and the history of the game that generally it's always been a pretty good football game. . . ."

"Let's talk to Mike, our first caller in Omaha. Hi, Mike, you're on with Coach Osborne."

"Yo, Tom, one question here."

"Okay."

"I want to ask you why you quit passing in the fourth quarter of last year's Oklahoma–Nebraska game. I was the last caller on the show last year, and I told you to continue to pass the fut-ball. I just want you to continue to pass the fut-ball when you get the lead this year."

"Okay. If I listened to you last year, we'd have won, wouldn't we, Mike?"

"Yeah, if you'd stopped passing . . . "

"That shows you how dumb I am. And I appreciate your

call, and I'll sure try to do it this year, okay?"

"—Continue, please."

"All right. We'll keep passing. The game may be over, and we'll be throwing, okay."

"Okay, let's talk to Steve now; Steve's in Wayne."

"Yeah, Coach Osborne."

"Yes, Steve."

"I just have a little, have a little comment here for ya. I would like to just say that you're a real inspiration to myself the way you present yourself, your coaches, and your players.

"Well, I appreciate that."

"That's not only for football but also for higher education and a responsibility toward the future and your players and the respect toward your opponent. You're a real asset to the city of Lincoln, the state of Nebraska, and to all college and university athletics. Good luck this season and throughout your coaching career."

"Appreciate that, Steve, thank you."

"Gretchen's our next caller in Lincoln. Hi, Gretchen, you're on."

"Hello, Gretchen."

"Hi!"

"How are you?"

"Fine!"

"Good. What did you want to ask tonight?"

"Ah, um, just wanted to ask if, um, if Tom would be happy if we would win Oklahoma."

"Well, that would make me very happy—how about you? Would you like that?"

"Yeah!"

"Okay, we're together on that one, thanks."

"All right, let's talk to Steve in Omaha."

'I just wanted to congratulate you on a fine season this year. You've done a fine job at Nebraska, and I hope you plan on continuing for many years to come."

"Well, I plan on it. You know, coaching is terminal, ah, ha, hopefully not in the immediate future, but, ah, ha, I'd like to stay with it for several more years. I enjoy it here. Certainly I enjoy the people of Nebraska and the support they've given us."

"Lots of calls on the line. The next one's from Chad out in North Platte. Hi, Chad, you're on with the coach."

"Hello, coach!"

"Hello, Chad. How are you?"

"Pretty good. I just wanted to tell you on Saturday whether you win, lose, or draw, I still think you're the best coach a football team could have."

"Well, I appreciate that, Chad. And I hope someday you'll come down and play for us. How old are you?"

"I'm almost twelve."

"Well, you see, you got about another five years to go. So we'll be countin' on you, okay?"

"*Okay!*"

"Okay, Chad, thanks for callin'."

"Okay, let's go back to Oklahoma, Oklahoma City. Tim's on the line. Hi, Tim, you're on with Coach Osborne."

"Hello, coach."

"Hello, Tim."

"How ya doin' today?"

"I'm doin' fine."

"That's good to hear. I just wanted to let you know there are Husker fans here in SoonerLand."

"Oh, I know there's a few of them. There's a few Oklahoma fans up here, too. But are you one of them?"

"Oh, I'm a Husker fan. I'll tell you how serious I am about it. I had a son born Saturday, and I had to get my, ah, Husker hat out and run it through sterilization so I could have it in the delivery room."

"Well, that's pretty serious."

"And I also work with a lot of people who are convinced that you're gonna be able to cover the spread this week."

"Well, I don't know even what the spread is. We just hope we can win."

"The line is running four points."

"Is that right? We'll try to do the best we can, and I think it will be a great ball game and it will be exciting. I appreciate your call."

Stevens: "I wonder who rounded it off. It was right at three-and-a-half this morning.

"All right, let's talk now to Diana in Lincoln. Diana, you're on with the coach."

"Yes, Tom, I am really . . . upset about the way so-called Husker fans are so critical . . . of your ability and coaching and in taking care of your players. And, ah, it's really sad that they're so critical. And I think you're doing a fabulous job, as far as I'm concerned, in my book of respect, you're No. 1."

"Well, I appreciate that. We haven't had too much criticism this year because we're undefeated, but, ha-ha, but it can come in a hurry. But when you're in a goldfish bowl you live with that. You understand that people are interested and they're going to be critical at times. But it just goes with the territory. We're doing the best we can. But I appreciate your call."

"Okay, time for one quick question from Mark from Omaha. Mark, go ahead, you're on with the coach."

"I guess I'm amazed at the amount of press this game is receiving. Is it very distracting to you, and at times don't you just feel like saying 'You know, I've said everything I can say about the game; let's just play it'?"

"Yeah, I'm tempted at times. But they got to fill so many columns. Ha-ha-ha. We'll keep doing the best we can. But I think it's about time to play the game."

10:30 P.M.

More than 1,200 partiers are packed like so many sardines into a tired-looking two-story building across the street from the Hilton Hotel, bopping and popping to the driving beat of the Pointer Sisters . . . George Michael . . . Anita Baker . . . Journey. Wednesday night is known as "Freak Night" in Lincoln, the one night a week players congregate en masse at whatever club is happening that season to let the air out of their football-only attitude, drink a few brewskis, and smile at the local talent and "freaks" who show up. And they always do. Gorgeous girls who just want to have fun with a football player and aren't necessarily averse to freaking with one player one week, another the next. It's an attractive proposition for both parties, particularly during Oklahoma week, it seems, when spirits are high—and so are hormone levels. Tonight at Mingles, your basic college haunt, a large pack of players are on hand—Broderick, Rod and Neil Smith, Steve Forch, Knox, Willie Griffin, Jeff Jamrog, Blakeman, Etienne, Lee Jones, Jon Kelley, Cartier Walker . . . all out to see what's cooking. The answer is: plenty. The mood is carnivorous in nature; man-eaters are everywhere. As a video replay of some earlier OU–NU tilt plays silently on a large video screen near the dance floor, the place teeters on the edge of a sexual panic, with consenting adults of all shapes and sizes prowling around, undressing each other with their eyes. The women arrive in tight little groups of two and three, dolled up, sexy. Blondes. Brunettes. Redheads. All with a hungry look that answers more questions than it asks.

Cartier Walker slides through the crowd rapping to a woman with a band of gold running through curly black hair. Forch cruises by with a couple of pitchers of beer in his hands. Lee Jones strolls by with a buxom blonde in braided hair. Rod Smith leans against one wall, catching the eye of a stunning long-stemmed blonde with a perfect Farrah Fawcett mane, the one who's been scoping him out ever since she walked in the door ten minutes earlier.

"I'd like to lay him," she says in everyday tones to a friend as she glides past Smith.

By midnight the place is on fire, beer flowing, the bar five and six deep, the dance floor putting off enough heat to launch the space shuttle. Rod Smith wanders by again, Cheshire-cat grin on his face. "Pretty crazy, isn't it?" he says. Yes, it certainly is. Being a Nebraska football player definitely has its advantages. Smith smiles once more; he wants to talk about the game. "It's gonna be electrifying," he says. "This is what you wait your entire career for."

Thomas pops in. His goofy smile suggests he's feeling no pain, yet somehow, even in this madness, his mind is fixed on the game; he's eager to send a message to a certain All-America tight end. "Keith Jackson," Thomas says, spitting out the name. "In the backfield. First play. My exact words." Then he's lost in the crowd, freaking out of there in a flash.

A drop-dead blonde with a consensus All–Big Eight body saunters past Smith, a man so clearly in demand he could have fathered ten children by now. No wonder this kid returns punts; he's cool under pressure.

"If you need something," he says to a visitor with a mischievous smile, "you let me know."

By 12:30, the crowd has thinned just enough to make mingling a real possibility. John Cougar Mellencamp's "Small Town" tumbles through the speakers as I touch the elbow of a blonde with a pretty shag.

"Ann?" I say.

Ann Waldron twists around, turning her back to a black man in a jaunty beret. I'm fine, she says, wasn't even sure I'd be coming over. Got off work kind of late. No, I haven't heard from Mike. Not in a while. "He's a good guy," she says. "I don't want to do anything to harm him."

A half hour later, the VCR brothers, Knox and Griffin, stroll out of the bar arm-in-arm with two blondes.

"This is just how it started the last time," says Knox, a $50 grin on his chin. No, make that $60.

THURSDAY

9:25 A.M.

The journalistic pace is clearly picking up. *USA Today* trumpets Game of the Century II by treating America to what might be called "Breakfast with Broderick," offering up a "Cornhuskers' Thomas Has All the Answers" headline over a tasty assortment of press conference quotes. Even Paul Harvey, the mahatma of radio, is digging the game; today he closes his commentary show on KRTI-FM (96.5) with a tale from Tyreese. "His teammates kept asking if the bricks were Beta or . . . VHS . . . This is Paul Harvey. Gooood Day!"

By 11:30 A.M. the Dow has dipped nearly nineteen points, but Christmas decorations are up, and so is the temperature, all the way to fifty-three degrees; and it's sunny, a damn fine way to spend a day. Except for one thing: the locals have already skipped ahead forty-eight hours and are talking about Saturday. Saturday this, Saturday that. And why not? Why, just this morning the first real-live Sooner fans showed up in town, chipper as can be, cocktails in hand, chattering among themselves. About what? Probably discussing the last three years.

In local news today the *Lincoln Journal-Star* ran a front-page feature on the strange doings expected in room 312-B at the Veterans Administration Medical Center come Saturday. That's where "Husker Bob" Rowe, sixty-five, arguably the No. 1 Big Red fan around, is recovering from a heart attack he suffered while walking down a downtown street after the Iowa State game on November 7. For the past nine years Rowe has come to Cornhusker games dressed from head to toe in red and white, carrying placards and playing with a puppet, and generally raising the spirit level in every section he ever so much as set foot in. But on Saturday Rowe will be on the outside looking in. Doctor's orders. "I'll put my red clothes on to watch," he told Kevin O'Hanlon of the *Star*, "if it's okay with the nurses."

Rowe will hardly be alone. Family and friends are coming over, and there is that avalanche of get-well cards to keep him company, plus his "Go Big Red" banner and the football autographed by the '87 Huskers.

"Everybody's been so nice," he says, "it makes me want to cry. I feel damn good, but I'm damn lucky."

So lucky that Rowe is already talking beer and point spreads. "I think we'll win by thirteen or fourteen points," he said. "But the crowd will have to help. Tell 'em to stand up and roar and cheer and scream." Which is just what O'Hanlon suggested Rowe might be up to in room 312-B.

The day's itinerary calls for a side trip to Hastings, in many ways the real MVP (Most Valuable Place) in Tom Osborne's life. It's a sturdy anchor for the hometown hero who still drives back to see his brother, Jack, his polar opposite, and his son, Mike, a handsome 6'4", 200-pound quarterback at Hastings College, and to visit his mom, Erma, a once vibrant and vivacious woman who now lives out her days in a world all her own, a distant place even her famous and loving son can't always reach.

The landscape on the ninety-minute drive west down I-80 is a succession of gentle, rolling slopes, farmland, and open space as far as the eye can see. Cattle graze peacefully in the

fields. The sky's a multicolored matrix of magenta, angry
blues, and yellow. Trucks roar down the interstate, rumbling
on to California.

Some sixteen miles outside of Hastings, signs for U.S. 281
south appear on your right, and not long after, as you follow
281 around to the left, toward town, you see the road sign
proclaiming this four-lane divided highway none other than
"Tom Osborne Expressway." A fitting tribute, for sure,
though no one is more aware of just how fleeting such fame
can be than the honoree himself: "A couple of 9–3 seasons
and that sign comes down pretty quick," he likes to say.
Chances are, if you live in the state, you've heard this joke
too:

Know the one thing you can't do on the Tom Osborne
Expressway?

No, what's that?

Pass.

1:00 P.M.

Arriving in Hastings, you coast down a slight decline past the
black silos and farm equipment and a local television studio
and down into town—one with a proud and special history all
its own.

A bustling industrial center back in the 1930s, Hastings
was populated by English-speaking immigrants from all over
Europe. In those days Hastings rivaled both Lincoln and
Omaha as a center of culture. Musicians and artists of national note regularly rode the railroad into town to perform
plays and concerts at the local liberal arts college.

Today Hastings hasn't changed all that much. The "Small
Town" label is as good as stitched all over the Ben Franklin
five-and-dime, the mom and pop shops like Dixie's House of
Sewing, the row upon row of clapboard homes lining numbered streets. But despite its relatively small population
(23,000), it's big city in mind and spirit. Independent. Open-
minded. Studied. Thanks largely to the dominant influence
of Hastings College, a private, picturesque Presbyterian col-

lege in the center of town, and the wisdom of businessmen
like Hal Lainson.

Lainson, formerly the chairman of the Hastings College
Board of Trustees for thirty-two years, is the bow-tied, bully-
backed leader of the Dutton Lainson Company, a 101-year-
old manufacturer of industrial winches and marine and
automotive parts. Even now, in what looks to be his seventies,
Lainson has the regal bearing of a law professor or govern-
ment ambassador.

On this day Lainson is sitting in his warm and wooded
office, behind an exact copy of George Washington's desk.
Grandfather clocks tick-tock in one corner, and antique
scales, chandeliers, mahogany furniture, and photographs
abound, making it easier for Lainson to travel back in time,
which he willingly does, through four generations of Osbornes. To the patriarch of the family, Tom Osborne, the pug-
nosed lineman on the Hastings College eleven who went on
to become a minister and politician; to Charles Osborne,
football star of the class of '30, war hero, hard-driving car
salesman, and budding businessman; to Tom and Jack, like
night and day in their outlook on life; and, finally, to Tom's
son, Mike, struggling to emerge from the long shadow of his
dad.

"The Osbornes were always people of great rectitude, well
regarded in this state," begins the white-haired Lainson.
"Their father, Charles, was a close friend of mine. He was in
the service, a captain in Europe during the war. Tom had a
perfectly normal childhood, excellent training, many oppor-
tunities. I think his success has come from his sense of values,
particularly about people. He's a person who respects people.

"The family was very open-minded. I don't mean to say
they were ever radical, because they weren't. But they were
people open to ideas, had a great sense of right and wrong,
and I think that still holds for Tom. They also had a feeling of
compassion for people.

"Tom's father was always a person interested in athletics.
As the boys came along, he gave them much companionship
and guidance in their sports development . . . Charles wasn't a

Monday morning quarterback completely, but certainly he had his say. But it was very bright, constructive criticism, analysis, and evaluation. It made Tom a very good coach.

"One of the unusual things about Tom was he went through high school and college and lived at home the whole time. He stayed in the family house. It gave Charles, who was a very skilled father, a longer time with the boys. Tom was about twenty-two years old when he left home."

And what of Jack? Lainson stirs a bit behind his desk. "Well, how would you like it if you were the younger brother of Tom? Get the idea? He's had a burden to carry. He wouldn't say that. Jack is a perfectly wonderful guy, everybody thinks he's just superb, but as a younger brother he was in the shadow or, I suspect, or at least I think psychologically he was."

"I've heard people say the same thing, that I was probably the better natural athlete," says Jack Osborne, relaxing in the cozy den of a showcase ranch home brimming with bric-a-brac and antiques. His boyish face is alive, eager to please, barely burdened by the advances of age. His hair, sandpaper brown—not red—falls forward in his face, making him seem even younger than his years. "I had a lot of tools that came naturally, but I didn't work nearly as hard as Tom," he says. "Tom worked hard. He was pretty dedicated with anything he got involved with. Schoolwork. Job. Athletics. If he was gonna do it, he was gonna do it right."

His voice leans toward Dennis Weaver's, a soothing sound that would go down easy at a board meeting or in a fishing boat or out in the fields, places Jack Osborne frequently finds himself these days. President of a company called Industrial Irrigation Inc., he's been running the family business his dad started (with the help of A. H. Jones) shortly after the car business slowed down in the early sixties, and from the looks of things Jack's done himself right proud: the spacious house; a bubbly, black-haired beauty of a wife (sixteen years of marriage) in Pamela Jean, who dresses more New York than Nebraska; a teenage son, Justin, who loves the Huskers and knows full well the meaning of respect. It's a happy life. A full

life. "I don't feel I've had to live up to anybody," says Jack. "I
always admired my father; I feel that same way about Tom.
I'm very proud of him; awfully pleased to be his brother. But
I've never felt there was any pressure on me to try and
achieve anything. In Hastings I think most people accept
Jack for who he is and Tom and Dad for who they are."

But just who his brother is has proved a mystery, even to
Jack. "He's a hard person to tell somebody about. You ask if I
know him well. Even as his brother, at times, I'm not completely sure I do. . . . I don't know what's behind his drive.
[But] there's nothing phony about it in any way. His ideas on
life, his morals, all those things are genuine. If that disturbs
people who look and poke and try to find a flaw, who feel he
might not be what he's perceived to be, well . . ."

The difficulties that plagued Tom's childhood—absent father, instant adulthood, insecurity—are foreign to Jack. The
three-year age difference, he says, spared him the trauma,
and he reached an understanding of his brother's anguish
only after reading his autobiography. "Growing up for me
must have been a lot easier than it was for Tom," says Jack.
"My impression after reading the book was that Tom perse-
vered. When Dad was gone, I just sorta bumbled along. Tom
took it personally. Some of that just rolls off some personalities; it sticks to the back of others."

February 13, 1984. Charles Osborne was driving back to
work when his heart called it quits. He'd had a similar attack
in 1969 but had survived and kept on smoking and putting in
the hours down at Industrial Irrigation, which is where he and
Jack had seen each other that morning. Charles had then
gone home and shoveled a little snow off the driveway before
stepping inside for some lunch. He was on his way back to
work, eight or nine blocks from home, when his chest tight-
ened up like a vise. Charles passed out and lost control of the
car; it ended up busting through the front door of a doctor's
office. It was Hal Lainson who first called Jack Osborne with
the news. Charles Osborne never regained consciousness.

A few years before the accident Jack had stopped by his parents' house on a Sunday afternoon to pull a few weeds around the yard and double-check on his mom. No problems. The next morning at 10:00 he called to check again. This time there was no answer. "I kinda assumed she was taking a nap or whatever," he says today. An hour later Pam called. Erma Osborne's speech sounded slurred, like she'd been drinking. She wasn't making sense.

"Something's wrong," Pam told Jack.

Jack's pickup raced the one-and-a-half blocks to his parents' home in record time. Through a window he saw his mother sitting slumped in a chair near the phone. Jack banged frantically on the door. Slowly his mother rose and wobbled over. *Something is wrong*, thought Jack. The door was locked. Dammit! Jack counted each second as his mother fumbled with the handle. Finally the door swung open.

"I don't know whether she realized anything was wrong or not," says Jack in hushed tones. "She started to talk, and things weren't right. We took her to the hospital, but she had deteriorated to the point where we weren't sure she was going to make it. Tom got out there that day. The doctors, when they came out, showed us an x-ray where an awfully large part of the brain had been completely shut off from blood. They said they didn't know what to tell us.

"She was a very independent and proud person, and when you end up in a situation where you have to depend upon someone for *everything*, it's awfully dehumanizing. She's paralyzed. She can't talk, she can't write, and yet she's very alert. There's no question as to whether she agrees or doesn't or understands.

"It has been hard for both of us. I think it bothers Tom an awful lot because he's not able to come and spend more time because of his job. He makes every effort to get out here. He'll drive out even if it's only to spend just an hour. I know it bothers him. . . . It's hard to lose a parent [Charles], especially when you've had good parents. And I almost consider Mom gone. That's a strange thing to say, but it's true, and I think we've got through it in pretty good shape."

5:30 P.M.

The clicking and clanging of thousands of pounds of iron swelled like a symphony in Boyd Epley's ear as he walked into the Nebraska Strength and Conditioning Center—a cavernous facility that he helped build—and smiled broadly at the sound.

As an accomplished pole-vaulter on the track team in the late 1960s, Epley set a school indoor record of fifteen feet as a junior. The next year, while recuperating from a back injury that would eventually end his athletic career, Epley developed a strong interest in strength and conditioning, so strong that he would come to be known as the father of collegiate strength training, a concept he helped develop back in 1970. Not long afterward he founded the National Strength and Conditioning Coaches Association and was elected the organization's first president. In 1980 he was voted the first Strength Coach of the Year. He later organized the nationally recognized All-American Strength Team and became a driving force in the construction of a weight training facility as big and impressive as the man-childs it produces.

Without question, no football team in this country—college or pro—takes more pride in its strength and conditioning program than the University of Nebraska. One look at the weight room and its attendant motto printed proudly on a sign—"Where the Best Athletes Come to Get Better"—tells you that. Where else can you find a Strength Museum cordoned off by red velvet ropes, separating such icons as the Original Husker Dumbbells and the Original Husker Preacher-Curl Platform (circa 1967) from the marveling masses who annually visit the complex? Visits due in large part to the promotional prowess of Epley, whose chiseled Chuck Connors–like features, technical expertise, and evangelical enthusiasm have made the phrase *Husker Power* an industry unto itself and earned the university which markets it thousands of dollars in extra income.

It was Epley who created the four-color 100-plus-page *Husker Power* magazine. Epley who thought of shirts, caps, and posters all bearing the magic words. Epley who organized the Husker Power Club, more than 1,000 members strong (each paying dues of $35) with all proceeds, thank you, supplementing Epley's "bare bones" overall budget of some $150,000, including the salaries of the dozen or so "supervisors" who patrol the complex.

And what a complex it is. As physical an image of Husker football as one can find. A huge spit-polished facility filled with 20,000 pounds of free weights, 125 workstations, a computer room churning out individual training schedules for 200 athletes, a Wall of Fame reserved for the names and faces of those who have set strength records at their respective positions. Yet all this pales in comparison to the most impressive sight of all. The very altar on which for years the entire program rested: the Record Platform, an elevated lifting area revered as the site of superhuman feats of strength. It dominates the facility the way Husker linemen have consistently controlled the college line of scrimmage, sitting, as it does, under four red and white Olympic-style rings. Inside the bottom ring, which in a sense supports the other three, are these words: "Combine Running, Stretching and Lifting—If you dare to be great."

At NU only athletes who have dared to do just that, who have reached extraordinary levels of strength—400-pound bench presses, 900-pound hip sled pulls, and 325-pound power cleans—are allowed to walk on, sit on, or even touch the platform. Organized demonstrations of Husker Power from this very spot, wild, frenzied affairs, have routinely left boosters and recruits limp at the sight of what man and muscle and machinery can achieve.

Epley has routinely proselytized about all this, about just what happens when another M-word, the mind, is put to work.

He preaches on about how coaches at Nebraska now recruit for height and speed. How he and his past and present assistants—many of whom have gone on to head-coaching jobs in college and the pros—eventually supply the weight and strength. How building a bigger, better Husker is a four-step process (that word again!), combining testing, evaluation, goal setting, and individual programs. How four times a year each and every player is tested and timed in the 40-yard dash, 300-yard shuttle run, vertical jump, seated shot put, agility run, bench press, and hip sled pulls, each and every result computer analyzed, ranked in one of seven categories (poor to superior), and printed out on a red and white Husker Power "Conditioning Profile." A profile scrutinized not only by weight-station supervisors but also by assistant coaches, Osborne, and even fans who can receive copies in various booster mailings.

This emphasis on speed and power, all the testing and retesting and the computer profiles, has spawned a new age of athletic measurement at Nebraska. The personal yardstick is no longer just sheer strength or power but something called an "Athletic Index," code for a complex, computer-adjusted size/strength/speed point rating based on a formula designed by a university statistics professor. The Athletic Index was instituted back in 1986, and the main reason behind the change, said Epley, was simple. "We wanted more emphasis on the workout, not the [strength] tests," he said. "This [the index] forces more work into the workout and gets away from performing on test day."

Oh, but what performances they were! Bench presses of 500 pounds. Squats of 700 pounds or more. Hip pulls of 1,000. Linemen weighing 285 pounds performing Jordan-esque vertical leaps of $39\frac{1}{2}$ inches. Nebraska at times resembled less of a football team and more of a powerlifting club. And that, in turn, placed tremendous pressure on "average" players to produce big numbers. As it turns out, it was such an environment—that of the platform, demonstrations, and testing, the vicious competition both on and off the field, the powerlifting mind-set that eventually permeated the squad—

that led Nebraska players closer and closer to the S-word. Not *strength . . .* but *steroids.*

Androgenic anabolic steroids are synthetic derivatives of the chief male sex hormone, testosterone. Medical experts believe, when used in conjunction with an exercise program, they enhance muscle growth, dramatically increase strength and endurance, and have been known to afford users a sense of well-being and invincibility, enabling them to train harder and recuperate from rugged physical exercise more quickly. Many of these experts, however, warn of the potential dangers of the drug: cancer, heart disease, hypertension, damage to the liver, kidneys, testicles, and other organs. Psychotic episodes, overly aggressive behavior, and major injuries have also been attributed to the drugs. Over and above any medical considerations, the sale or purchase of anabolic steroids without a prescription is illegal in the U.S. and is considered a felony in several states. Use of the drugs has also been banned by the International Olympic Committee and the NCAA.

In a concentrated effort to slow the dramatic rise in the sale and use of steroids at all levels of sport, from junior high and up, the Civil Division of the U.S. Department of Justice, in cooperation with U.S. Customs, the Food and Drug Administration, the FBI, and local law enforcement agencies, in 1985 instituted a nationwide crackdown on steroid traffickers in this country. As of October 1987 some sixty individuals in ten federal districts had been prosecuted and fined more than $1 million.

Reports of steroid use by Nebraska's football team first surfaced publicly just about the time of the federal crackdown. Between December 1985 and October 1987 at least five stories linked various members of the football team to steroid use. To wit:

▶ Husker lineman Todd Carpenter (6'6", 300 pounds) was reported in the December 9, 1985, issue of *Sports Illustrated* to have bought $280 worth of steroids from a convicted trafficker while at NU. The next week in *SI* the same trafficker, Tony Fitton, stated that he had sold steroids to "several" Huskers in 1983 and '84 and advised them on ways to pass school-sponsored urine tests. Potentially even more damaging, Fitton was quoted as saying that after receiving a "frantic call" from one Husker player, he Federal-Expressed a dozen tablets ("enough for four people") of an aggression-building steroid, methyl testosterone, to that Husker on the eve of the 1984 Orange Bowl.

▶ In March of 1986 the Smith-Pete bottle-of-steroids-in-the-dorm-room incident became public.

▶ In October of the same year Switzer was quoted as saying of UCLA, "They're not like Nebraska. They haven't discovered steroids yet." Switzer subsequently told Osborne he "felt bad" about the statement—but did not retract it.

▶ In January 1987 Steinkuhler told *Sports Illustrated* that he had used steroids during both his junior and senior years at the school (1982–83) as had, he claimed, at least half a dozen other Huskers. "It was my decision, and I made it," he said. "I wanted to be the best I could be."

▶ In May 1987, shortly after being drafted as the No. 1 pick of the Dallas Cowboys, middle guard Noonan (6'4", 280), the only Husker ever to achieve "superior" status in all the Athletic Index categories, was reported to have been one of the twenty NFL draft selections who tested positive for anabolic steroids in testing conducted at the league's scouting combine in January. Noonan said he'd used the steroids only briefly—to build himself up after becoming ill at the Japan Bowl. "I had never tried them before," he said. He also said he hadn't been aware the NFL would be testing for steroids at the combine.

From the outset Osborne has publicly declared himself "dead set" against steroids and has taken aggressive action to discourage their use. In August 1984—"long before we had a gun to our head," he says—NU became one of the first Division I schools to institute random testing for steroids. Epley has also jumped on the antisteroid bandwagon. "I don't see any place for steroids in college football at all," he said.

Osborne has been equally aggressive with the media, criticizing those who reported Nebraska steroid stories for "sin-

gling out" his program. He went so far as to release overall
test results that showed no positive steroid-test results by *any*
NU player in 1984 and '85 and just one positive test in
1986—one steroid user caught in three years. Yet even Osborne wasn't naive enough to believe that figure was totally
accurate. "I think there's no question over the years we've had
some guys who have taken steroids," he admitted privately.
"[But] what I would feel bad about is if a whole team over a
long period of time is indicted. We have a pretty good work
ethic. . . .

"But I want everyone to understand what our position has
been and is now . . . that we're going to do everything we can
to eliminate this problem."

Yet a problem is exactly what anabolic steroids have been—
for years—at Nebraska. According to four former players and
two prominent steroid dealers who say they regularly supplied
drugs and advice to team members from 1982 to 1986,
steroids have been—despite Osborne's objections—a fact of
athletic life at the school since the early 1980s, one former
team dealer going so far as to describe the use as "massive,"
estimating perhaps as much as 85 percent of the 1983 and
'84 team had at least experimented with the muscle-building
drugs.

At the very least the depth of the usage problem is disturbing, especially in light of these developments:

▶ In addition to Steinkuhler, two-time Lombardi-Outland
  winner Rimington, considered one of the greatest linemen
  in college history, is said by sources to have regularly used
  steroids.
▶ In 1985 and '86 the FBI and FDA reportedly conducted a
  wiretap investigation into local dealers believed to be
  supplying the team.
▶ One team dealer brazenly solicited new clients right on the
  floor of Epley's strength complex, bragging that he, not
  Epley, built the Huskers.
▶ Steroids were suspected by both the team trainer and
  doctor as contributing to postoperative complications that
  nearly cost former two-time All–Big Eight linebacker Marc

Munford (6′2″, 230 pounds) his life following serious knee surgery in late 1985.

It all began, says a former player, with the weightlifting boom that hit the West Coast in the late 1970s and echoed back to Nebraska around 1980. "It [steroid use] went from nonexistent to high single digits on the team," says the player. "Mostly [by] offensive line and a few other individuals." Says a former grad assistant, "In 1980–81–82 the coach and players got concerned. It [the use] really exploded."

If so, one of the people who helped light the fuse was a former Nebraska student (1980–83), a bodybuilder by the last name of "Nelson." Sitting in an Arizona restaurant one afternoon, Nelson, a strapping six-foot blonde in his late twenties, who asked that his first name not be divulged, explained how he dealt steroids to several team members for two years beginning in October 1982. It all began, he said, with friendships struck up while working out in the strength complex—until it was discovered he wasn't a football player and was forced to leave the facility. "I'd ask them what they were using," he said. "A lot of guys who were buying didn't know what they were doing." Nelson did. He had started using steroids at age eighteen, and by 1982, at the age of twenty-three, he had discovered a solid gold steroid connection—a local emergency room doctor who was making direct purchases from a Long Island, New York, pharmaceutical house. In October of '82, says Nelson, he began supplying steroids to the team via three people—Carpenter, who would set the school record for the seated shot put (38′3″) in 1985, and two local bodybuilders, Jay Hall and Mark Sullivan.

Hall was a cocky cousin of linebacker Munford; Sullivan was a weight-room supervisor at a local racquet club. Both Sullivan and Hall had reportedly tried out for the team at some point but failed to make the squad. Both had been linked by several sources, law enforcement and others, to steroid dealing. (Sullivan, while aware, he said of team usage—"I know for sure they [the team] are [using]," he said, during a brief meeting in Mingles, "and I have a pretty good idea who it is [supplying]"—denied any direct involvement with steroids; Hall said, "I never supplied anything to the team. That was all rumor. I knew a lot was going on, but I was never involved." Asked if he had ever used steroids, Hall replied, "I don't want to comment on my personal use. You have to use your imagination. I'm a competitive body-builder.")

Nelson said that about "six or seven" times a year, most often during spring ball and again in July and August right before the season started, he would order $2,000 worth of steroids from his medical sources, double the price, and sell the drugs to his team connection. A typical team order, according to Nelson was "twenty bottles of Dianabol (500 tablets per bottle), ten cases of testosterone (100 bottles per case), fifteen cases of deca-durabolin (ten bottles per case), five to ten bottles of Winstrol, a cutting drug, and some Anavar." Nelson says he knew the steroids were "most definitely" going to the team because Sullivan, Hall, and Carpenter—"my main guy"—told him so. Or other NU football players told him they were using.

"I met with Carpenter at least twenty times, and he purchased large amounts of steroids from me," said Nelson. "Carpenter just had a big mouth. I'd ask him, 'Where's all this stuff going?' and he'd say, 'the football team.' Hall would say things like 'I made those guys' or 'I made that boy,' referring to his cousin, Munford."

A former Husker noseguard who was on the squad from 1983 to 1985 recalls bumping into Hall one day in the strength complex. The player said he was shocked by the rampant use of steroids on the team—"God, I know at least fifty guys or more that used them," he said—but was even more shocked when Hall put the hook into him right inside the weight room. "He tried to get me to use them [steroids]," the player said. "He put the pressure on. He talked to a lot of players, telling them 'I can build you up.' He came directly up to me and said, 'People think Boyd Epley builds the Huskers. But I built the Huskers.'" Asked about this, Hall said, "That's pretty funny. I can't remember saying that."

Munford nearly died when his kidneys failed following routine knee surgery in late 1985. NU's head trainer George Sullivan said back in 1986 that both he and team physician Dr. Samual Fuenning had associated the kidney dysfunction with possible steroid use. "Certainly that came to me, yes, you bet," said Sullivan. "The orthopedic surgeon talked to Marc about it. He denied it."

Nelson, who had his own problems with the police, finally left Hall, Sullivan, and Carpenter behind in the spring of 1985, shortly after he and Carpenter argued over the purchase of $1,700 worth of steroids. A law enforcement source says that Carpenter had conspired to purchase 8,000 to 9,000 units (ninety bottles) of steroids from Nelson, but the deal somehow went sour, and Nelson's apartment was eventually broken into and searched by some NU football players. "They [the steroids] were here," says Nelson, "but they didn't know where to look." Carpenter later tried to run Nelson and his motorcycle off the road; he subsequently faced a third-degree assault charge—later dropped—one of many such police-related incidents involving the Husker lineman. (Lancaster County court records reveal that from August 1982 through February 1987 Carpenter had been cited for twenty-four different offenses, everything from crossing intentionally against a signal to numerous parking and moving violations to checks written against insufficient funds to assault.)

Carpenter, who was dismissed from the team in 1986 for reasons that were not specified by Osborne, denied ever purchasing steroids from Nelson or using them. Asked if he had ever tried to run Nelson off the road, Carpenter said, "I wouldn't say that was true. No."

Had he ever trailed Nelson, driven a car, and been the subject of an assault charge?

"Yes," he said.

Asked if this incident had anything to do with steroids, Carpenter replied, "You're talking about the way a guy rides his motorcycle."

Nelson's subsequent departure to a Sun Belt city had little effect on the local steroid market, because arguably the largest—and most knowledgeable—steroid dealer in the country was wired into the football program.

By late 1984 Tony Fitton, in his mid-thirties, a native of Rochdale, England, two years off the Auburn University campus where he had served as a strength coach, was up to his thick neck in anabolic steroids. Arrested at Atlanta's Hartsfield International Airport in 1982 with some 200,000 tablets of anabolic steroids in his possession, Fitton pleaded guilty to a misdemeanor controlled substance charge and was placed on probation. But that was hardly the beginning. Fitton's course had been charted twenty years earlier in the foothills and local gyms of the Pennine Mountains, 200 miles northwest of London.

According to U.S. District Court records, Richard Anthony Fitton was first introduced to powerlifting at the age of fourteen. A year later, thanks to his father's influence and handiwork, young Tony had a place to lift—the local youth club. At seventeen he weighed 260 pounds and had won both British junior and senior weightlifting titles and established several teenage records. One British newspaper ran an article calling him Britain's strongest schoolboy.

In 1969 Fitton entered the administrative side of a then-fledgling sport. A year later he was named manager of the ten-man British team that challenged the U.S. in the first international powerlifting meet. A year after that he both coached and managed the British entry in the World Power-lifting Championships. He began competing again in 1973, winning the superheavyweight title two years later. In 1976 he briefly held the world record in the 242-pound class with a squat of 815 pounds. Three years hence, Auburn University was developing a National Strength Research Center, and through his association with Terry Todd, one of the directors, Fitton was hired as a coach and liaison to the university. In 1981, following a dispute with Todd, Fitton left the center to coach Bill Kazmaier, who subsequently won three NBC-tele-vised "World's Strongest Man" competitions.

It was during this period that Fitton, traveling to meets all around the United States and Europe, started selling steroids

in king-size quantities, primarily, according to federal prose-
cutors, out of mail-order companies set up in Opelika, Alabama, just down the road from Auburn University.

On November 12, 1984, at the U.S.-Mexico checkpoint
near Tecate, California, Fitton's rental Ford was stopped and
searched by customs agents. Discovered hidden under the
backseat and in trunk panels and three pieces of luggage
were 2,090 boxes of Dianabol plus other prohibited vitamins.
Phil Halpern, as assistant U.S. attorney in San Diego who
prosecuted the case against Fitton, recalls this was no ordi-
nary bust: "He may have been the biggest dealer in the world.
Fitton deals at the highest levels. He was one of the major
distributors in the country for the last five years. He traffics
not in every state, but in any state. His major customers were
gym owners, fitness centers, and colleges. Fitton is important
because he has contacts." Fitton was eventually convicted
and sentenced to four and a half years in prison and five
years probation for offenses that included two counts of
illegal trafficking in anabolic steroids.

During an interview one day in San Diego, Tony Fitton's
soft British lilt fairly danced in the air. "Society wants the
biggest, meanest, most aggressive, most winningest football
teams there is," he said. "They don't think about how they
become that way. They forget players aren't as American as
apple pie. But, in fact, they are. They are taking anabolic
steroids. That is part of America now."

Mixing the realism of "anabolics are a fact of life" with what
might be called bewildered remorse—"I'm sorry, but what
the heck was my crime?"—Fitton offered some sharp insight
into the growing specter of steroid use by athletes in sport, at
a time, mind you, long before steroids became a stock item
on the sports pages. During his days of dealing Fitton, who in
1987 was out of prison and attempting to start a powerlifting
magazine, said he counseled athletes or strength coaches
from Virginia, Maryland, Baylor, Temple, South Carolina,
and Towson State, but for "perspective" Fitton chose to talk
about just one school—the University of Nebraska.

"They [Nebraska] have to open their eyes to what's going on," he said. "The peer pressure, the pressure to win, to please your father. You want to succeed, you want to do good—that's the way it goes.

"Guys were about to be cut, suddenly they're gaining weight, putting on eighty, ninety pounds on their bench [press] in two months. You know what's going on. It's a moral decision they make if they want to play."

Fitton said "contacts in Lincoln gyms" led him directly to the team. "I got people referred to me," he said. "They [the players] all sounded like responsible, sensible people. I enjoyed working with them."

In 1983 and '84, Fitton said, he counseled and sold steroids to at least three Huskers—Steinkuhler, All–Big Eight offensive tackle Mark Behning, and Noonan. He says he also dealt with Hall and Sullivan for about six months in 1982–83—"Hall did some pretty good buying, Sullivan too"—and, on occasion, Carpenter, whose name was one of ninety-six found on a sales ledger belonging to Fitton, a ledger seized as evidence in Fitton's steroid case. Carpenter denied knowing Fitton or buying steroids, to which Fitton replied: "He's an irresponsible dipshit; he went along with steroids because everyone else was doing it."

Steinkuhler's buys, says the dealer, were for personal use—about $100 a month in 1983. Fitton estimated from the size of their "regular" purchases, that Behning was fronting for "four or five" guys and Noonan for "two or three." Of Noonan, Fitton said, "He'd call, and we'd chat about ideas, programs, methods. He seemed a bit more with it." The middle guard purchased "a couple of [eight- to ten-week] cycles, two or three times at least in 1983–84.

"Noonan was serious about being a damned good football player and about getting stronger," Fitton said.

Questioned about Fitton and steroid use in September 1986, Noonan replied, "I don't know who that is. I never use steroids."

One of Fitton's more shocking recollections of his Nebraska days was that "frantic call" he received on the eve of the 1984 Orange Bowl from an NU player asking for methyl testosterone. The player, not revealed in the *SI* story, turns out to have been Behning.

The 6'7", 290-pound Behning, a second-round draft choice of the Pittsburgh Steelers in 1985, was perhaps Epley's ultimate "creation." To appreciate just how far Behning had come, all one had to do was check the cover of 1984–85 *Husker Power* publication. There was Behning, hands on hips, military-erect, posing in a red "Husker Power" tank top as Epley, jackhammer in hand, pretended to be blasting his body from stone. "Chiseled to Perfection" read the caption. Inside the front cover were dramatic "before" and "after" photos of Behning, the kind you see in weight-loss ads. On the left a faded black-and-white photo of the flabby freshman. On the right a four-color cover shot (minus the jackhammer), the accompanying caption describing how Behning had raised his bench press from 280 to 470 pounds, increased his vertical jump by 11½ inches, and improved from 550-pound hip sled pulls to 900 pounds.

Behning, said Epley, was perhaps the most goal-conscious Husker ever; he ached to improve on every test every time. "Testing became very important to Mark," Epley said. "To make those strides every time. Sometimes that pressure is self-imposed."

Fitton said that as a junior, Behning was ordering so many steroids and asking for so much advice, "I assumed he was a coach, not a player. He was responsible, with an air about him that was dedicated."

Behning and his agent have declined in the past to answer questions about his alleged steroid use despite repeated requests for comment.

It seems now that as far back as 1981 Nebraska coaches were worried about steroid abuse. Height-weight ratios were moving off the charts; players were recording abnormal gains in size and strength almost overnight. Back in 1986, puffing on his ever-present pipe, trainer Sullivan identified Behning, Steinkuhler, Noonan, Munford, 1982–83 star fullback Mark

Schellen (5'8", 230, pound for pound the strongest Husker ever), 1986 offensive tackle Keven Lightner of vertical jump fame, and 1985-86 offensive guard Ron Galois (6'2", 275 pounds) as players who, at one time or another, were "all suspected" of steroid use. All, says Sullivan, were tested. All, he says, passed. "We ask them if they're using steroids," said Sullivan. "If they say no, and they all do, then we check so they can prove us wrong." (Lightner, according to a police source, was kicked out of a local gym early in 1986 after the gym manager saw him injecting a substance believed to be steroids into his buttocks.)

The news that Osborne was checking—instituting random testing in August 1984—sent tremors through the team. "The only worry they had at Nebraska was when they introduced drug testing," recalled Fitton. "They wanted to make the team. People don't want to appear worse than last year. There is nothing worse than going backwards." No one was more uptight, it seems, than Behning, who went so far as to question coaches about what "testosterone ratios" the school would use in its testing. "I knew he [Behning] was a little antsy about the time we started testing," remembered Osborne. "He asked some questions. . . . Mark may have been involved, I don't know. But we had no evidence." Especially after Behning passed every test, thanks in large part to Fitton, who acknowledges he counseled Behning and several other Huskers "a lot" on ways to conceal their steroid use.

The testing lab Nebraska had chosen was American Institute for Drug Detection in Rosemont, Illinois. In 1986 American president Don Shattuck rated his company's equipment and procedures as "comparable" to the United States Olympic Committee, but acknowledged that his company tested not for all anabolics but for only eight of the most common, "a good fundamental anabolic profile," as Shattuck described it. Fitton and Dr. Mauro di Pasquale of Toronto, who has written a series of steroid-related booklets entitled *Drug Detection and Use in Amateur Sports*, considered companies like American, while solid in their detection of common street drugs such as marijuana and cocaine, severely limited

in steroid expertise and technology. Only the USOC-accre-
dited labs like the ones in Los Angeles and West Germany
have the equipment necessary to conduct sensitive steroid
testing. "They [American] could easily make mistakes," said
Fitton.

Is it possible to use masking drugs and pass an American-
administered steroid test?

"It's possible," said Shattuck.

Few thought it possible that Dean Steinkuhler would admit
to using steroids. But in a January 5, 1987, article in *Sports
Illustrated* the 6′3″, 273-pound right guard, a three-year
starter for NU, the second player picked in the '84 draft, and
a rock at right tackle since he signed with Houston, spoke
openly about his steroid use.

One day in December, 1986, the shaggy-haired Steinkuhler
sat peacefully in the players' lounge of the club's training
facility, the top half of his blood-red Oilers sweats ripped at
the collar, just enough, it seemed, so his king-size neck could
expand when he breathed. "I thought about it last night," he
said, "whether I would talk to you. I thought, ah, fuck it, get it
out, so I don't have to worry about it coming up again. That
way I don't have to worry about it every time something
comes up."

That "something" was, obviously, steroids, Steinkuhler's
drugs of choice during his junior and senior years at Nebraska, drugs he continued to use, he said, until he hurt his
knee late in '84, his rookie season with the Oilers. "That
[using steroids] could have had something to do with it, and I
had heard that with injuries and steroids you're slower to
recover."

Steinkuhler had grown up the son of a gas station owner in
tiny Burr, Nebraska (pop. 110), where he starred on the local
eight-man football team, playing five positions. His senior
year he was named Defensive Player of the Year in the state by
the *Journal-Star*, which went a long way in convincing NU
coaches he could play at the Division I level. "I got the last
scholarship," recalled Steinkuhler. He was a 6′3″, 225-pound

fullback-defensive lineman upon arrival at school and was quickly switched to the offensive line, where he grew to a natural 260 by his junior year. But then the scale stopped moving. Weight gains were measured on the fingers of one hand. "Sometimes you expect quicker results, and that's one of the reasons I wanted to do it," said Steinkuhler of his steroid use. "I really didn't get any pressure from anybody, not from the coach. It was my decision, and I made it. I wanted to be the best I could be. I thought I was a good enough athlete, but I thought I needed something that could put me over the hump."

To obtain the drugs Steinkuhler went to a "friend" on the team. "I bought the first ones from that friend," said Steinkuhler. "That's how I learned to do it. We talked. I asked him if he could get some for me." Steinkuhler declined to disclose the name of the friend for personal reasons, but a source close to Steinkuhler identified that friend as Rimington, the 6'2", 280-pound center who would win the Outland and Lombardi awards in 1982. (Rimington, now playing for the Philadelphia Eagles after several seasons with the Cincinnati Bengals, has in the past denied using steroids.)

Steinkuhler said he initially tried methyl testosterone but quickly rejected the drug because of his rough reaction. "Not a good drug," he said. "It makes you real moody, violent; you want to kill somebody." He laughed a tiny laugh.

His steroid education continued, thanks to conversations with other teammates—Schellen, Behning—and some calls to Fitton, after which Steinkuhler said he switched to Dianabol, better known as D-ball, the bread-and-butter drug for those interested in rapid increases in size and strength. "I saw instant results from that," he said. An immediate weight gain of fifteen pounds. A fifty-pound boost in his bench press to 350. And a new compulsion to train. "I never really gained *that* much strength," he said, "but it really gets you fired up about working out. You see the results. You recover faster. It helped me mentally. I had longer workouts. It just puts you in a state of mind."

His most pleasurable state, anabolically speaking, came

after "staking," or taking three drugs at once: Dianabol; Anavar, a powerful, orally administered steroid; and an injectable testosterone. During a typical six-week cycle, Steinkuhler said, he would consume thirty Dianabol tablets, half a dozen Anavar pills, and a 1-cc injection of liquid testosterone a week. Money for such purchases came from his wife, Sue, who wasn't all that pleased about supporting her husband's habit. Said Steinkuhler, "She used to tell me, 'Why take the risk?' She really didn't care for it."

Steinkuhler said he knew of "four or five—no, five or six" other Husker linemen using steroids during his junior year, and just two linemen his senior year, though he believes steroid use on that squad "kinda took off." His rationale for the low numbers was that steroid use was a private matter, "not something you really talk about; you don't sit around drinking beer, talking about steroids."

Steinkuhler was asked about winning the Lombardi and Outland. Did he feel that he had cheated in any way, that his honors had been tainted by the fact he used steroids? "No," he said, "because basically it came down to my workouts. Nobody can ever take that away from me."

Was it the right thing to do? Steinkuhler leaned closer to his questioner.

"Looking back, I can't say it was the right thing to do," he said. "I can't condone it. I don't feel great. I let myself slip that way. I kinda prided myself on what I had done. I didn't smoke pot. I didn't snort cocaine.

"The worst thing about this is my dad. I don't want to lose any respect that I've gotten. I was hoping I'd never have to tell him, but he's gonna find out. The worst thing is what people will start to say about Nebraska. But it's everywhere. Things have happened I'm not proud of. But like I said, I wanted to get this off my back."

Nelson says he also lightened his emotional load back in 1985 when the FBI and the Food and Drug Administration began working with him to investigate interstate steroid trafficking around NU. Nelson said for eighteen months, until at least mid-1986, the FBI wiretapped calls placed from a

Lincoln gym to an Arizona dealer who had been supplying a team contact with some $500 a month in steroids. To date no local arrests have been made, and the Justice Department won't comment on past, present, or future investigations. "There's been no kind of public disclosure or acknowledgment of any kind of a Nebraska case regarding the university or anything else," said a Justice Department spokesperson.

FRIDAY

11:37 A.M.

After 364 days of what-ifs and how-abouts, Countdown to Kickoff has officially begun, putting a spring in everyone's step. Gone is the buttoned-down business atmosphere; in its place is a holiday excitement colored by an outbreak of Christmas red: sweaters, ties, jackets, socks, dresses, carnations—you name it. Even the day's lead stories are upbeat: little nineteen-month-old Jessica McClure is leaving the hospital one month after being rescued from an abandoned well in Texas; Sonny Crockett, actor Don Johnson's alter ego, is marrying smoldering Sheena Easton on "Miami Vice" tonight. And after months of political speculation, former governor Kerrey announced his plans to run for the U.S. Senate in 1988. At a Democratic luncheon in Omaha Kerrey had thrust two running shoes skyward and declared, "There is no turning back," all the while pledging to "do battle" on national issues.

The most pressing national issue? Game of the Century II, of course.

Over at the student bookstore a video replay of the '71

189

game draws a crowd comparable to the one waiting to see
Tom Cruise's new hit movie playing down the street. Meanwhile, all over the state, from Kimball to Kennard, from
Springview to Superior, suitcases are being packed, engines
started, car doors slammed. As the pilgrimage, as it has every
weekend for years, begins anew; season-ticket holders taking
off on 600-, 700-, 800-mile journeys to join in the celebration.

Arriving too are dozens more media types—*Sports Illustrated*'s gifted college football writer Rick Telander among
them. Telander had checked into the Cornhusker late Thursday night after spending the previous two days in Norman
checking out the Sooners. A former second-team All–Big Ten
defensive back at Northwestern and the eighth-round draft
pick of the Kansas City Chiefs in 1971, Telander, thirty-eight,
had won raves for writing that showcased both sensitivity and
wit. A *Sports Illustrated* staff writer since 1981 (he started as
a special contributor to the magazine in 1976), the handsome Chicagoan was now considered one of the most versa-
tile and popular writers on *SI*'s staff.

Telander had arrived in stylish fashion, flying in on the
Sooners' charter, and although he and Switzer weren't drinking buddies by any stretch, the OU coach had evidently
appreciated Telander's restraint and open-mindedness when
Switzer's integrity was occasionally called into question.
"Barry must like me," laughed Telander. "I didn't call him a
criminal in my last story."

As a writer Telander was clearly captivated by Switzer's
charming personality, his tolerant way of dealing with athletes, particularly blacks, and, of course, his storytelling. "He
told me this one story, about how he found Charles Thompson. I about died laughing," said Telander during dinner late
Thursday night. "Barry was out at some grand opening for a
car dealership in Oklahoma City a couple of years ago when
he sees this group of break dancers right on the street. Said
the leader was doing the damnedest things he ever saw. He'd
drop to the floor, spin around, get up on his head, fall down
again. Unbelievable stuff. So Switzer asked somebody, 'Who's

that dude?' And the guy said, 'That's Charles Thompson.'"

"Charles Thompson, the Lawton High quarterback?" asked Switzer.

"Yeah," somebody said.

"Holy potatoes," said Switzer, walking right over and introducing himself to what he likes to call a "great, great" athlete.

Telander said that in preparation for writing about Game of the Century II he'd spent Wednesday night reviewing a videotape of the original classic. "What a trip," he said. "It's a lot of slow white guys and Johnny Rodgers for Nebraska and Greg Pruitt for Oklahoma." Telander felt Osborne still hadn't come to complete grips with the black athlete issue. "They keep using the word *speed* around here," he said. "In college football it's just a euphemism for the word *black*. What we're seeing now is almost the Reverse Slave Theory. Slow white guys blocking for 5'6" break dancers. It's the break-dance theory of college football."

Just before practice Osborne and Taylor meet briefly outside the players' lounge, the hallway jammed with fans. Friends, students, fathers, sons, all gathered 'round, soaking up some pregame psych, hoping to catch a glimpse of a Husker or two. Exiting the players' lounge after his final pregame press conference, Osborne had run headlong into the crowd. He politely signed footballs and autographs for anybody who asked—and many did—before spotting Taylor.

"How'd you do?" said Osborne.

"Got an A," said Taylor, smiling at a reporter before adding, "I'd better."

Calculus? Art history? No, in addition to the daily demands of school and practice, quarterbacks at Nebraska must pass Professor Osborne's advanced course on signal calling. Each and every week during the football season NU quarterbacks are tested on the game plan. Situational play calling. Reading defenses. Reaction. Audibles. And this week's assignments were unusually complex; the Huskers would run eighteen different offensive sets on Saturday—nine left, nine right—more than most games and the most against an Oklahoma team in years.

At least Taylor would have all his weapons. At the press conference Osborne pronounced the team in "pretty good shape," citing the recovery of defensive tackle Smith, wingbacks Brinson and Hendley Hawkins, and I-backs Clark and Kelley. Other news: Turner Gill would lead chapel service the next day, and the prospect of Game of the Century II had brought dozens of ex-Huskers out of the woodwork. "Players I haven't seen for years are coming to the game," said Osborne.

Predictions, Tom?

"I'm not predicting a victory," he said. "But I think we've got a good chance to win. I really believe we're going to play well."

2:00 P.M.

Dave Gillespie is drowning in blue chips. Not that he's feeling any pain, mind you. Standing on the sidelines of an empty Memorial Stadium, the Huskers' second-year on-campus recruiting coordinator is surrounded by thirty of the finest high school football players in the land. Most are here on an "unofficial" visit, meaning, according to NCAA rules, they have paid their own way to Lincoln. Such is the status of this game and the Husker program.

Gillespie, a man with a crisp military manner, came up through the ranks to earn his position: three-year letterman as an I-back at NU in the mid-1970s, assistant coach at Lincoln High, head coach at Hastings High for three years before accepting a grad assistant post at NU in 1985. A year later he moved into recruiting full-time, his days and nights a never-ending search for the player of the '90s. "We're looking for the best athletes," says Gillespie. "Speed has really become the name of the game."

The recruiting game at NU is limited, literally, by nature. "We do a lot of research, and the two reasons we don't get kids are weather and locale," Gillespie says. "But our feeling is those are two things we can't do anything about. So we worry about the things we can control." Consequently, the positive is pushed: Osborne's image, fan support, the winning tradition. Like everything else under Osborne, it's a process. The country is divided into nine areas with future Huskers targeted in their sophomore or junior year. Once identified, they receive a steady stream of low-key videos, letters ("20 Reasons to Attend Nebraska"), and phone calls. Always the phone calls. Osborne may lead the nation in long-distance bills. "He's very conscientious," says Gillespie. Each recruit is allotted at least two or three calls from the head coach, between eight and ten minutes each. In addition Osborne will personally visit the home of the top sixty or seventy recruits—as many or more "home visits" as any college coach in the country. All conducted in Osborne's homespun style. "He's not an exploitive person, an expressive person," says Gillespie. "He doesn't want to act like he's hard-selling the program. That's not him."

No, it's not, but don't think for a minute Nebraska can't raise a recruit's eyes faster than a 5:00 A.M. reveille when it wants to. The use of Learjets tells you that. So does the recruitment of Aaron Emanuel. For his on-campus visit, Osborne took a private jet out to Los Angeles, where Emanuel, who ran for 4,807 yards and fifty-four touchdowns at Quartz Hill High School in Palmdale, California, was whisked off to a nearby airport in a white chauffeur-driven Cadillac limousine. "I was impressed by him [Osborne]," said Emanuel. "He didn't try to impress you. He told me I was the type of back for his offense, that I would fit in pretty good."

Upon arrival in Lincoln, Emanuel received the standard tour: the stadium, weight room ("Boyd gets them pretty pumped up," says Gillespie), academic center, a basketball game, and the dinner and party thing. Only in Emanuel's case he dined with then-Governor Kerrey and his then-girlfriend, actress Debra Winger. For some recruits it's magic. But for some big-city kids Lincoln is, well, still Lincoln.

"Pretty slow," said Emanuel. "Not my type of place." He eventually chose USC and became the Trojans' starting tail-back.

By mid-afternoon Nebraska has wrapped up its final prepa-rations, leaving the stadium turf to the hundreds of fans and former players who mingle casually among the team. There's Broderick over at the 20-yard line posing for pictures, then strutting off the field as two grade-schoolers hand him a set of plastic keys. A fired-up Black Shirt defense huddles around McBride, their inspirational leader, listening and watching as OU players slowly begin to drift onto the surface for the start of their practice.

Suddenly the crowds part. Breezing onto the field in a golf cart is Switzer. His left knee, injured by a freak sideline hit during OU's 17–13 squeaker over Missouri the week before, is stretched out over the front portion of the Cushman cart. Stacked in the back are Holieway and a pretty blonde, ob-viously enjoying the ride. The cart stops abruptly near mid-field. Switzer remains seated, signing autographs and holding court for the curious, of which there are many.

Across the field, near the west sideline, Oklahoma's 6'4", 198-pound senior strong safety David Vickers, a certifiable sock-rocker, is deep into pregame analysis by Brent Mus-burger of CBS, in town for the play-by-play duties. Brent is looking rather dapper at the moment, something out of Sherlock Holmes in his houndstooth cap and trench coat. A few moments later, hustling away from the Vickers interview, Musburger says the outcome of the game itself is something of a mystery. "Everyone now is saying tight defensive game, edge Nebraska," he says. "It's one of those games that always seems to have weird, weird endings, trick plays.

"Oklahoma gives me the same vibrations all the time—they're loose and ready to play. I did not expect the young-sters here to be so loose. I was surprised. I think this is going to be their year."

One of the final factors on any pregame checklist is always

the character of the two head coaches. How will they handle the pressure? React to adversity? Motivate and relate to their players? For years the consensus among the media and even some die-hard Husker fans—right or wrong—was that Switzer held a big advantage over Osborne as a game-day coach. That somehow Switzer's cocksure nature and ass-kickin' attitude got transferred to his players, especially at critical times in crucial games. The kind of man who recruits break dancers and bozos named Boz and three days before a Game of the Century can pour piss and vinegar all over his opponent and not give a good goddamn. "Why they think they're going to beat the snot out of us I don't know," he told Telander on Thursday in Norman. "They ain't scored but 3 touchdowns in 3 years against our defense. . . . Clothes, hair—what the hell does that have to do with winning? Earrings? Sunglasses? Does any of that tell you whether a player is a great athlete, what kind of competitor he is?"

Nebraska, on the other hand, was perceived as fearing the big game. Osborne's critics contended his exhaustive preparation and placid personality left his team long on technique but woefully short on emotion and guts at game time.

At his press conferences on Friday afternoon coaching character held true to form as Osborne kept it all in place, his emotions in a deep freeze. At his, Switzer, in contrast, was warm and witty, a man without a worry in the world. "I'm not uptight about this game at all," he said after OU's practice. "It doesn't bother me at all. I want to win it just as much as Tom does, but if we lose, what the hell, I'm gonna go back to Norman, Oklahoma. I'm not gonna get to go bird huntin' next week because of this leg, but I'll find something I like to do.

"This game is where we want to be," Switzer continued, "and how we want to be there. Back in August, when we started two-a-day practice, we wrote down a goal on the board in our coaches' dressing room that was 10–0 on November 21, in Lincoln, Nebraska. How we arrived is really irrelevant. We're where we want to be.

"I know we have a good football team. We have the type

players who are very competitive and really play to the challenge. This football team is hungry. . . . Emotion isn't gonna give Nebraska an edge in this game. Talent does. What you do on the field counts, not emotion. We're not talkers. The only one who talked is in the Northwest right now playing for Seattle.

"We got the same team except for Bosworth, the same secondary. We gotta play the running game. We gotta play the play-action pass. We know what their bread and butter is, we've looked at it a bunch. We've practiced against it a bunch. We know what plays they'll run. They know what plays we'll run. It just gits down to who gits it done the best."

Switzer squirmed a bit on the plastic seat, stretching his bum knee, wrapped in a heavy harness. Someone asked about the injury. "The leg?" said Switzer. "Ah, it's all right. It bothered me the first night, but after that, no problem. It's just hell putting on your underwear is all."

Chip Williams would beg to differ on that last point. Actually he enjoyed slipping on his long johns, some red tights, his, ah, cape, and parading around Memorial Stadium. All for a good cause, mind you. That cause officially being Husker football. Which Williams, er, "Huskerman" turned out for on Friday afternoon, adding a sense of the surreal to the old-fashioned, rabble-rousing Pep Rally of the Century held just outside the Student Union. Williams, thirty-five, a lean, athletic-looking auto detailer by trade, stood on a fountain adjacent to the union—red cape blowing in a stiff breeze—and shivered slightly as dusk and, finally, darkness settled in. "I've been a Nebraska fan for twenty-five years now," he said. "I've got the fever just like everyone else here."

So it seemed. Hundreds of students, faculty, moms and dads, their children, and football stars past and present crowded the plaza, all yelling and screaming with the kind of "Everybody's All-American" enthusiasm that seemed to die out on college campuses years ago. But not at Nebraska. Never has, never will. One look at the "Go Big Red" banners, the bonfire, the pink-cheeked cheerleaders, booming pep

band, "Live at Five" camera crews, the punkers and businessmen all shouting "Hus-ker Pow-er, Hus-KER POW-ER!" told you
that. So did the spirited demolition of the "Switzermobile"—
two bucks a shot—and the poetry reading by an NU vice
chancellor of student affairs, a man who snickered when he
said the limerick he was about to read had been penned by
"T. S. Osborne," the distant cousin of you-know-who.

> There once was a team coached by Barry
> That took on a task quite scary,
> They came into our house,
> With a fire hard to douse,
> Then found Christmas in Tempe quite merry.

The speeches came next. Jerry Tagge, star QB of the '71
team, Everybody's All-American himself that year and later a
seven-year pro in the NFL with the Packers, set the tone right
out the chute.

"I hate Oklahoma," he said.

Brinson and Lee Jones then grabbed the microphone to
urge the crowd to "pump it up" tomorrow.

"You know where we're headed!" yelled Jones.

"Orange Bowl!"

"Yeah," smiled Jones.

"We're gonna pay back Miami for what they did in '83,"
yelled assistant coach George Darlington above the din.
"We've had two great weeks of practice, and we've been
waiting one whole year. We're ready."

So was Chip Williams.

He said he'd tried out for the team as a punter back in '79,
but a knee injury ended that dream early. In 1981 ("Irving
Fryar's sophomore year") he stumbled on the "Huskerman"
idea when a Halloween costume of silk and velvet made "by a
lady friend" caught on. "The fans like it, you know," said
Williams. So much so that for three years Williams said he
took to leading the Huskers out on the field before each home
game, a practice that was cut short when a fan got hit by a
frozen orange thrown from the stands and the university
started cracking down on security. But Williams, not to be

denied, went ahead with his shtick anyway, the result being an arrest and charges of criminal trespassing. "All the football players get off, and I get charged," he moans. He planned to plead guilty until the presiding judge informed him that he faced five years in jail and a $5,000 fine. He opted for a jury trial. Then he showed up as his alter ego.

"Well, Mr. Williams," the judge said with a smile, "it looks like you want to make things difficult."

Williams never got around to explaining exactly what the court's decision was, saying only that the judge hadn't led the league in leniency that year. "I think he got some pressure from the university to keep this asshole off the field," says Williams. A sentiment, Williams reveals, often shared by his wife, Kathy: "She doesn't like me doing this. She wishes I'd stop."

But this *is* Big Red football, so he can't or won't, believing that somehow a grown man dressed in a cape, tights, cutoff sweatpants, red NU visor, and, of course, those long johns ("I'm no fool," he said. "I may be crazy, but I'm no fool.") makes a difference. And from the looks of the little children wandering up and clutching the cape, pointing to the smiling man with their red and white pom-pons, smiles as wide as Neil Smith's wingspan, maybe he does, maybe he just does.

5:40 P.M.

The fever continues to rise, and with it the Dow, which seems somehow tied to pregame excitement. The 30 Industrials are rising too, up 18.24 on the day. Downtown resembles spring break in Lauderdale or Daytona Beach, packed with partiers, college kids, and out-of-towners getting their game faces on, joining the fraternity of other college towns—the Austins, Ann Arbors, and College Stations of the world, places where football is King and Friday night one long coronation.

Over at the Cornhusker, eighteen-year-old Jeff Kinney patiently awaits the return of this father, Jeff Sr., from the rally. Talk about kings. In addition to rumbling for 174 yards (on 31 carries) against the Sooners in Century I, Kinney Sr.

slammed across the goal line like the Fourth Armored Division for the game-winning touchdown—his fourth score of the day. Mr. Reliable, they called him. Reliable enough to break tackles like twigs, to run over would-be tacklers who found themselves holding shreds of a long torn and tattered jersey.

At 6'4", 190 pounds, it was obvious the younger Kinney had a lot of the old man in him. The blonde hair. The straight answers. A senior at Wheaton North High School near Chicago, where his dad now worked in security sales, Jeff, a quarterback/defensive back, said he had helped his team to the Class 5A state championship the year before and was now fielding recruiting offers from places like Indiana, Illinois, Iowa State. And, of course, Nebraska, where he was on a recruiting visit.

"My dad must have introduced me to 500 people since we got here," he said.

Did he want to follow his father's path and play here?

"Yes," said Jeff Kinney, Jr., "I do. But there'll be a lot of pressure, that's for sure." (He eventually wound up at Illinois.)

The son is asked a question. "It was like business with them," he said of his father's famous team. "Old philosophies, old-fashioned football. They didn't talk. They just went in, played hard, and did their best.

"My dad likes coming back here every year, I think he does," continued Kinney. "When we come down here, it's so different. Other games you wonder what you're going to do. Here everybody is talking about the game. It's totally different."

Makes you proud to have a father who played here, doesn't it?

Jeff Kinney, Jr., looks you straight in the eye before he answers.

"Yes sir," he says. "It sure does."

SATURDAY

7:42 A.M.

The streets are deserted now, a raw, 39-degree chill in the air.
Inside of an hour, however, the city stirs in earnest. At The
Cornhusker Hotel a distinguished gray-haired Okie steps into
an elevator sporting an OU jersey and jeans, a pretty blonde
on one arm, binoculars and overcoat on the other. Kickoff is
still seven hours away. "Gonna get there early today," says
the Okie. "Gonna need all the help we can get today."

By nine the red coats are out, roaming the streets, window-
shopping, saying howdy to other friendly folks decked out in
scarlet hats, ties, scarves, socks, pins . . . even matching
husband-wife ensembles. Over at Jan Drake's Garden Cafe a
little boy, no more than nine, complains to his parents, gift-
wrapped in red, how "boring" it is to watch these two football
teams play every year.

"Think so?" says his mother.

"Well, not really," says the son.

"And don't forget, son," explains his father, "it helps the
Lincoln economy."

That it does. To the tune of some $3.3 million every

201

football weekend, a boon to the hotels, restaurants, bars, and even, certain enterprising college fraternities.

11:20 A.M.

At the corner of R and 14th streets, a half dozen "frat rats" are engaged in a spirited game of half-court hoops, as spirited as one can be while sweating off all the hops and grains they poured down their throats at last night's pregame primer. Behind the court, inside the vine-covered manse, some seventy-five Phi Gamma Delta "brothers" reside in various states of consciousness.

Because the house and its adjacent parking lot abut one of the university's busiest corners, parking on said lot can fetch a hefty price, a thought not lost this morning on Sean Halligan, Aaron Kull, and Will (The Grimace) Varicak.

"Up earlier than I've been all week," says Will, draining a Diet Pepsi and waving in two Chevys and a Ford—at $5 a shot. Kull chimes in proudly, noting the house bagged about 400 bucks at the last home game, thanks, in part, to the brothers' ability to wedge cars in at such odd angles that some have to be *lifted* out of the lot after games. But hey, that's the beauty of college, and, come to think of it, so is today's upcoming "primer" with those gorgeous Kappas. And how about those fifty OU brothers who are in town for the showdown!

A customized Chevy van cruises by, a white "No. 1" finger wagging in the back window.

"Fuck Oklahoma," mutters Will.

Another car with an Oklahoma plate passes by.

"Fuck Oklahoma," mutters Will, who's definitely got that line down pat.

Another OU supporter stops, rolls down his window, and cautiously checks the parking rates. "Charge them extra and see what happens," whispers Kull.

"How much?" asks the driver.

"Ten bucks," says The Grimace.

"I'll take it."

Kull, a freshman, shares a deep laugh with his buddies as

he leans back against an aging MG. Kull (rhymes with pool) is looking quite coolish himself today in his Tom Cruise *Risky Business* shades, faded jeans, and a Herbie Husker T-shirt, the one that shows ol' Herb pissing across the state line into Oklahoma. Kull had crossed a few state lines himself to enroll at Nebraska, growing up, as he did, in the affluence of Bloomfield Hills, Michigan, hanging around with the son of GM president Roger Smith, playing some high school soccer. After high school his parents, natives of Fremont, Nebraska, urged their son to rediscover his roots. "They brainwashed me," laughs Kull. "They said, 'Come down to Nebraska, see what it's like.'" Cool, thought Kull. Now he says, "I love it here."

High Noon

The distant sound of a bass drum echoes like cannon fire across campus. On the Memorial Library steps scalpers have already set up shop, whispering ticket prices—"Sixty dollars each," says one—to a passerby. Up the walkway a bit an old man bends behind a tree and offers two 40-yard-line seats for $100 each. All around Game of the Century II T-shirts and sweatshirts are selling like sno-cones in the Sahara, the grounds around the stadium brimming with merchants hawking everything from helium balloons to plastic keys to NU football caps. The downtown streets and campus have the feel of a big country fair, turning Lincoln, Nebraska, into truly a rare sporting treat.

12:40

A crowd builds outside Gate 2. The first few bars of "Boomer Sooner" fill the air before stopping seconds later.

"That's why they make that song so damn short," quips one Husker fan. "So everybody in the damn state can sing it."

1:10

Osborne hits the field for the first time with defensive ends coach Tony Samuel at his side. Oz looks every bit the head coach, covered in red from tip to toe. He leaves Samuel and moves off by himself, alone with his thoughts, just the way he likes it, walking east to west, cutting the field in half horizontally, pausing every ten yards or so to check the turf for wetness. *No stone unturned.* He moves slowly, methodically along the west sideline, then out through the south end zone and into the locker room.

1:20

Welcome signs and banners have sprouted up in the sun: Kansas Cornhuskers. North Texas Nebraskans. Alaskan Nebraskans. Canada Loves Nebraska. Californians for Nebraska. Even Notre Dame Sisters for Nebraska.

1:30

Press box. Pregame media sentiment is leaning in favor of the hosts.

1:55

"Our House" is almost full now, roaring as the public address announcer utters his first "Nebraska" of the day. The game officials enter; they have plugs in their ears. Five minutes later Switzer and Osborne, the yin and yang of college football, meet and shake hands warmly at midfield. On the sideline you can feel the frenzy in your feet.

"Well, I guess they're all here," says Osborne as he reaches the Nebraska sideline.

"Good luck, Tom," I reply.

2:10

The "Go . . . Big . . . Red!" chants are deafening now, out of control. The band, colors, sights, and sounds, all folding together into one big buzz. Oklahoma takes the field, led by strongside linebacker Dante Jones, a "Raw Dog 50" towel hanging off his hip. A dozen Husker recruits snap pictures and stare proudly at the teams.

Another chant.

"Whose House?"

"Our House!"

"WHOSE HOUSE?"

"OUR HOUSE!"

2:20

Nebraska leaves the field for the final time. Air horns and a mighty roar accompany the Huskers' departure. Thomas, the Sandman himself, is the last one in, lingering long enough to wave an index finger high to the sky before low-fiving cornerback Marvin Sanders as they disappear together under the South stands.

2:34

The seniors show first, pouring through a path formed by band members and half-crazed students. Honorary captain Von Sheppard, a talented wingback out with a knee injury, leads the way. Brian Washington is next, then the Jones boys, Keith and Lee, then Tomjack, Blakeman, and the rest of the farewell class, all honored one by one. Taylor and the bulk of the underclassmen follow. In keeping with his sense of the dramatic, Thomas is the last man on the field. He's half-mad with emotion, spinning and twirling, flinging his arms around before, finally, whipping a set of plastic keys high up into the stands, into His House, sending the vast majority of the 76,663 fans on hand—the single largest home crowd in the history of NU football—into a screaming lather.

"Let's do it now!" screams Forch.

As his players pound pads and butt heads, Osborne straddles the sideline in silence. Slowly he flips the toggle switch for his headset back and forth, checking and rechecking his field-to-press box communication. For 75 percent of the game he will be talking with offensive line coach Tenopir and backfield coach Solich, calling plays, checking strategy, attempting to stay one or two plays ahead of the action—and Switzer. Unlike some coaches, Osborne shuns computer-generated play-calling charts. His moves are intuitive, chess-like, purposely lacking in emotion. ("I don't think you can call plays and make decisions and be emotional," he says.)

2:45 P.M.

But *emotional* is the operative word as sophomore kicker Chris Drennan of Cypress, California, drives his foot into the football at exactly 2:45 P.M. The weather is a gift from above—sixty degrees and gloriously sunny. On the first offensive play of the day, OU's Thompson steps behind center, tight end Jackson split out wide to the left, far away from Broderick "In the Backfield, First Play" Thomas. The crowd's still in a tizzy, so much so that "King Charles VI" (as the towel hanging from his belt attests) asks for time. The referee agrees. (Thompson will later explain he used that time-out to his "advantage," to show the defense "I was in control, [that] this guy isn't as dumb as he looks.")

Finally the crowd settles down. And so does Oklahoma. Over the next six minutes Thompson moves the Sooners smartly down the field behind an offensive line that weighs 1,400 pounds tackle to tackle. All the way down to the Nebraska 9-yard line. Then Thompson hands off to Anderson—fumble! Linebacker Etienne smothers the muff at the 8.

On the sidelines Mark Blazek yanks off his helmet and talks sense to a trio of teammates. "We've been hurtin' ourselves," he says. Ten feet away Thomas stuffs a white towel deep into the corner of his mouth; it's the color of courage as he pulls it out.

After an exchange of punts it's Nebraska's turn to find an offensive rhythm. A quick pass from Taylor to reserve wing-back Richard Bell gains 11 yards. A quarterback draw nets 15. I-back Jones—off a key block from Heibel—gains 7 on a critical third-and-two.

Taylor again. This time his scrambling ability turns a busted double-reverse pass into an 11-yard gain, down to the Sooners' 31. A holding penalty. Back to the 41. Then Jones, running with a fire in his belly, speeds 16 yards down to the 25. Jones again. Around right end. Big blocks from All-America right guard John McCormick and the gritty Heibel. Nobody's gonna catch Jones. Touchdown! Nebraska draws first blood, 7–0.

"That's the way to run it!" Taylor tells Jones as they jog off the field. "That's the way!"

The second quarter opens with Melton ordering up a quick defensive huddle. He warns Thomas to "stay put," to stop pursuing OU backs like some dime-store detective; he's setting himself up for a reverse or counter. "But I want to *move*," pleads Thomas. So does Oklahoma. But the Sooners are sputtering. Lost fumbles (2) and poor field position (4 of their first 6 possessions began inside their 26-yard line) have them talking to themselves.

Near the NU bench, Rich Glover, Lombardi and Outland winner in 1972, and a one-man wrecking crew in the '71 game (22 tackles), pulls middle guard Pete aside. "You've got to come across the line of scrimmage at a better angle," says Glover. As Pete walks away, Glover turns and says, "But this isn't the time for coaching. It's a time for *playing*."

And play the defense does.

"We're doin' it, man! We're doin' it!" screams Forch after another short defensive series.

"All right, people," said Glover, settling things down, "let's keep working."

Melton calls another meeting. "Good job, Neil," he says to defensive tackle Smith. "We gotta go out and bust ass, bust ass. We do that, and everything will be cool."

"They're fuckin' scared," screams Smith as the meeting breaks up. "The motherfuckers are running outside all the time."

Halftime. Nebraska 7, Oklahoma 0. Tom Osborne is half-way home.

On the fourth play of the second half, Huskers' ball, third

and 10 from their own 20, Taylor fires a pass over the middle to Brinson. The ball is tipped by cornerback Derrick White and intercepted by free safety Rickey Dixon, who dances 24 yards down to the Huskers' 13. Two plays later, Anthony Stafford speeds around right untouched, and it's all tied, 7–7.

"That's all right," Osborne tells his team. "Let's go, let's go."

"Damn," mutters Etienne, pacing the sideline in solitude.

"We gotta play ball, man!" screams Smith, whose plaintive appeal reflects the game's shifting emotional edge—now swinging back strongly in favor of Oklahoma. You sense an "Oh, no, not again" feeling on the Huskers' sideline. Unfortunately it turns out to be true. As Osborne, McBride, and many others have predicted, the Sooners begin wearing the home team down inside. The ol' one-two punch (huge offensive line, blinding backfield speed) takes its toll as Pete and Murray are blocked time and time again by OU's interior line. Cracks in the defensive line widen. Etienne and Forch are having to make far too many tackles. But still the Huskers hold.

Nebraska's offense is also struggling, stymied by a proud and punishing Sooner D. "Let's go back to blocking the old way, okay?" says Osborne during one sideline huddle. When that doesn't work, he quickly shifts strategy: "We need to protect better," he tells the offensive line late in the quarter. "We're gonna start passing."

No sooner has Osborne delivered that pitch than Thompson shovels one of his own to Patrick Collins, who cranks around the corner and heads off to the races. Sixty-five yards later it's Oklahoma 14, Nebraska 7. A minute remains in the third quarter.

"We'll come back," Etienne says.

"Stay up," Rod Smith tells Jones.

"What's a touchdown? What's a touchdown?" yells Blazek, attempting to rally the troops.

The fourth quarter opens on a dismal note—Dixon picks off another Taylor pass. The junior quarterback is having one of his erratic afternoons. Back on the bench, wingback Brin-

son turns when someone shouts, "Hey, Brinson, come 'ere."
It's a boozy college kid. "You gotta play, man, play to win,"
says the kid. Brinson, who for some reason is wearing a Gucci
hat instead of his helmet, reaches out and shakes the guy's
hand.

On the very next offensive series, with 12:56 to play and
Nebraska still in it, Taylor fades back into his own end zone
and fires a 55-yard bullet down the middle of the field. It
arrives in traffic just over Brinson's right shoulder at the OU
45-yard line. A difficult catch. One requiring unusual concentration. And Brinson doesn't make it. The crowd lets out a
groan as Brinson repairs to the bench, chin on his chest.

"Hey, man," says a teammate. "Where'd it hit you? Shoulder pads? Helmet?"

All Brinson can do is shake his head—minus the Gucci cap
now—and gingerly rub the fingers of his left hand.

Midway through the fourth quarter OU's R. D. Lashar adds
a short field goal. It's 17–7 now, time ticking away. Thomas
sits alone, talking via telephone to the defensive coaches
upstairs, before he slams down the receiver in disgust, swear-
ing softly under his breath. "We'll come back," says Etienne,
sitting beside him. Thomas just shakes his head. From the
stands a lone voice calls out: "It's not over yet, guys."

But it is. The defense, on the field all day, is dragging.
Memorial Stadium sounds almost empty as a glassy-eyed fan
with a pockmarked face pushes up against a short fence that
separates the field from the stands. *Osborne!* he yells
through a rolled-up program. His tone is ugly. Threatening.
Strangely, security guards pay no notice, even after the fan
deftly hops the waist-high divide and melts into the sideline
crowd. Ten seconds later he's standing between a CBS cam-
eraman and the chain gang—five feet from the head coach.
Security is notified. The man is quickly and quietly removed.
Osborne, it appears, never notices.

With 2:59 remaining and Taylor throwing at will, he tosses
his third interception of the day. Blinking back tears, he
struggles to the sideline, head swaying from side to side.
Osborne remains mute, hands dug deep in his red pockets,

grinding away on his gum. Taylor looks skyward as if to ask "Why me? Why now?" Moments later the final gun sounds.

For a brief moment Taylor is alone as he limps his way across the field to the locker room. Then a coed runs up and gives him a teary hug. Fans pass by and pat his shoulder. Near midfield, Osborne jogs up from behind and pulls the disconsolate quarterback toward him in a fatherly fashion seconds before they're both swallowed by a large but cheerless crowd. "You're still No. 1 to us; keep your head up, Steve," someone shouts.

The chant "Mi-am-mi! Mi-am-mi!" builds in the Sooner rooting section in the west stands. OU rooters unfurl a king-size banner that reads "Hey, Steve Taylor, A Closed Mouth Gathers No Foot."

Taylor keeps his mouth closed the entire trip to the locker room, the only sign of just how empty and hollow he must feel expressed in one angry act of emotion—the bashing of his helmet against the locker room door.

"Jinxed," mumbles a sweat-soaked player.

"It's so sad," replies a fan.

Not over in the OU locker room, it isn't. Now the Sooners are talking, labeling Nebraska's pregame noise a major mistake. "Makes the win all the sweeter," crows defensive end Darrell Reed. "They talked and talked, but they never backed it up. Adds OU guard Mark Hutson, "When you talk trash before a game and then don't back it up, I would have to think you'd be a little bit disappointed, a little bit embarrassed."

On the field two middle-aged souvenir hunters rummage around the Nebraska bench. But since there's nothing left to steal, they settle for a Coke cup full of ice water, turning to toast one another as if it were champagne. How appropriate. For indeed, it has been a vintage year for Oklahoma.

To his credit, Osborne pulls no postgame punches. The numbers tell the story: 419 rushing yards for Oklahoma, six times what the Husker defense had averaged in its previous nine games. Collins, 131 yards. Thompson, 131 yards. Anderson, 119 yards. Nebraska gained just 235 yards in total offense (300 below average), 144 of that 235 coming on its first and last drives of the game. In between, diddly. "I would say that of the losses I've been associated with, this was the most disappointing," Osborne says, his voice barely a whisper. "I feel halfway apologetic, but I don't know what to apologize for." He looks lost, like a lottery winner suddenly told he's one number off. Drained and dazed, he says, "We just got whipped, just got whipped." But still Osborne is alert enough to quiet any second-guessing by the media. "No," he says when asked about Taylor's poor play, the 6-of-18 passing, 54 yards rushing on 18 carries. The 3 interceptions. "No, I don't think there was too much pressure on Steve. He's had better days, he's had worse days. When you're not controlling the line of scrimmage, it's very, very tough to play quarterback."

A back door swings open. A yellow-jacketed bowl official moves in, interrupting Osborne's thoughts to "announce" that Nebraska has been invited to Tempe to play Florida State in the Fiesta Bowl. Talk about strained. The jacket mumbles something about how sorry he is Nebraska has lost but how he's looking forward to having the Huskers and their "great fans" show up in Tempe.

"I'm sure they'll be there," says Osborne.

Off in a quiet corner of the players' lounge, McBride 'fesses up to the obvious. "The speed factor is still there," he says. "Speed in the backfield. Speed in the secondary. Speed all over. . . . In simple terms they're a better football team than we are on both sides of the ball. For some reason we were flat. We didn't play as emotional a football game as last year." He shakes his head. "It was just one of those old-time rear-end shots—a real butt-kicking. Their line is what they say it is . . . you give their backs a little crack, two feet wide—boom!— they're through it. Oklahoma, by all rights, gave us a legitimate beating. It wasn't a fluke or anything like that."

Steve Taylor takes a couple of deep breaths before beginning. In his hand is a towel. "On a Mission" it reads, a gift from his girlfriend, Kelly Bell. But the mission today was impossible, and Taylor hasn't, as yet, figured out what went wrong. Only that it hurts. "It's tough," he says. "I said a lot of things before the game. I still feel that way. They shouldn't have beat us. We all wanted to win. We were confident. For some reason I feel we didn't play the way we could have." He swallows hard. "We had momentum, the athletes . . . the time was right. We just didn't make it work today.

"This is my third year," he says. "I've got one more year to beat Oklahoma. . . . Now I've got to eat my words. It's difficult to accept; it really is. It's going to be hard to live with knowing what the papers will be like in this crazy town."

He stops to compose himself. The room waits. Seems like he has something else on his mind. "I know I'm a winner," he says. "I know I showed great poise. Maybe it's something else, I don't know. Luck. But they didn't beat us because they wanted it more than us. I wanted it *bad*."

So did Thomas. Whereas three days before a bubbling, wisecracking kid had predicted victory, this time around Thomas looks more like a survivor of an earthquake or airplane disaster, unable to focus, wracked by grief. He sits stone-faced in the interview chair, tears glistening in his eyes. Blinking them back. Blinking them back. Thirty seconds pass. "It's hard," he begins. "My feelings are hurt. I don't know where to go."

What about the taunting? Had it backfired?

Thomas stiffens. "I know I gave 110 percent," he says. "I played football, okay! The whole defense played football today. My teammates gave 110 percent. It's something, I guess, we couldn't control. . . . This is more than a game. I'm not going to go out and kill myself. I may feel like that now. . . . I'll probably go home and just cry. I'll probably just wake up tomorrow and live my life."

Almost an hour later, after a classy Keith Jones, styling in a calf-length denim coat, offered some pointed postmortems ("We do have a better football team; Oklahoma played a better football game"), Thomas still hasn't left the lounge. He's alone now, just him and a writer he'd met during the week. Flip, flip, flip. Sitting on a couch, mindlessly turning pages in a discarded game-day program. Flip, flip. He stops at page 40, staring at the names and faces on OU's roster.

"I'll probably go home, play with my dogs, talk to Steve, look at the game again, see what went wrong. Try to get on with the next day," he says in a whisper. "Thank God, I guess it's a blessing. We're still livin'. My knee's not busted up. There are some bright things.

"I think I am a human being, a role model. I'm hurting for Steve. I look at these guys [in the game program], you know I'm gonna see them again. I just hate that we couldn't bring these people, our fans, the Big Eight championship. Because they're the ones who make it so much fun."

SUNDAY
NOVEMBER 22, 1987

7:13 A.M.

"Sooners Steal Keys to NU 'House,'
No Magic Is Needed, Switzer Says"

"Sooners Ransack 'Our House'"

"Taylor 'Must Eat Words'
Unconvinced OU Is Better"

"Sooners Lower Boom on Top-Ranked NU"

"Sooners: Huskers' Pregame Talk
Simply Whistling in the Wind"

Headlines of heartache. Words to cry by. Twelve losses in the last sixteen years. Four in a row. Questions without answers. Sentences that read "The loss meant the 30 seniors introduced before the game leave Nebraska without . . . a victory over Oklahoma." A state is numbed, in mourning, its spiritual leader at a loss to explain what happened, yet in-

215

stinctively, impulsively looking inside for answers. "I guess I have to look at myself as a coach," Osborne tells the local paper. "Apparently I didn't get them that well prepared to play."

By 10:00 in the morning a quilt of quiet has covered the campus; the revelry so real and joyous twenty-four hours earlier seems a meaningless memory now. But while others pine for what might have been, Osborne pushes on. The process continues. The family wagon is already parked out-side South Stadium. There's so little time to lose. The agony of yesterday already replaced by the realities of today—Colorado, NU's final regular-season opponent of the season and anything but a pushover. The year before in Boulder, the Buffalos had stunned the then-third-ranked Huskers, 20–10, ending a 12-game losing streak in that city dating back to 1960. "This is a moment in our program we'll always cherish," CU coach Bill McCartney gushed right after that game.

Now, after more than twenty-five years of coaching, fifteen as the head man, what moments will Tom Osborne ultimately cherish? A big win over Oklahoma? His valiant 2-point try against Miami? The graduation of hundreds of student-athletes? The Academic All-Americas? The men he's made? Certainly not the news that some players on his teams sold their tickets for thousands of dollars. Or were paid to play. Or smoked and snorted cocaine to get high and swallowed and injected steroids to build strength. Or lied to NCAA investigators. Or violated NCAA rules. Or fought with police. And certainly not, in the end, the realization that one of the classiest college football programs in the country has had its fair share of problems and sins, if you will, just like just about all the others. Can Tom Osborne accept these facts, institute change, and power—no, *speed*—his Huskers forward? Or will the need to protect and punish prevail?

And finally, can Tom Osborne escape the catch-22 of coaching? Can he continue to survive in a system where the pressures and the power, like the number of missions in Joseph Heller's classic novel, keep increasing, and every time the biggest fish in the bowl wants to stop swimming, to tread water just a bit, he faces the chilling prospect of how much less powerful—how much less loved—will he be if 10-2 becomes 9-3 or, horrors, 8-4? One play. One player. The drums of discontent beat louder and louder.

Those are the questions, it seems, that cry out to be answered before the Big Red Machine lays claim to another decade of dominance.

EPILOGUE

The ninety-ninth consecutive season of Husker football proved one of acute pain and promise to Tom Osborne and his troops. The 1988–89 campaign officially ended on a desultory note on January 2, 1989, in the Orange Bowl in Miami, where the Huskers had come with high hopes of avenging the bitter loss to the Hurricanes exactly five years earlier. It didn't happen. The 'Canes completely dominated the Huskers, 23–3, holding the visitors to just 135 total yards. "We just got beat by a better team," said Osborne, whose Huskers still finished 11–2.

Nebraska had reached the Orange Bowl and South Florida on arguably its biggest high since the helter-skelter days of the "Scoring Explosion." In a game Osborne proudly declared "belonged to our defense" Nebraska had shattered the four-year-old "jinx" and stuffed Oklahoma, 7–3, in Norman on November 19. The win was Nebraska's 11th of the season (against one loss), the most since the glory days of '83, and it earned the school its first outright Big Eight title since that season. It was doubly rewarding because it came under some of the most miserable of conditions: a biting rain, winds of thirty miles an hour, and a windchill factor of nine degrees. But after Steve Taylor capped an 80-yard opening drive with a 1-yard sneak for a touchdown, Thomas, Etienne, and the rest of the Black Shirts dug in, and that was all she wrote, folks, as Oklahoma, averaging 367.9 yards on the ground, gained just 98 and failed for the first time in 62 games to score a touchdown. What's more, on the final play of the game, the Sooners' break-dancing quarterback, Thompson, was hit so hard he broke both the tibia and fibula in his right leg.

The win left Nebraska a perfect 7–0 in the conference and ranked sixth in the country. Only a 41–28 loss to UCLA in the third week of the season kept the Huskers out of the national championship picture. But overall, UCLA or not, it had been a sensational season, one that had opened almost three months earlier in East Rutherford, New Jersey. There the Huskers had dusted off Texas A&M, 23–14, in the Kickoff Classic, as Terry Rodgers gained 65 yards on just 10 carries. After that game Taylor, the game's MVP, was quoted in the *New York Times* as saying he'd "learned his lesson" about trash-talking. "I learned [it] last year when we lost to OU," he said.

"It was painful for about a day," he added. "I had to eat some crow. But I am a very confident person. That was last year. We're going to do our talking on the field this year."

And they did—loud and clear. In the home opener they pummeled Utah State, 63–13, before stumbling and playing their only bad quarter of the season, the first against UCLA, in which the Bruins scored 28 points on their way to a 13-point victory. Then, led by Taylor and a surprise starter at I-back, junior Ken Clark, Nebraska rolled past Arizona State (47–16), Nevada–Las Vegas (48–6), Kansas (63–10), Oklahoma State (63–42), Kansas State (48–3), Missouri (26–18), and Iowa State (51–16) before slipping by Colorado, 7–0, thanks to 165 yards from Clark and his 2-yard touchdown plunge. That left only the Norman Conquest to complete a memorable regular season.

Afterward the awards rolled in. A record 13 Huskers earned All-Big Eight honors of some kind, including outside linebacker Thomas who led the team in ten defensive categories and was the overwhelming choice as Big Eight Defensive Player of the Year. He finished second to Alabama's Derrick Thomas in the Butkus Award for best linebacker and runner-up to Auburn's Tracy Rocker for the Lombardi Award. Not that Thomas, a consensus All-America, found that vote total much to his liking. "Rocker's a 1; I'm a 10," he said one evening while flying back to Lincoln after filming a Bob Hope Christmas special. "I'm one of the top two, three players in the draft. Those other guys aren't even top ten. But that's okay. I'll be gettin' mine soon, come draft time."

Taylor, for his superlative efforts, was selected consensus All–Big Eight quarterback for a second straight year. He finished his career with a school-record 62 touchdowns (32 rushing, 30 passing), third in career total-offense yards, sixth in passing, fifth in touchdown passes, and the most yards rushing (2,125) of any NU quarterback in history. By the end of the season, however, you couldn't ask him how he felt about it; he had learned his lesson so well he'd stopped talking to the national press. In February, without waiting for the NFL draft, he followed the path of his idol, Gill, and signed a three-year contract with the Edmonton Eskimos of the Canadian Football League. (Gill had played for two years with the Montreal Alouettes before a series of concussions ended his career in 1985. He went on to play baseball in the Cleveland Indians and Detroit Tigers organizations.)

Safety Mark Blazek was honored as the Toyota/CBS Leader of the Year. The senior co-captain, who lost his starting free safety spot to Tim Jackson of Dallas, finished with a 3.96 average in social science education and spoke of applying to law school.

Osborne was named Big Eight Coach of the Year for the fourth time. For the sixth time in the last eight years he won 10 or more games, upping his career coaching percentage mark to .815. He was said to be trying to slow down but showed no sign of it. On his office desk were books with names like *Running for Therapy* and *How Humor Reduces Stress.*

Terry Rodgers, after gaining more than 100 yards against

Arizona State, hurt his knee in practice and was lost for the remainder of the season.

Off the field, however, discipline and drug use still posed problems. Prior to spring ball, Osborne announced seven players would be held out of drills for "academic and discipline" reasons. The seven were Brinson, Fryar, Clark, tight end Chris O'Gara, freshman fullback Randy Williams, and defensive linemen Ray Valladao and Kent Wells. Osborne declined to provide specifics, saying only that his decision was "cautious" in light of new university regulations that precluded students on academic suspension from making up classes in summer school—a longstanding Husker tradition.

Moreover, Williams, a blue-chipper from Oklahoma, had been arrested in January and charged with felony theft involving $300 worth of radar equipment. Charges were subsequently dismissed. And several starters were rumored to have dabbled with drugs. Finally, according to court records, Thomas was still having police problems. He was cited in May for speeding (sixty-nine in a fifty-five zone) and in June for "discharging an air, gas or spring operated gun in such a manner as to endanger the safety of persons or property." Three weeks later that charge was dismissed.

Food for thought:

▶ Eighteen of NU's 22 starters in the Orange Bowl hailed from outside Nebraska, from places like Texas, California, Kansas, New Jersey, Wisconsin, Missouri, Louisiana, Colorado, and Iowa.

▶ Twenty-two of the twenty-four scholarships awarded at Nebraska in 1988 went to out-of-state recruits, an all-time high. Included were players from Bellevue, Washington; Chandler and Mesa, Arizona; Brandon, Florida; Bell Gardens, Anaheim, and Fontana, California; and Columbia, South Carolina, as Nebraska continued to widen its talent search.

▶ Had Nebraska beaten Miami, it could have conceivably jumped from sixth to second in the national rankings. As it was, NU dropped down to tenth, barely keeping Osborne's Top 10 ranking streak alive. One bowl game. Eight poll places. That's the margin of error in college football these days.

▶ In December the NCAA completed its inquiry and slapped OU with a stinging three-year probation for "major violations," including offering cash and cars to recruits and giving airline tickets to players. The Sooners were banned from bowl games for two seasons and blocked from live coverage for one season. The NCAA Committee on Infractions stated that for "at least several years, the university has failed to exercise appropriate institutional control" over the football program.

Within a four-week period in January and February the roof fell in at OU. On January 13 defensive back Jerry Parks was arrested and charged with shooting with intent to injure a teammate during a late-night argument in the football dorm. A week later three OU players—offensive tackle Nigel Clay, tight end Bernard Hall, and running back Glen Bell—were arrested and charged with raping a twenty-year-old woman in the same players-only dorm.

Then, on February 13, the stunner: quarterback Thompson, King Charles himself, just days after lecturing grammar school children on the dangers of drug use, was arrested and charged with selling seventeen grams of cocaine to an undercover FBI agent for $1,400 on January 26. If convicted, Thompson, the Sooners' leading rusher, could receive twenty years in prison and $1 million in fines.

"This is the most difficult situation I've ever had to face in my life," said Barry Switzer.

How difficult became painfully apparent on June 19, 1989, when a troubled Switzer tearfully resigned as head coach.

"I will never coach at another institution," he said at a Norman, Oklahoma, press conference. "I will never coach at another college level. I promise you that.

"It's no fun anymore. I'm drained. I don't have the energy to compete in this arena today. The time has come for new leadership."

AFTERWORD

Wednesday, April 26, 1989, 7:00 P.M.

The captain of United Airlines flight 495 informs a cabin teeming with business travelers—plus a couple of red coats—that as soon as he signs off on this tire change, we'll be winging our way from Chicago to Lincoln. "It's a beautiful day down there," he explains. "Clear skies. Good visibility. And are you ready for this? Ninety-six degrees!"

By 9:00 P.M. and the arrival of 495 the temperature has dipped to a balmy eighty-four and the Lincoln skyline is bathed in the twinkling glow of downtown lights, a reddish hue visible above the stadium where the gigantic neon N glows brightly in the night. Football is also in the air, for on Saturday, April 29, twenty days of spring practice will officially conclude with the annual Red–White intrasquad game, a sneak preview of a fall campaign that will commemorate Nebraska's hundredth season of football, a season that opens September 9 at home against Northern Illinois.

Northern Illinois? We know. Fact is, the Huskies (not Huskers) are just one of four cushy nonconference opponents (Utah, Minnesota, and Oregon State round out the quartet)

225

that have stirred considerable local debate—and a tepid ticket response. One columnist has already predicted NU will open 5–0 (lowly Kansas State follows in the first Big Eight game) and rise to 8–0 (beating borderline Missouri, Oklahoma State, and Iowa State) before running into legitimate action against Colorado in Boulder. NU will also play 7 of its 11 regular-season games at home this year, giving rise to speculation that Osborne has fully realized national championships are won by teams with perfect records entering the new year; rugged, preconference competition is nice, but one loss and you're out of it these days.

Of course, still others suggest NU may need half a season to rebuild a team that lost 12 seniors, including 10 All–Big Eight performers, and find a suitable replacement for three-year starter Taylor at quarterback. The top three candidates—senior-to-be Gerry Gdowski of Fremont, Nebraska, and prospective sophomores Mickey Joseph of New Orleans, Louisiana, and Mike Grant of Valrico, Florida—have less than two games of experience between them. Gdowski, 6'0", 190 pounds, is cut from the mold of Husker quarterbacks of old— Jerry Tagge, Travis Turner, and Clete Blakeman spring immediately to mind. A heady kid who can run a little bit and throw a little bit, Gdowski doesn't make crucial mistakes. Joseph (5'11", 175 pounds) and Grant (6'2", 200 pounds), on the other hand, symbolize the style of athlete—instinctive, elusive—that Osborne has courted of late to compete with OU, Miami, and Notre Dame come bowl time. But in the case of both players, they are also, at least at this stage, erratic—a word that doesn't fit into Osborne's gridiron vocabulary.

By Friday, after another ninety-degree day, the week-long heat wave has finally broken, leaving the afternoon temperature in the high fifties. At practice about 130 prospects— some more suspect than prospect—bend and stretch their limbs, easing out the kinks before tomorrow's final scrimmage. It's a loosey-goosey kind of day, one Osborne seems to enjoy. Hands pressed deep into his red coaching shorts, he casually strolls the field, chatting it up with players and assistants. He looks more relaxed, the pain and strain of the regular season and the incumbent recruiting pressures washed away—at least temporarily. "The season can really wear you out," he had said on Thursday. But behind the scenes, behind the smile, at least one incident suggests Osborne may be as uptight and reactionary as ever, burrowed more deeply into his bunker "us against them" mentality than ever before, particularly when it comes to the media.

To wit: After NU's embarrassing 23–3 loss to Miami in the Orange Bowl, a game in which the Huskers were completely stifled on offense, *World-Herald* sportswriter Lee Barfknecht, who has covered the team with distinction for the last seven years, quoted some unidentified NU players in a column in which he, among other things, questioned the predictability of the team's offense. Barfknecht preferred not to discuss Osborne's reaction to the piece, but others say the beat writer received a three-page, single-spaced letter in which Osborne criticized him for quoting unnamed players, before refuting each and every *opinion* Barfknecht had expressed. Perhaps most telling as to Osborne's sensitivity these days was the letter's final paragraph. In it Osborne reportedly said he would "take steps" to ensure that the access to players that would allow such a column to be written would cease. Soon after, the NU Sports Information Office instituted a new football team interview policy: writers covering the team are no longer allowed to conduct pre- and postpractice interviews outside the locker room or in the weight room—traditional areas of conversation. And in the future all interviews had to be cleared through the SID office. Told such measures would make it very difficult for some writers to meet early deadlines, in effect cutting off some readers from NU football news, Osborne stuck to his guns.

In addition, NU's football philosophy of recruiting more and more out-of-state blue-chippers—particularly urban blacks—continues. In February the team announced it had signed twenty-two new recruits, nineteen from outside the state (including seven from talent-rich Texas), the majority of them black student-athletes from cities like Camden, New Jersey, St. Louis, and Houston. The prize catch may have

been Derek Brown, a 5'8", 175-pound senior from Servite
High School in Anaheim, California. Brown, a tailback, was a
member of *USA Today's* first-team All-America squad.

Moreover, the ever-increasing number of black athletes on
the squad seems to have further strained the city's social
fabric. Local businesspeople and sources close to the team
say they sense growing unrest among local high school players and the Lincoln community over the influx of blacks at
the expense of local scholarships and playing time. Resentment is also said to be rising in local bars, where the fraterni-
zation is often closer—and more volatile. "In Omaha, it's
different," says the night manager of one popular local night-
club. "Here, it's a culture clash. The athletes, for the most
part, are gentlemen, but as far as race goes, this town is split
right down the middle."

Mingles is no longer the hot spot of social activity, the
crown passing smoothly to Celebration, the consistently
popular dance club. Popular enough to find quarterback
Taylor dropping in at 12:20 Saturday morning. Pausing on
the winding staircase leading to the lower-level club, Taylor
says he is thrilled to be heading off to Edmonton and the CFL
and that he has purposely skipped many of the NFL's predraft
workouts because he wasn't sure what the league's attitude
was toward black quarterbacks. "Just look what happened to
Rodney Peete," he says in reference to the USC quarterback
who was expected to be drafted in the first or second round
and was finally tabbed in the sixth round by Detroit. "Got to
take care of yourself now," adds Taylor.

Taylor, as it turns out, was one of seven NU players drafted
by the NFL on April 23. The most celebrated local pick was
Thomas, selected in the first round (sixth pick overall) by
Tampa Bay. In true Thomas fashion, he began wearing an all-
leather warm-up suit, toting around a cellular phone, cruising
the town in his customized Mercedes and Jeep, and signing
his name "$andman." Other Huskers drafted . . . defensive
tackle Pete (fifth round, Detroit), safety Tim Jackson (ninth,
Dallas), tight end Todd Millikan (tenth, Chicago), defensive
tackle Willie Griffin (eleventh, Tampa), and Taylor (twelfth,

Indianapolis). Cornerback Charles Fryar (Pittsburgh) and 1987 star Rod Smith (Kansas City) both signed free agent deals.

Signing is exactly what Taylor is doing by noon on Saturday. Seated at a folding table ninety minutes before the spring game is to begin, Taylor is besieged by a young crowd of eager autograph hounds, all thrusting pen and program in his direction. Taylor inks away ("To Mark—Good Luck, Steve Taylor"), at $3 a pop, the proceeds passed to a local antidrug program, just part of a day-long Drug Free Nebraska rally organizers have planned.

By game time some 25,000 red-clad rooters raise their voices as hundreds and hundreds of kids, enough to fill every summer camp in the state, roam the stands and ring the field, hoping to catch a pregame handshake or autograph. The atmosphere is less enthusiastic but more familial than on a fall afternoon; this clearly is Kids' Day, a rare opportunity to hero-worship in person, to touch, to live the dream. Which is kind of how the underdog White squad (comprised of second- and third-string players) must feel after rebounding from a 14–0 first-quarter deficit to tie the Red (first- and fourth-stringers) 21–21 at half.

During intermission, thousands of kids swarm onto the field to take a drug-free pledge. Governor Kay Orr moves to the microphone and makes two predictions. "First," she says, "Tom Osborne will deliver a great Cornhusker team this year." Huge cheers. "And second, we're going to keep drug dealers out of Nebraska." After Orr leads parents in a drug-, alcohol-, and tobacco-free pledge, one that brings a mild response, Osborne approaches the microphone just as the governor says, "It's a great pleasure to introduce our No. 1 coach . . ." The name is drowned out in wild cheers. If Osborne's popularity has diminished at all, it's not evident today. "I want to thank you all for coming," he says, "and I want to thank all you young people for bringing your parents."

Osborne turns to introduce Thomas. The linebacker was some two hours late for his autograph session ($andman posters $5, autographed pictures $3), but that's history now as Broderick, dressed in a camouflage-colored, all-leather warm-up, a tiny cross dangling from his left ear, steps front and center to implore a hushed stadium to "never say yes to drugs." By Churchill standards it isn't much, but the crowd goes crazy, kids swarming to the most popular Husker ever like bees to honey. For the next two hours Thomas sits at a table near the west stands and signs away, a crowd ten-deep pressing in. When the game ends, Thomas smiles as he says, "I think I done signed enough for half the people in here." (Little did his fans know that there was a warrant out for his arrest, stemming from a bounced $72 check Thomas had written to a liquor store in November 1988.)

The final game score reads White 40, Red 28, the first such upset since 1981. Grant has a huge day (157 yards rushing on 19 carries) and stamps himself a legitimate contender at quarterback. Joseph is also dazzling at times. At one point he scrambles out of the pocket to his left, avoids a heavy rush, and fires a perfect 39-yard touchdown pass that hits senior split end Morgan Gregory in stride. But in the Osborne system, the chess match, steadiness and a minimum of mistakes mean more. And for every good move Grant and Joseph make at this point, they seem to take two steps back (touchdown . . . interception or a bad read on an option). So, come fall, in all probability, the even hand of Gdowski will be under center, at least in the beginning. (He had a solid spring game: 4 of 9 passing for 45 yards and 1 score and 5 rushes for 23 yards.) The real question involving the quarterbacks will undoubtedly come later in the season against Colorado, Oklahoma, and in a bowl game. In the final three games of 1988–89, against CU, OU, and Miami, NU combined for a total of just 17 points, raising questions as to whether the speed and big-play prowess of a Joseph or Grant might fare better against a relentless Top 10 defense.

But that's all fodder for the fall. On the final Saturday in April all Nebraska players share the same pedestal. One has only to witness the postgame scene to remember that.

Hundreds of children and their parents swarm onto the

spongy turf of Memorial Stadium like locusts, surrounding red and white jerseys (it doesn't matter whom), begging for attention. Second- and third-teamers like outside linebacker Travis Hill and strong safeties Freeman White and Curtis Cotton are hemmed in; even No. 15 in white, not even listed in the game program, is the idol of a dozen children's eyes. For an hour the people stay. Walking the sidelines. Kid's chasing kids, running imaginary post patterns, tackling each other in glee on this field of dreams, pretending to wear the sacred scarlet and cream.

"Dad, Dad," pleads a feisty four-year-old boy near midfield. "Kick it to me. Kick it to me." The ball is invisible, but the dream is not. "Dad. Dad. Kick off. Let's kick off." And Dad does, chasing happily downfield after his son. Thirty yards away, a young teenage girl, a future NU cheerleader, perhaps, asks her father to "watch me do a cartwheel on this line."

And in the east stands a towheaded boy named Josh, with a runny nose and the most free of spirits. Sitting on a concrete step surveying the action, he instinctively thrusts a tiny fist into the clear, crisp afternoon air.

"Go football," screams Josh.

Go, indeed. But in Nebraska the burning question these days remains *where?* To a national championship? To days of greater stress and strain? To the model program of the 1990s? In this centennial season and beyond, only one man will shape that future, and even he, for a change, doesn't have all the answers.